Thomas Hardy

Tess of the d'Urbervilles

EDITED BY GEOFFREY HARVEY

Consultant editor: Nicolas Tredell

D0884944

ICON BOOKS

Published in 2000 by Icon Books Ltd.,
Grange Road, Duxford, Cambridge CB2 4QF
e-mail: info@iconbooks.co.uk
www.iconbooks.co.uk

Distributed in the UK, Europe, Canada, South Africa and Asia by the
Penguin Group: Penguin Books Ltd., 27 Wrights Lane, London W8 5TZ

Published in Australia in 2000 by Allen & Unwin Pty. Ltd.,
PO Box 8500, 9 Atchison Street, St Leonards, NSW 2065

Consultant editor: Nicolas Tredell
Managing editor: Duncan Heath
Series devised by: Christopher Cox
Cover design: Simon Flynn
Typesetting: Wayzgoose

ISBN 1 84046 174 8

Printed and bound in Great Britain by
Biddles Ltd., Guildford and King's Lynn

Contents

Focuses on three important studies that indicate the continuing invigorating contribution of theory and promise an exciting future for *Tess of the d'Urbervilles* criticism. Includes extracts from Marjorie Garson's fluent Lacanian study of Hardy's anxiety about dissolution; Joe Fisher's fascinating materialist reading of Hardy's subversive hidden text; and Peter Widdowson's stimulating essay examining Hardy's deconstruction of character, which reveals him as our post-modern contemporary.

A NOTE ON QUOTATIONS

In the text of the Guide, page references given to quotations from *Tess of the d'Urbervilles* appear in brackets. The quotations have been amended to follow the Oxford World's Classics edition of the novel, edited by Juliet Grindle and Simon Gatrell, first published in 1988 and reissued in 1998. This text is that of their authoritative Clarendon edition, published in 1983.

Editorial ellipsis within a sentence or paragraph is denoted by a row of three dots. A row of six dots denotes the omission of either a paragraph break, or of one or more paragraphs.

INTRODUCTION

TESS OF THE d'Urbervilles is one of the most popular novels ever written, and has produced a vast body of criticism, astonishing in scope and encompassing virtually every critical and theoretical development since its publication. There are also issues unique to Tess of the d'Urbervilles, which make the history of its criticism complex and fascinating: among them the intensely personal relation between Hardy the author and the character Tess; Hardy's creation of the fictional county of 'Wessex' and its peculiar relation to 'real' history; his defiant addition of an ambiguous subtitle to the novel; and the extraordinary circumstances of its publication. These have been taken into account in the selection of critical texts for this Guide. Other criteria are comprehensiveness and quality for, as the Guide will reveal, Tess has attracted some of the most brilliant criticism of the twentieth century. This Introduction begins by discussing the context within which the novel was produced, including salient features of Hardy's life and writing career, and the material conditions of publication, and then offers a brief preliminary overview of the text's critical history, in order to indicate the scope and organisation of this Guide.

Hardy's reputation as a novelist had been made with the resounding success of Far from the Madding Crowd, which was serialised in the Cornhill magazine in 1874 and went on to be a bestseller. The introduction into Hardy's fiction, with the appearance of this novel, of the idyllic pastoral county of 'Wessex' appealed to the jaded taste of metropolitan readers. As well as its curiosity value, 'Wessex' came to be regarded by humanist critics as a timeless place that revealed the permanent truths of human nature. And in spite of their reservations about Hardy's inclusion of improbable and sensational elements, in due course critics made Far from the Madding Crowd a benchmark of Hardy's realism, so that by the 1880s he had inherited the mantle of the great realist and historian of rural life, George Eliot.

Tess of the d'Urbervilles, serialised in the Graphic in 1891 and published in the same year by Osgood, McIlvaine, is also set in Wessex. It is Hardy's penultimate major novel. After the hostile reception afforded Jude the Obscure following its appearance in 1895, he abandoned fiction for poetry. The gestation of Tess had been a long process, and we know from The Life of Thomas Hardy, his autobiography ghosted by his second wife Florence, and from other sources, that several experiences went into its composition. The opening of *Tess* was suggested by Hardy's overhearing a drunk on a street corner of a Dorset town singing about his Norman ancestry and family vault; he had noted the decline in social status of the Hardys; and had heard a paper read about the Turberville family buried over at Bere Regis. Details such as the blood stain on the ceiling when Alec is stabbed, and the piercing and haemorrhaging of the horse Prince, are drawn from reports in a local newspaper, the *Dorset County Chronicle*. Tess herself, it has been speculated, may owe something to Hardy's cousin Tryphena Sparks, while she also answers to Hardy's description of a girl he once saw. And Tess's death draws on his experience of witnessing the execution of a woman he knew called Martha Browne for the murder of her husband. Hardy also redeployed themes from his earlier fiction: the prior engagement of the woman, which repels her second suitor; relationships that transgress class boundaries; and the familar story of seduction and abandonment. And there are less tangible influences, such as Hardy's interest in folktale, philosophy, science, Shelley's poetry, the paintings of J. M. W. Turner and mythology.

Hardy's later novels are influenced by his growing preoccupation with contemporary social issues, such as the New Woman debate, and although his discussion of the fallen woman question in *Tess of the d'Urbervilles* was not in itself new or daring, his treatment of it was. Hardy had for some time been on a collision course with Mrs Grundy[1] and in both *Tess* and *Jude* his earlier skirmishes with censorship developed into open warfare. *Tess* has a quite extraordinary publishing history, which has profoundly influenced subsequent criticism. First commissioned as a serial entitled 'Too Late, Beloved!' (its original title had been 'The Body and Soul of Sue') for a Bolton newspaper syndicate – a Christian firm called Tillotson & Son – it was rejected on moral grounds after Hardy declined to alter his manuscript. *Murray's Magazine* similarly found it too sexually explicit and turned it down, as did *Macmillan's Magazine*. In the *Life*, Hardy claimed that he could not afford to forgo the income from serialisation and bring out the novel in volume form, and he recorded how instead he cynically mutilated his manuscript to accommodate the conventional expectations of magazine editors, replacing Tess's seduction and her illegitimate child by a mock marriage ceremony. Hardy's anger at this necessity may be gauged by an essay, 'Candour in English Fiction', that he had written in the *New Review* in 1890, where he laments the damage done to novels in England by the power of censorship. Hardy's bowdlerised version of *Tess* was finally taken up by the *Graphic* and published in twenty-four instalments. But two substantial excisions were published separately in the same year, 'The Midnight Baptism' in the *Fortnightly Review* and 'Saturday Night in Arcady' (Chapters 10 and 11 of *Tess*) in the *National Observer*. These were reincorporated into the first edition of the novel, published by Osgood,

McIlvaine in 1891. What really drew down upon Hardy's head the wrath of the Grundyists was not simply his inclusion of dubious material, but his combative posture in adding the provocative subtitle to the first volume edition of *Tess*, 'A Pure Woman Faithfully Presented by Thomas Hardy'. However, the problems did not stop there, for Hardy could not leave his text alone. He made revisions for the 1892 single volume edition, and as late as the 1912 Wessex edition he decided finally to incorporate the incident of the dance at Chaseborough. *Tess of the d'Urbervilles* is thus an unstable and problematic text.

In spite of mixed reviews, *Tess* was a runaway success, and has remained phenomenally popular worldwide. Within a month the first print run had gone, and the reprinting was similarly quickly sold out. Several editions and reprints followed, and this novel alone made Hardy financially secure for life. For instance, he made the then considerable sum of £400 in a single year from the issue of a paperback edition in June 1900. Between 1900 and 1930 *Tess* was reprinted some forty times. It was filmed in America in 1913 and 1924, but there was a long gap until Roman Polanski's controversial version of *Tess* appeared in 1979. In 1998 a successful television production was made by the BBC.

Tess of the d'Urbervilles brought Hardy almost universal fame. The young architect from Dorset who had frequented the art galleries and theatres of London in the 1860s, and had essayed writing poetry in his free hours, was now lionised by fashionable society. Hardy noted that the Duchess of Abercorn explained to him how she grouped her guests according to their view of Tess's character, in order to avoid their almost fighting across her dinner-table. However, it was a society towards which Hardy, as an outsider, felt intensely ambivalent. His frequent visits to the houses of aristocratic ladies disturbed his wife Emma, who did not accompany him. Their marriage, which had not produced children, had ceased to be a happy one and at this period was in decline. Emma's religious mania made her husband's agnosticism offensive to her; she bitterly resented his attraction to women; and she had a limited comprehension of the pressures under which a famous writer laboured. In his turn, Hardy seems to have become emotionally estranged from her.

After publishing *The Well-Beloved* serially in 1892, Hardy embarked on what was to be his final novel, *Jude the Obscure*, in which his relationship with Florence Henniker may have contributed to the characterisation of Sue Bridehead. Hardy was at the height of his powers as a novelist, and at the peak of his anger with establishment society. *Jude* was published serially in *Harper's New Monthly Magazine* from December 1894 to November 1895, and the reviews were damning. Novels about women, marriage and sexual equality were fashionable in the 1890s, but Hardy's was a ferocious critique that also encompassed social class, the educational system and the Church. Distressed by the reaction to the novel, Hardy gave up fiction for poetry, and after Emma's death in 1912 produced out of his grief some of the finest poetry in English. In 1914 he married Florence Emily Dugdale, and continued to develop as one of the major poets of the twentieth century. Hardy had been born in 1840. His life spanned the Victorian and early modern periods, and in his later years, until his death on 11 January 1928, he enjoyed an unchallenged position as the Grand Old Man of English Letters.

The opening chapter of this Guide offers a selection of contemporary reviews of *Tess of the d'Urbervilles* by, among others, the novelist, Mrs Oliphant, the formidable Richard Holt Hutton of the *Spectator*, the poet and critic Sir William Watson, and the American academic critic, W. P. Trent. The reviews offer a variety of sharply conflicting opinion, including the derogatory comments of Andrew Lang, which polarised critical reactions, and Mowbray Morris, which drew a personal response from Hardy himself. These early reviews, some of them acutely perceptive, discern those issues that recur in *Tess* criticism: Tess's 'purity', the novel as tragedy, the nature of Hardy's 'Wessex', the voyeuristic treatment of the heroine, Hardy's realism, his pessimism and his failures of style.

Chapter two examines *Tess* criticism up to 1949, a period during which a more leisurely evaluation of the novel took place. It demonstrates the establishment of the liberal humanist approach, together with the extension of critical interest into broader areas. The first major Hardy critic was the Catholic poet, Lionel Johnson, to whom so many subsequent critics return in their essays. Other studies explore the influences of Victorian science and culture on Hardy's 'philosophy', for instance Harvey Curtis Webster; the response to Hardy of contemporary modernist writers, such as D. H. Lawrence and Virginia Woolf; and the appropriation of Hardy by Lord David Cecil as the great tragedian and chronicler of essential Englishness for wartime Britain. There is also Donald Davidson's evaluation of Hardy as a writer of folk mythology, and David J. De Laura's well-known essay on 'the ache of modernism'. This period may be seen as culminating in Albert Guerard's provocative reassessment, following Morton Dauwen Zabel, of Hardy as an anti-realist and modernist writer, which marked a watershed in the criticism of *Tess*.

Although the influential critic, F. R. Leavis, had earlier dismissed Hardy as a significant novelist, his reputation attracted the serious attention of some major critics in the 1950s, a period when the influence of New Criticism and Marxist criticism began to make themselves felt. Chapter three of this Guide explores both of these strands: in John Holloway's persistent examination of Hardy as a Victorian sage; Dorothy Van Ghent's brilliant probing of the richly symbolic texture and mythological-realist structure of *Tess*; the humanist Marxist critic Arnold Kettle's urgent analysis of this novel as social thesis and moral fable; and Douglas Brown's more traditional historical approach to the novel's society.

In the 1960s and 1970s, the period which occupies chapter four, *Tess of the d'Urbervilles* criticism was dominated by humanist formalism, which produced some outstanding insights. Roy Morrell's existential humanism is embodied in his demolition of the New Critical approach. Very different are Tony Tanner's dazzling examination of the novel's patterns of imagery, and David Lodge's close interrogation of Hardy's style. There is also Richard Carpenter's intensive study of the way in which the text is structured by mythology; Dale Kramer's subtle reading of *Tess* as a subjective tragedy; and Ian Gregor's comprehensive and enormously intelligent revelation of the novel's underlying rhythms. Alongside these, and to some extent informed by humanist ideology, there continued the valuable historical approach of Raymond Williams's stimulating essay on *Tess*, and the work of Merryn Williams. At the same time genetic criticism developed from J. T. Laird's seminal work on Hardy's progressive shaping of the text; and Mary Jacobus combines a feminist and materialist approach to his textual revisions in a splendidly argued essay.

Chapter five records the impact on the study of *Tess of the d'Urbervilles* of the tidal wave of theory that swamped British and American culture in the 1980s. *Tess* was regarded even more overtly as a text to be fought over by competing ideologies, and criticism of the novel was revitalised by a variety of new departures that produced exciting readings. The best of them are considered here: Rosemary Sumner's approach through the psychological writings of Freud and Jung; J. Hillis Miller's challenging deconstruction of the text; Penny Boumelha's seminal feminist reading, and Patricia Ingham's feminist study of the text's language and syntax; John Goode's passionate materialist interpretation; J. B. Bullen's elegant scholarly examination of the mythological structure in *Tess* based on the influence of the painter J. M. W. Turner and solar worship; and Simon Gatrell's innovative textual biography, relating Hardy's changes to *Tess* to the evolution of his thinking. In the final chapter of this Guide, a period during which the momentum of *Tess* criticism appears to have slackened, though with no diminution in quality, three readings of *Tess* are selected to represent the place of this novel in our time: a penetrating and fluent Lacanian study by Marjorie Garson; Joe Fisher's intriguing materialist reading of Hardy's subversive hidden text; and Peter Widdowson's stimulating assessment of Hardy as a post-modernist writer.

Since its publication over a century ago, *Tess of the d'Urbervilles* has exerted a hold on the imagination of its readers and offered a unique challenge to critical interpretation. Testimony to its elusiveness is the variety of sharply divergent opinions included in this Guide. The publication of *Tess* was surrounded by controversy, and its criticism over the years has been marked by fierce partisanship. Taken together, these essays by some of the most outstanding critics contribute to our growing understanding of a text that has become a cultural icon.

CHAPTER ONE

Controversy and the Reviews: 1891–2

HARDY WAS very thin-skinned when it came to criticism. The tone of a comment he made about it in 1908 is angry and defiant: 'But criticism is so easy, and art so hard: criticism so flimsy, and the life-seer's voice so lasting.'[1] He suffered under the lash of several of his reviewers.

Richard le Gallienne, who reviewed *Tess of the d'Urbervilles* in the *Star* on 23 December 1891, was an aesthete and a member of the Rhymers' Club,[2] who wrote under the pseudonym 'Logroller'. His review of *Tess* offers a good insight into the kind of presuppositions that reviewers brought to the novel, and it is reproduced in full, apart from summaries of the plot:

- On an evening in the latter part of May, a middle-aged man was walking homeward from Shaston to the village of Marlott, in the adjoining Vale of Blakemore or Blackmoor. The pair of legs that carried him were rickety, and there was a bias in his gait which inclined him somewhat to the left of a straight line (p. 13).

When a novel begins so, who needs to be told that we are once more in Mr Thomas Hardy's 'Arcady of Wessex', that villages with all kinds of quaint cider-sounding names lie about us, Bulbarrow, Nettlecombe-Tout, Dogbury, High Stoy, Bubb Down, and that here all roads do not lead to Rome, but to Casterbridge. The devoted student of Mr Hardy would also immediately recognise him by a less pleasing token in this passage. Who else, except maybe Mr Meredith, would describe the unsteadiness in the walk home of an aged tippler as 'a bias in his gait which inclined him somewhat to the left of a straight line'? But this is only a trifling example of a defect in Mr Hardy's style which is continually making one grind one's teeth, like 'sand in honey'. One cannot call it euphuism, because euphuism tends to 'favour and to prettiness'. It seems rather to come from sudden moments of self-consciousness in the midst of his creative flow, as also from the imperfect digestion of certain modern science and philosophy, which is becoming somewhat too obtrusive through the apple-cheek outline of Mr Hardy's work. For example, the little boy talks to his sister, 'rather for the pleasure of utterance than for audition' (p.35); a wooer at a certain hot moment entreats the wooed – 'Will you, I ask once more, show your belief in me by letting me clasp you with my arm?' (p.74). Another lover, trying to persuade Tess that his marrying her cannot hurt his family, says, 'it will not affect even the periphery of their lives' (p. 194), and, later on, when the time has come to forgive, he asks – 'How can forgiveness meet such a grotesque prestidigitation as that?' (p.226). And when Mr Hardy would tell us that Tess had forgotten that children must be expected from their union, he says that she had been 'forgetting it might result in vitalizations that would inflict upon others' (p.239), etc. Mr Hardy continually delights in those long Latin and Greek words that seem to be made of springs rather than vowels. Think how absolutely out of colour in Arcadia are such words as 'dolorifuge', 'photosphere,' 'heliolatries', 'arborescence', 'concatenation', 'noctambulist' – where, indeed, are such in colour? – and Mr Hardy further uses that horrid verb 'ecstasize'.

Don't let anyone say that these are small matters. The more beautiful the rest of the work the more jarring such defects as these. Why, one of such words is as destructive as an ounce of dynamite in any dream-world, more especially so in Mr Hardy's 'Sicilian Vales'. If, as I, you hold it no exaggeration to describe Mr Hardy as our modern Theocritus (of course a Theocritus in prose), think how the flute and the pipe would stop with a shriek before words of such 'terrible aspect'. They could not more potently destroy our illusion if they were steam-whistles, and this they are constantly doing, like the 'Doctor' in the rhyme, constantly making us dance out of Wessex – yes, 'into France', among other places; for study of French authors seems to be having a strong influence on Mr Hardy's work just lately. Realism as a theory seems in danger of possessing him at times, though happily but intermittently. In that part of realism which is not theory but a necessary artistic instinct, Mr Hardy has always been strong.

However, despite those dreadful words, and despite the painful 'moral', the noble, though somewhat obtrusive 'purpose', *Tess of the d'Urbervilles* is one of Mr Hardy's best novels – perhaps it is his very best. The beautiful simplicity of his style when, as usual, he forgets he is writing, the permeating healthy sweetness of his descriptions, the idyllic charm and yet the reality of his figures, his apple-sweet women, his old men, rich with character as old oaks, his love-making, his fields, his sympathetic atmosphere – all these, and any other of Mr Hardy's best qualities you can think of, are to be found 'in widest commonality spread' in *Tess*. The motive of *Tess* is one of those simple (and yet how cruelly tangled) sexual situations round which 'the whole creation moves', and in which Mr Hardy delights to find 'the eternal meanings'. Mr Hardy has heretofore been more inclined to champion man the faithful against woman the coquette, but in *Tess* he very definitely espouses 'the cause of woman', and devotes himself to show how often in this world – all, alas, because the best of us is so conventionalised – when men and women break a law 'the woman pays'. Of course it is a special pleading, because a novel might be as readily written to show how often a man pays, too. Indeed, was not *Middlemarch* such a novel? It is noticeable that most of these books against men are written by men, and that *Middlemarch* is the work of a woman. Such is the gallantry of sex, and such its ironical power . . .

Tess is the most satisfying of all Mr Hardy's heroines. She is by no means so empty-headed as they are wont to be, but, like her sisters, she is a fine Pagan, full of humanity and imagination, and, like them, though in a less degree, flawed with that lack of will, that fatal indecision at great moments . . . So 'the woman pays'. Thus you see the plot is the plot of Mr H. A. Jones,[3] but the hand is the hand of Thomas Hardy. One would venture further and breathe 'Shakespearean', concerning the women, but the adjective is so apt to be misunderstood.[4] □

Le Gallienne's reference to *Middlemarch* is an indication of how George Eliot dominates Hardy criticism, while the simultaneous allusions to the popular contemporary playwright, Henry Arthur Jones, who dramatised social themes, and to Shakespeare, suggests le Gallienne's genuine ambivalence towards *Tess of the d'Urbervilles*. Although the general tone of his review is supercilious, he appears to be endorsing the novel, but his attitude to the 'Arcady of Wessex' is both idealised and patronising; that of one of the Londoners Tess speculates about at the railway station. Le Gallienne ignores Hardy's treatment of the grimmer aspects of 1890s Dorset, because as his references to 'Arcadia' and to Theocritus (a classical writer of formal pastoral) reveals, he detects in them a contemporary threat to this secure literary world. Whereas Theocritus balanced the ideal and the real in his portrayal of the life of Sicilian shepherds, Hardy espouses the theoretical realism (or rather naturalism) of modern French authors, with their emphasis on biological and socio-economic determinism, and on objective documentary observation. One of the schisms in contemporary reviews is exposed precisely here, for it is exactly this feature of *Tess* that D.F. Hannigan later praises so highly in the *Westminster Review*.

The anonymous reviewer for the *Pall Mall Gazette* (31 December 1891) also alludes to this 'last Wessex tale' in order to record his disappointment at the way the 'rustic geniality' of *Far from the Madding Crowd*, present in the opening chapters of *Tess*, descends into tragedy. Clearly Wessex has become so firmly established in the minds of reviewers as a fictional locale, that it can be invoked as a criterion for critical judgement. Hardy's characters are enthusiastically endorsed as being 'pure Wessex'. And again the realistic, detailed descriptions of landscape and nature are praised. It is a warm review, and a perceptive one. It laments the unfortunate necessity that forced Hardy to publish his novel so idiosyncratically and is sympathetic to his probing of the causes underlying what is described as 'peculiarly the Woman's Tragedy!'.[5] It also endorses his ability both to create tragedy through the artistic shaping of a simple tale and to combine a modern exploration of the contemporary ethos with the universal. Indeed Hardy's modernity is validated by a comparison with Ibsen.[6] The criterion of psychological realism and probability also comes into critical play, as so often in the early reviews – Angel is 'too fastidious', while, somewhat unusually, Alec's passing conversion is regarded as being sufficiently common among sensualists to be seen as a convincing episode.

Like the first readers, reviewers were divided about Hardy's presentation of Tess. Clementina Black the novelist, who reviewed *Tess of the d'Urbervilles* for the *Illustrated London News* on 9 January 1892, is clearly in the pro-Tess lobby. She praises the novel's moral earnestness and offers a mildly proto-feminist defence of Tess as an example of the worthy and vulnerable woman, who is most at risk in contemporary society. She asserts Tess's claim for equality with men and evaluates her life on its own terms, For Black, the novel's condemnation of tyrannical social convention deliberately challenges the closed mind of the complacent reader. The three paragraphs quoted below omit a summary of the novel:

■ . . . The conventional reader wishes to be excited, but not to be disturbed; he likes to have new pictures presented to his imagination, but not to have new ideas presented to his mind. He detests unhappy endings, mainly because an unhappy ending nearly always involves an indirect appeal to the conscience, and the conscience, when aroused, is always demanding a reorganisation of that traditional pattern of right and wrong which it is the essence of conventionality to regard as immutable. Yet more, of course, does he detest an open challenge of that traditional pattern, and *Tess of the d'Urbervilles* is precisely such a challenge.

Mr Hardy's story, like *Diana of the Crossways*,[7] is founded on a recognition of the ironic truth which we all know in our hearts, and are all forbidden to say aloud, that the richest kind of womanly nature, the most direct, sincere, and passionate, is the most liable to be caught in that sort of pitfall which social convention stamps as an irretrievable disgrace. It is the unsuspicious and fundamentally pure-minded girl in whom lie the noblest possibilities of womanhood, who is the easiest victim and who has to fight the hardest fight . . .

. . . The wholesome life of the dairy farm, and the wonderful pictures of changing aspects and seasons, the descriptions of three or four solitary walks, remain with us like bits of personal experience. Perhaps no other English writer could have given precisely these impressions. Yet these, characteristic as they are, are not the essence of the book. Its essence lies in the perception that a woman's moral worth is measurable not by any one deed, but by the whole aim and tendency of her life and nature. In regard to men the doctrine is no novelty; the writers who have had eyes to see and courage to declare the same truth about women are few indeed; and Mr Hardy in this novel has shown himself to be one of that brave and clear-sighted minority.[8] □

In contrast to Clementina Black, the reviewer for the *Saturday Review*, in a piece published on 16 January 1892, pours scorn on *Tess*. (Hardy decided it was George Saintsbury and never forgave him.) He offers a contemptuous parody of the story and dismisses the 'terrible dreariness of this tale, which, except during the few hours spent with cows, has not a gleam of sunshine anywhere'.[9] What he finds particularly distasteful is something that was to be taken up by many later critics, namely Hardy's dwelling on Tess's sexuality. The reviewer complains that 'It is these side suggestions that render Mr Hardy's story so very disagreeable, and *Tess* is full of them'.[10]

A week later, this view was counterbalanced by Richard Holt Hutton's review in the *Spectator*, of which he was joint editor. A distinguished critic and writer of theological works, Hutton has the perspicacity and breadth of mind to recognise great fiction while, as a Christian, recoiling from the picture of the universe it presents. Hutton is an early example of the many critics who in different ways have reacted against Hardy's 'pessimism', and also against his assertion of Tess's 'purity'; including his fellow-Christian reviewer Mrs Oliphant. He begins his review by acknowledging the power of *Tess*, but finds abhorrent its metaphysical thrust:

■ Mr Hardy has written one of his most powerful novels, perhaps the most powerful which he ever wrote, to illustrate his conviction that not only is there no Providence guiding individual men and women in the right way, but that, in many cases at least, there is something like a malign fate which draws them out of the right way into the wrong way. Tess of the d'Urbervilles is declared by Mr Hardy to be 'a pure woman', and as he has presented her, we do not doubt that her instincts were all pure enough, more pure probably than those of a great number of women who never fall into her disgrace and shame. She was, of course, much more sinned against than sinning, though

Mr Hardy is too 'faithful' a portrait-painter to leave out touches which show that her instincts even as regards purity, were not of the very highest class . . . On the whole, we deny altogether that Mr Hardy has made out his case for Tess. She was pure enough in her instincts, considering the circumstances and the class into which she was born. But she had no deep sense of fidelity to those instincts. If she had, she would not have allowed herself time after time to be turned from the plain path of duty, by the fastidiousness of a personal pride which was quite out of proportion to the extremity of her temptations and her perils. It is no doubt true that her husband behaved with even less fidelity to her than she to him. Perhaps that was natural in such a pagan as Mr Hardy depicts him. But we cannot for a moment admit that even on his own portraiture of the circumstances of the case, Tess acted as a pure woman should have acted under such a stress of temptation and peril. Though pure in instinct, she was not faithful to her pure instinct. We should, indeed, say that Mr Hardy, instead of illustrating his conviction that there is no Power who guides and guards those who are faithful to their best lights, has only illustrated what every Christian would admit, that if fine natures will not faithfully adhere to such genuine instincts as they have, they may deteriorate, and will deteriorate, in consequence of that faithlessness.[11] □

But as Hutton continues, the critic speaks in spite of the theologian, and he enthuses over Hardy's tragic power, his realistic portrayal of a rural community and his psychological truth, both in his exploration of Tess's states of mind and his understanding of Alec d'Urberville's conversion; though like other reviewers, he picks Hardy up on his style, its pedantry reminding him of 'George Eliot in her scientific mood':[12]

■ While we cannot at all admire Mr Hardy's motive in writing this very powerful novel, we must cordially admit that he has seldom or never written anything so truly tragic and so dramatic. The beauty and realism of the delineations of the life on the large dairy-farm; the sweetness and, on the whole, generosity of the various dairymaids' feelings for each other; the vivacity of the description of the cows themselves; the perfect insight into the conditions of rustic lives; the true pathos of Tess's sufferings; the perfect naturalness, and even inevitability, of all her impulses; the strange and horrible mixture of feelings with which she regards her destroyer, when, believing that all her chance of happiness is over, she sells herself ultimately for the benefit of her mother and brother and sisters; the masterful conception of the seducer as a convert to Antinomianism, and the ease with which his new faith gives way to a few recitals by Tess of her husband's ground for scepticism (with which, however, we are not favoured); the brilliant description of the flight of Clare and Tess, and of the curious equanimity with which Tess meets the consciousness of having committed murder, seeing that it has restored her for five days to her husband's heart – are all pictures of almost unrivalled power, though they evidently proceed from the pantheistic conception that impulse is the law of the universe, and that will, properly so called, is a non-existent fiction. We confess that this is a story which, in spite of its almost unrivalled power, it is very difficult to read, because in almost every page the mind rebels against the steady assumptions of the author, and shrinks from the untrue picture of a universe so blank and godless . . .[13] □

Andrew Lang, a versatile, prolific writer and Greek scholar, reviewing the novel in February 1892 for the *New Review*, also admits that he is not *'en rapport'* with Hardy, contrasting him with his revered Homer and complaining of his bitterness of mood, though Lang concedes that the fault may well lie with the reviewer. He takes exception to Hardy's famous concluding phrase, 'the President of the Immortals . . . had ended his sport with Tess' (p. 384), and protests:

■ I cannot say how much this phrase jars on one. If there be a God, who can seriously think of Him as a malicious fiend? And if there be none, the expression is meaningless.[14] □

Hardy was stung by Andrew Lang's review of *Tess*, so much so that he responded by referring in his Preface to the fifth edition of the novel to the objections of a certain 'great critic', and in particular to his condemnation of Hardy's alleged exclamation against the gods.

Friends too, such as the poet and *Academy* reviewer, Sir William Watson, were uneasy about the expression of bitterness in *Tess*. However, his review is notable for its uncompromising assertion that the novel is a 'tragic masterpiece'. After the by-now ritual cavilling at Hardy's use of excessively academic phraseology, Watson stresses the universality of experience that the novel offers, and testifies memorably to its personal impact on him as a reader. Using the benchmark of psychological realism, Watson is alert to the narrative problem of the reader's identification with Angel Clare because of the author's apparent sympathy with him, and our concomitant easy condemnation of Alec d'Urberville. But Watson points out that Hardy's manipulation of the reader's response is complex and masterly because, at the moment of Clare's cruel rejection of Tess, our anger against him is balanced by our sympathetic perception of his nature as 'consistently inconsistent'. In the extracts below, Watson begins by making an implicit comparison with Shakespeare, goes on to define the novel's tragic experience and its effect on the reader, discusses the problematic characterisation of Angel Clare, and notes Hardy's moral anger:

■ In this, his greatest work, Mr Hardy has produced a tragic master-piece which is not flawless, any more than *Lear* or *Macbeth* is . . . . . . Fortunately, however, *Tess* is a work so great that it could almost afford to have even proportionately great faults . . . Powerful and strange in design, splendid and terrible in execution, this story brands itself upon the mind as with the touch of incandescent iron . . . The great theme of the book is the incessant penalty paid by the innocent for the wicked, the unsuspicious for the crafty, the child for its father; and again and again this spectacle, in its wide diffusion, provokes the novelist to a scarcely suppressed declaration of rebellion against a supramundane ordinance that can decree, or permit, the triumph of such wrong. The book may almost be said to resolve itself into a direct arraignment of the morality of this system of vicarious pain – a moral-ity which, as he bitterly expresses it, 'may be good enough for divinities', but is 'scorned by average human nature'. Almost at the outset, this note of insurrection against an apparently inequitable scheme of things is struck, if less audaciously, upon our introduction to the Durbeyfield household:

All these young souls were passengers in the Durbeyfield ship – entirely dependent on the judgement of the two Durbeyfield adults for their pleasures, their necessities, their health, even their exis-tence. If the heads of the Durbeyfield household chose to sail into difficulty, disaster, starvation, disease, degradation, death, thither were these half-dozen little captives under hatches compelled to sail with them – six helpless creatures, who had never been asked if they wished for life on any terms, much less if they wished for it on such hard conditions as were involved in being of the shiftless house of Durbeyfield. (p. 28)

In one way and another, this implicit protest against what he cannot but conceive to be the maladministration of the laws of existence, this expostulation with 'whatever gods there [*sic*] be'[15] upon the ethics of their rule, is the burden of the whole strain.

. . . Truly a stupendous argument; and in virtue of the almost intol-erable power with which this argument is wrought out, *Tess* must take its place among the great tragedies, to have read which is to have per-manently enlarged the boundaries of one's intellectual and emotional experience.

Perhaps the most subtly drawn, as it is in some ways the most per-plexing and difficult character, is that of Angel Clare, with his half-ethereal passion for Tess – an 'emotion which could jealously guard the loved one against his very self' (p. 193). But one of the problems of the book, for the reader, is involved in the question how far Mr Hardy's own moral sympathies go with Clare in the supreme crisis of his and Tess's fate. Her seducer, the spurious d'Urberville, is entirely detestable, but it often happens that one's fiercest indignation demands a nobler object than such a sorry animal as that; and there are probably many readers who, after Tess's marriage with Clare, her spontaneous disclosure to him of her soiled though guiltless past, and his consequent alienation and cruelty, will be conscious of a worse anger against this intellectual, virtuous, and unfortunate man than they could spare for the heartless and worthless libertine who had wrecked these two lives. It is at this very point, however, that the masterliness of the conception, and its imaginative validity, are most conclusively manifest, for it is here that we perceive Clare's nature to be consistently inconsistent throughout . . .

The reader pities Clare profoundly, yet cannot but feel a certain contempt for the shallowness of his casuistry, and a keen resentment of his harsh judgement upon the helpless woman – all the more so since it is her own meek and uncomplaining submission that aids him in his cruel punishment of her . . . . . .

There is one thing which not the dullest reader can fail to recognise – the persistency with which there alternately smoulders and flames throughout the book Mr Hardy's passionate protest against the unequal justice meted by society to the man and the woman associated in an identical breach of the moral law. In his wrath, Mr Hardy seems at times almost to forget that society is scarcely more unjust than nature. He himself proposes no remedy, suggests no escape – his business not being to deal in nostrums of social therapeutics. He is content to make his readers pause, and consider, and pity; and very likely he despairs of any satisfactory solution of the problem which he presents with such disturbing power and clothes with a vesture of such breathing and throbbing life.[16] □

The prolific novelist and reviewer Mrs Oliphant, whose novels frequently deal with the problems associated with being a woman in Victorian society, writing in *Blackwood's Magazine* in March 1892, might have been expected to be sympathetic to Tess, but she was not. Though she turns to *Tess of the d'Urbervilles* from her review of Mrs Humphry Ward's *David Grieve*[17] with some relief, her pugnacious and witty essay, which contains moments of real perception, confesses to being hampered by a number of things in her endeavour to appreciate *Tess*. Though Mrs Oliphant recognises the power of Hardy's art, she frankly admits that his writings are simply not to her taste: the 'one thing upon which there is no discussion.'[18] By identifying the novel as a 'bold romance',[19] she ignores the whole dimension of its social realism, and this position is reinforced by her stated preference for 'cleanly lives and honest sentiment',[20] for a kind of idealism in other words. Although she clearly responds strongly to Hardy's art and to the power of his imagination, even her enthusiasm for his rural society is clouded by an idealising impulse, plus a touch of contempt. She describes Wessex as a 'very primitive country',[21] and its rustics are treated to a patronising comparison with those of George Eliot. In Hardy's Wessex the 'hard labour' of the fields is part of the countryside's charm for the metropolitan consumer of fiction.

Behind this idealising tendency lies the idea of the novel as a legitimate form of moral instruction, and this prompts her objection to Hardy's treatment of the infant Sorrow, which runs counter to literary stereotypes such as that offered in Elizabeth Barrett Browning's *Aurora Leigh*.[22] Mrs Oliphant regards Hardy as presenting an alternative sordid reality, which she identifies as stemming from the modern *fin de siècle* creed, developing out of the scientific rationalist philosophy of enlightenment. But at the core of this Christian reviewer's objections to *Tess* is Hardy's scepticism. Like R.H. Hutton and Andrew Lang, she finds his godless universe unacceptable. Confessing her own Christian meliorist view of moral and material evolution, she rebuffs Hardy's muddled quarrel with God.

Like other reviewers, Mrs Oliphant's main aesthetic criterion is plausibility. In contrast to Sir William Watson's subtle understanding of Angel Clare, she condemns his portrayal as incredible on the grounds that he is not a man's man but feminised. And similarly, while she admires the power and passion of the novel, it fails as a 'bold romance', as she has defined it, because the heroine's actions are not credible, particularly her return to Alec d'Urberville, where Mrs Oliphant detects the polemical strategies of the indignant novelist. And then there is the discreditable mode of publication, with which the following extracts commence:

■ . . . We have a great many objections to make to *Tess*. The fact that what we must call the naughty chapters have had to be printed surreptitiously, in what we presume ought to be described as elderly Reviews, while the rest has come out in the cheerful young newspaper open to all men, is of itself a tremendous objection to our old-fashioned eyes. But with all this, what a living, breathing scene, what a scent and fragrance of the actual, what solid bodies, what real existence, in contrast with the pale fiction of the didactic romance! We feel inclined to embrace Mr Hardy, though we are not fond of him, in pure satisfaction with the good brown soil and substantial flesh and blood, the cows, and the mangel-wurzel, and the hard labour of the fields – which he makes us smell and see. Here is the genuine article at least.

Here is a workman who, though he has his lesson hidden beneath his apron, is an artist first of all, and knows how to use his colours, and throw his shadows, and make us feel the earth under our feet . . . . . .

. . . The girl who escapes from her fellow-servants in their jollity by jumping up on horseback (and how about the horse? does that fine animal nowadays lend itself to such means of seduction?) behind a master of such a character, and being carried off by him in the middle of the night, naturally leaves her reputation behind her. 'At almost any other moment of her life she would have refused such proffered aid and company', Mr Hardy says, 'but coming as this invitation did at the particular juncture, when fear and indignation at her adversaries could be transformed by a spring of the foot into a triumph over them, she abandoned herself to her impulse, climbed the gate, put her toe upon his instep, and leapt into the saddle behind him' (p. 71). Thus poor Tess yields not to any impure suggestion, which is the last thing to be thought of in such a case, but to those mingled motives of vanity and excitement which have so large a share in this kind of moral downfall . . .

. . . And the unfortunate child thus brought into the world is also a most powerful agent in fiction. Generally it has been supposed by the story-teller to be a means of redemption for the fallen woman. One remembers how Mrs Browning treats it in *Aurora Leigh*, elevating and developing the being of the girl Marian, who is a still greater martyr than Tess, by the revelation of maternity and the glory of the new life. But the philosophy of enlightenment and the *fin de siècle* has nothing to do with such imaginations. Naturally a new creed must treat such a situation in a new way, especially when the principles of that creed are indignation (against whom? unhandsomely we are given to understand that it is against God – but then when there is no God?) and wrath, and have no sympathy with the everlasting reconstruction which another philosophy perceives to be going on for ever in the moral as well as in the material world . . . . . .

. . . We can at our ease gently deride David Grieve for being feminine, for he is the creation of a lady. But before Mr Angel Clare we stand aghast. What is he? Had he, too, been framed by a woman, how we should have smiled and pointed out his impossibility! This is how a man looks to the guileless feminine imagination, we should have said. But before the name of Mr Hardy we can only gasp and be silent. The thing must be male, we suppose, since a man made it, and it is certainly original as a picture of a man . . . . . .

We have not a word to say against the force and passion of this story. It is far finer in our opinion than anything Mr Hardy has ever done before. The character of Tess up to her last downfall, with the curious exceptions we have pointed out, is consistent enough, and we do not object to the defiant blazon of a Pure Woman, notwithstanding the early stain. But a Pure Woman is not betrayed into fine living and fine clothes as the mistress of her seducer by any stress of poverty or misery; and Tess was a skilled labourer, for whom it is very rare that nothing can be found to do. Here the elaborate and indignant plea for Vice, that it is really Virtue, breaks down altogether. We do not for a moment believe that Tess would have done it. Her creator has forced the rôle upon her, as he thinks (or says) that the God whom he does not believe in, does – which ought to make him a little more humble, since he cannot, it appears, do better himself. But whatever Mr Hardy says, we repeat that we do not believe him.[23] □

Reviewing *Tess of the d'Urbervilles* for the *Quarterly Review* (April 1892), Mowbray Morris found himself in a unique position because, as the editor of *Macmillan's Magazine*, he had earlier declined the manuscript for publication as a serial. In his derogatory review, after giving the reader a parodic account of the action of *Tess*, Morris summarises it thus: 'It is a queer story and seems to have been published in a queer manner'.[24] Morris notes smugly that some of Hardy's chapters that did not appear in the *Graphic* serial had to be 'relegated (as "episodic sketches") to other periodicals whose editors presumably take a more liberal view of their duties towards their neighbours, or whose readers are more habitually adult'.[25] This contemptuous review represents the most extreme antipathy to Tess's character and career. Morris is unable to countenance Hardy's powerful evocation of her sexuality, and is ironically unaware of the degree to which he implicates himself as consumer/voyeur when he says:

■ . . . Poor Tess's sensual qualifications for the part of heroine are paraded over and over again with a persistence like that of a horse-dealer egging on some wavering customer to a deal, or a slave-dealer appraising his wares to some full-blooded pasha . . .[26] □

Hardy's reaction to this is recorded in his notebook:

■ *Good Friday*. Read review of *Tess* in *The Quarterly*. A smart and amusing article; but it is easy to be smart and amusing if a man will forgo veracity and sincerity . . . How strange that one may write a book without knowing what one puts into it – or rather, the reader reads into it. Well, if this sort of thing continues no more novel-writing for me. A man must be a fool to deliberately stand up to be shot at.[27] □

An American perspective of *Tess of the d'Urbervilles* is offered by W. P. Trent, of the University of the South at Sewanee, Tennessee, later

Professor of English at Columbia University. His comment on *Tess* forms part of a longer review of Hardy's fiction in the *Sewanee Review* of November 1892. He feels that the sharply conflicting opinions of critics and readers of *Tess* make objective criticism difficult. Particularly he wished to avoid being drawn into a debate about the author's ideas. While recognising that Hardy has 'written a novel with a purpose', the 'power and movement' of the story obscure its underlying aim, which is revealed 'only when we read a review of it'.[28]

In a wholeheartedly enthusiastic essay, Trent boldly sets aside the debate about Tess's 'purity' and more boldly still the critics' 'chorus of praise and blame' for the novel, which to him seem 'beside the point'.[29] He sees the profound and entirely credible character of Tess as 'the greatest character in recent fiction'.[30] Like Sir William Watson in the *Academy*, but even more unequivocally, Trent stresses the elemental and universal nature of Tess, her stature as a heroine worthy of Shakespeare, and the intensity of tragic experience that makes her story profound. But, unlike previous reviewers, for Trent the novel's artistic triumph transcends Hardy's 'pessimism', and at its core incorporates a particular humanistic value:

■ . . . we see little use in arguing whether or not Tess was really pure. We may see some excuse for her second fall, another may not. But what no one can fail to see is that in Tess Mr Hardy has drawn a great character, nay, his greatest character, and we venture to say the greatest character in recent fiction. She seizes one at once and never looses her hold. What does it matter to us, from the point of view of art, whether she is pure or not, provided she does not repel us? There is here no allurement to sin, no attempt to make wrong right, no disposition to paint vice in the colours that belong to virtue. We see in her only a beautiful earth-born creature struggling against a fate too strong for her, a fate that brings her to a dishonoured grave, and yet not a fate that will cut her off from the peace and joy of another world than this. She is elemental, this peasant's daughter with the blood of a Norman noble in her veins. She has the elemental freshness, the odour of earth, that Mr Hardy's other peasants have, but she has also an elemental strength and nobility that they have not. This elemental freshness, this elemental strength and nobility, make her a woman fit to set in the gallery of Shakespeare's women – which is but to say that she is a creation of genius that time cannot devour. Her story is pure tragedy – the greatest tragedy, it seems to us, that has been written since the days of the Elizabethans – it lacks 'the accomplishment of verse', but at least it is told in the strongest and purest prose. If this be true, how vain to call it a horrible book? As well call the *Othello* horrible . . . Mr Hardy may take his leave of us with a pessimistic fling, but he succeeded malgré pessimism in producing a great work of art. He must have kept his eye fixed upon the nobleness, the pathos of his heroine's life, he must have seen a rift in the black sky above her, he must have sunk his realism in idealism, his pessimism in optimism, oftener than he was perhaps aware of ... ...

But *Tess* has merits that lie apart from the power of characterisation and of dramatic presentation which its author so constantly displays. Never has Mr Hardy's knowledge of nature stood him in better stead than in the descriptive passages which here and there break the tense thread of the action. They have the effect that all description should have in a novel, of heightening the impression which the author is endeavouring to convey by means of his characters and their actions. We read them only to plunge once more into the narrative of Tess's adventures with a sense of the impotence of nature to avert the doom of her choicest creation. At times it seems as if this modern Englishman were really a Greek endowed with the power of personifying the trees and streams past which his heroine glides, just as he seems to be a Greek in his never-ceasing sense of the presence of an inexorable fate. In fine, the Hardy of this novel is the Hardy who has charmed and impressed us before, but also a Hardy of heightened and matured powers – a master of fiction.[31] □

Meanwhile the feud with Andrew Lang, ignited by Hardy's comments in the Preface to the fifth edition of *Tess*, was fanned by Lang's rejoinder in which he engages in a lengthy explanation, in *Longman's Magazine* (November 1982), of his essential criticism of the novel. Unlike *Clarissa* or *Père Goriot*, or *Madame Bovary*, Lang asserts, Hardy's novel is not credible, partly due to its faulty style (again discovered to be similar to George Eliot's). Andrew Lang's antagonism prompted some reviewers to take sides, including D. F. Hannigan in the *Westminster Review* (December 1892) in an extended and strongly personal attack on Lang, who is characterised as a moralist seeking for the Ideal in literature:

■ Comfortable critics of this sort cannot sympathise with the temptations, the struggles, the miseries of a noble but half-darkened soul like that of poor Tess Durbeyfield. Mr Hardy himself has vigorously dealt with the 'genteel' reviewer in the preface to the fifth edition of the novel, and most rational persons will be inclined to think that Mr Lang cuts a very sorry figure under the lash of the novelist's just resentment ...[32] □

In another very interesting paragraph, Hannigan begins by asserting that the best critics put their own predilections aside and apply to a work under review impartial standards of judgement (as we saw, for example with Richard Holt Hutton). He then goes on to praise Hardy for including in *Tess* elements of scientific rationalism, and creating a naturalism that goes beyond even the conscious, hard-won realism of George Eliot. Strikingly, Hannigan places Hardy on a par with the great naturalist, Balzac:

■ . . . [*Tess*] is a monumental work. It marks a distinct epoch in English fiction. From beginning to end it bears the hall-mark of Truth on every page of it. It is a more impressive narrative of crushing facts than George Eliot's *Adam Bede*. It is more deep and poignant than anything that either Zola or Guy de Maupassant has written. It is a work worthy of Balzac himself . . . [33] □

As ever, George Eliot remains the standard for reviewers, and like earlier critics Hannigan notes that stylistically Hardy falls into similar faults, but he dismisses this minor complaint by asserting Hardy's assumption of the mantle of the great realist, and at the same time his radical departure from her:

■ There are spots on the sun. The fact remains that *Tess of the d'Urbervilles* is the greatest work of fiction produced in England since George Eliot died . . . [Hardy] has revolutionised English fiction. [34] □

These contemporary reviews regard Hardy's dominant subject as being the creation of Wessex, with its focus on the peasantry of the south-west of England. They identify his pessimistic conception of life, his tragic vision, and his debts to Greek drama. Along with this goes the universal nature of his characters, his scenes and his landscapes. Some reviewers detect a Shakespearean quality in his work; others already perceive him as modern; while still others find in this heir to George Eliot the essential quality of realism – an allegiance to the ordinary, the natural, the believable and the true. Underlying all this is an endorsement of Hardy's humanism, which the reviewers construe as involving opposition to the industrial and the urban. But they are also preoccupied with what they specify as flaws: surrealistic plotting, artifice, the melodramatic, the sensational and the violent, improbable characterisation, and an intermittently pedantic style.

Allowing for differences of emphasis, these broad critical perceptions established some of the commonplaces that governed Hardy criticism during the last decade of the nineteenth century and well into the twentieth. However, as the following chapter will demonstrate, the post-Victorian assessment of *Tess of the d'Urbervilles* was also characterised by tentative exploration and a widening critical focus, which marked a serious endeavour to evaluate a novelist who was perceived increasingly as eluding categorisation.

CHAPTER TWO

Post-Victorian Stocktaking: Evaluation and Consolidation: 1894–1949

CRITICAL REACTION to *Tess of the d'Urbervilles* immediately following the close of Hardy's career as a novelist has to be viewed in the context of his final work, *Jude the Obscure*, which was published in 1895. Even more outspokenly controversial than *Tess*, it was perceived as subversive and degenerate for its frank discussion of the status of marriage in Victorian society, its attack on restrictive social conventions, its criticism of the class-bound exclusivity of the higher education system, and its brooding over the nature of morality and spiritual faith. Hardy had already had to hack the novel about for serialisation in *Harper's New Monthly Magazine* to placate Mrs Grundy, and its publication aroused a whirlwind of protest. By this time Hardy had had enough. He had reached the limits of what he could express in fiction, and there was no financial obstacle to a return to the writing of poetry.

Then began a long period up to 1949, during which critical studies appeared that viewed *Tess of the d'Urbervilles* in the context of Hardy's fictional *oeuvre*, including the gloomy and iconoclastic *Jude*. Setting out to evaluate Hardy's stature as a novelist, they are tentative and exploratory, and tend to consolidate as areas of enquiry those issues in *Tess* that had attracted the attention of its first reviewers.

However, the first book-length studies of Hardy, Lionel Johnson's *The Art of Thomas Hardy* and Annie Macdonnell's *Thomas Hardy* came out in 1894, before *Jude the Obscure* was published. Annie Macdonnell's book is impressionistic and critically naïve, but Lionel Johnson's work on Hardy's fiction has stood the test of time. A poet, a member of the Rhymers' Club, and a friend of W. B. Yeats, Johnson was also a Catholic convert and, like Richard Holt Hutton and Mrs Oliphant, his Christian belief colours his writing. Although his highly intelligent study quarrels with Hardy's ideas and narrative strategy, it is acutely responsive to the novel's tragic power and raises fundamental issues that later critics were to return to frequently. Johnson's rewarding discussion of *Tess of the d'Urbervilles* forms part of a book that explores aspects of Hardy's art in an urbane and leisurely manner, offers an illuminating and judicious assessment, and ushers in a period, up to the First World War, during which Hardy's reputation as a novelist was consolidated.

Claiming to have read the novel 'some eight or ten times',[1] Johnson admits to being mastered by the book's grandeur of conception and its human tragedy. From his early reference to the *Oresteia*,[2] it is clear that his critical reference point is Greek tragedy, and also the tragic theory of Aristotle. However, Johnson finds Hardy's narrative procedures in *Tess* awkward, particularly his interventions in its tragic experience – his refusal to allow tragic facts to speak for themselves:

■ ... **Either the story should bear its own burden of spiritual sorrow, each calamity and woe crushing out of us all hope, by its own resistless weight: or the bitter sentences of comment should be lucid and cogent ...** [3] □

Johnson also laments Hardy's inartistic introduction of topics that gesture towards philosophical debate:

■ ... **But it is useless to attempt a combination of methods: when the reader is following the fortunes of Tess, he hates to fall into some track of thought, which leads him to the debateable land, where he must listen to Aristotle and Rousseau, Aquinas and Hegel, Hobbes and Mill, Sir Henry Maine and Mr Herbert Spencer.[4] It is a question of manner: things, intolerable in one manner, are delightful in another ...** [5] □

Not only that, Johnson also anticipates many subsequent critics when he objects impatiently that Hardy's narratorial interjections are both diverse and confusing:

■ ... **But Mr Hardy is not content to frame his indictment, by the stern narration of sad facts: he inserts fragments of that reasoning, which has brought him to his dark conclusion. They are too many, too bitter, too passionate, to be but an overflow, as it were, from his narration: they are too sparse, too ironical, too declamatory, to be quite intelligible. After enjoying their grimness, I want definitions of *nature, law, society,* and *justice*: the want is coarse, doubtless, and unimaginative; but I cannot suppress it ...** [6] □

Lionel Johnson's argument proceeds by summarising and paraphrasing Hardy's comments scattered throughout the novel on the Wordsworthian view of 'Nature's holy plan' (p. 28) (further references by critics to Hardy's anti-Wordsworthian stance in *Tess* may be found on pp. 43, 58, 132 and 161 of this Guide), and noting his views of the world as a 'psychological phenomenon' (p. 91), of an 'unsympathetic first cause' (p. 158), of the suffering of children for their fathers' sins, and of the fiendish, sportive, unjust treatment of Tess by fate (p. 384):

▪ I know not, who can lie under a stronger necessity to realise the sorrow of the world, than a Catholic: but he lies under no obligation to abnegate his reason: and I cannot, with all the will in the world, to understand Mr Hardy's indictment, understand one word of it. Making all allowance for mere sentiment, and all deductions for mere passion, I can see in it but a tangle of inconsistencies. What is this 'Nature', of which or of whom, Mr Hardy speaks? Is it a *Natura naturata*, [nature created] or a *Natura naturans*, [nature creating]? Is it a conscious Power? or a convenient name for the whole mass of physical facts? . . . [7] □

Hardy's statement is found to be 'a tangle of inconsistencies' and Johnson goes on, with severe logic, to worry about the matter of Tess's relations to nature and to society:

▪ . . . And Mr Hardy's praise of nature is in the very dialect of the eighteenth century: the suggestion, that on a desert island, away from censorious eyes, Tess would have felt innocent and unashamed, is worthy of Rousseau. Nature alone has essential laws: society has but expedient laws; 'arbitrary', in the sense that they are *only* expedient. Such seems to be Mr Hardy's position. Now, the misfortune of Tess, her seduction, was in conformity with Nature, as a simple, physical occurence: it was out of conformity with Society, because it broke a social law, necessary, if arbitrary: but a state of Nature precedes a state of Society, and has therefore deeper, wider, larger laws: Society, then, was but prejudiced in favour of its own well-being, when it condemned Tess: therefore Society was unjust, preferring its necessary laws of expediency to the great fundamental laws of Nature. Tess, from fulfilling against her will her natural function, was driven on by iron forces, till at last she committed murder: she could not help herself: why was she hanged, unless to amuse God? True, she was at first haunted by a sense of guilt: but conscience is a conventional thing, the utilitarian product of racial experience: it merely meant, that her misfortune, though nothing in the sight of Nature, belonged to a class of acts prejudicial to Society: true, she yielded at the last to her old seducer; but that was in despair, and to help her family; she was but *vulning* [wounding] herself, as heralds say of the pelican in her piety; and, once more, since the rabbits and the pheasants would have seen no harm in it, why should she, merely an animal, higher in the scale of physical development?

It is perplexing: some one, some thing, must be to blame. It cannot be Nature, because you cannot blame an abstraction: it cannot be Society, unless you would have it commit suicide: it must be God.

Like flies to wanton boys, are we to the gods:
They kill us for their sport . . . [8] □

Johnson contrasts Hardy with Aeschylus, whose tragic drama lacks Hardy's bitterness because he has faith in divine justice. As one might expect, given his Catholicism, Johnson's main ground of disagreement with Hardy turns out to be metaphysical. He objects to the dominance of contemporary scientific rationalism, to Hardy's emphasis on determinism as the mainspring of the tragedy in *Tess*, and particularly to the biological determinism which issues in Tess's 'inherited nature', which leads her first to strike and then kill Alec d'Urberville:

■ But, winning and appealing as she seems, there remains in the background that haunting and disenchanting thought, that upon the determinist principle, she could not help herself: she fulfilled a mechanical destiny. There is nothing tragic in that, except by an illusion: like any other machine, she 'did her work', and that is all . . .
    The tragedy of Tess does indeed rouse in us 'pity and fear': it does indeed purge us of 'pity and fear': but with what a parody of Aristotle! . . . Upon Mr Hardy's principles, there was no real struggle of the will with adverse circumstances, no conflict of emotions, nor battle of passions: all was fated and determined: the apparent energies of will, regrets of soul, in Tess, were but as the muscular movements of a dead body: 'Simulars' of freedom and of life. Our pity and our fear are not purified merely: they are destroyed, and no room is left for them . . . 'All this passion, sorrow, and death, inevitable and sure, to come upon one poor girl, whose struggles were ordained by the same force, that ordained their vanity! Is there no tragedy in that?' I can find none: I can find in it nothing, but a reason for keeping unbroken silence. Least of all, do I find in it an excuse for setting up a scarecrow God, upon whom to vent our spleen.[9] □

However, argues Johnson, although the author's control of his own text is fallible, *Tess of the d'Urbervilles* does not finally depend for its effect on textual consistency. It is entirely possible to reconstruct the novel's tragic experience and meaning by ignoring Hardy's intrusive 'ideas' and narrative voice, by appropriating the novel's imaginative core and rejecting its polemic (which is pretty much what Richard Holt Hutton did):

■ . . . But without changing a single incident of the story, it is possible to reject Mr Hardy's moral: read it apart from his commentary, and it loses nothing of its strength: rather, it gains much. Tess is no longer presented to us, as predestined to her fate: she once more takes the tragic place . . . like Maggie Tulliver,[10] Tess might have gone to Thomas à Kempis:[11] one of the very few writers, whom experience does not prove untrue. She went through fire and water, and made no true use of them: she is pitiable, but not admirable.[12] □

The criticism of Lascelles Abercrombie (*Thomas Hardy: A Critical Study*, 1912) is more typical of its period than that of Johnson. In some respects an impressionistic study, it endorses Hardy as a writer of great tragedy and makes the by now ritual reference to Greek drama. Abercrombie marginalises those dimensions of the novel that deal with life in nineteenth-century rural society in order to foreground his own humanistic concerns:

■ . . . Tess is described, in the title of her history, with challenging defiance, as 'a pure woman faithfully presented'; but the protest for which this prepares us, is not uttered against the stupid logic of society. That, to be sure, is pilloried; but much more than that; Tess's tragedy is a specimen syllogism in the cruel reasoning of universal fate. Her tortured life, unnecessarily sensitive, is nothing but the symbolic language wherein the premisses of fate are quietly and ruthlessly worked out; and it is the useless fact that she is sensitive – that fate, for its rapt arguing with itself, has invented the medium of human life, utterly careless that it is a medium exquisitely tormented by the processes of this transcendent reasoning – it is this useless fact which stirs Hardy to fill the record of her life, not with pathos or pity, but with irreconcilable indignation against the prime, tragic condition of life . . .[13] □

In the process of striving to identify what he calls the epic motive of *Tess*, Abercrombie develops an illuminating perception about the conflictual nature of Hardy's imagination:

■ . . . It is decidedly uncommon in a work of art, such intense and personal regard on the part of the author for his own creation; and it is likely that this is what upset, and perhaps still upsets, the critical balance of some readers. But this noticeable dualism in *Tess of the d'Urbervilles* is exceedingly important for the conveying of the epic motive of the whole book – the dualism of a merciless, unhesitating tragic imagination, and an impotent fervour of charity for its central figure; charity that seems always desiring to protect this figure from the steady, injurious process of the imagination which conceived her, yet can do nothing but painfully watch her destruction . . . [14] □

And this 'epic motive', Abercrombie argues, is worked out in terms of the book's form; the way its central conflict between Tess's will to enjoy and the willed circumstances that operate against this contributes to the novel's unity of purpose and statement:

■ . . . From first to last, *Tess of the d'Urbervilles* is one relentless onward movement. The human narrative, the surrounding nature, the accompaniment of intellectual and emotional significance, all weave inextricably together, and go forward dominated by a unity of purpose; they unite in a single epic statement, formidable in its bare simplicity, of the conflict between personal and impersonal – the conflict which is the inmost vitality of all Hardy's noblest work.[15] □

By 1916, when Henry Charles Duffin's book, *Thomas Hardy*, was published, Hardy's eminence as a novelist was assured. Like so many early critics, Duffin's critical allegiance is to simple photographic realism, credible characterisation, classical tragedy and a humanistic underpinning of Hardy's idealisation of human nature. Interestingly however, he also engages with the contemporary debate about nature and nurture, and contrasts Hardy's emphasis on biological determinism with George Bernard Shaw's polemical demonstration of the power of environment:

■ . . . Hardy's making Tess the offspring of the father we have seen and the mother we are shortly to see reminds us of Candida and the equally impossible Burgess.[16] But whereas Shaw's point is that education and environment can obliterate heredity, Hardy's is that in the absence of such education and meliorative environment heredity is everything . . . [17] □

After tracing this idea in the text, Duffin concludes:

■ . . . Tess herself is the most sublime figure in Hardy, combining supreme beauty with a nobility that elevates the whole conception of human nature. And yet she is not, like Marty South,[18] flawless: she has the *harmartia*, the fatal weakness, necessary to give tragedy a rational if not a moral basis . . . [19] □

Alongside these general studies of Hardy's achievement there started up avenues of enquiry of a more specialised kind, which laid foundations for later critical explorations. Helen Garwood's *Thomas Hardy: An Illustration of the Philosophy of Schopenhauer*, published in 1911, examines

Hardy the philosopher and focuses on his conception of the Immanent Will. In 1922 Joseph Warren Beach published a study of Hardy's narrative art, *The Technique of Thomas Hardy*, while another area of investigation was opened up in 1927 by Mary Ellen Chase with the appearance of *Thomas Hardy: From Serial to Novel*. Characteristic of Chase's procedures is her chapter on *Tess of the d'Urbervilles*, where she compares the text of the first edition with that of the serial version that had appeared in the *Graphic*. For the sake of analysis she divides *Tess* into a series of 'incidents'. This, for instance, is her conclusion to her study of 'incident seven', Tess's confession to her mother of her seduction by Alec d'Urberville:

■ Finally, in view of the preceding facts, I assume that the serial version of incident seven is a makeshift, substituted in place of the book version, unwillingly, no doubt, and, I must think, without sufficient care by Hardy, who must have known that it lacked in itself sufficient motivation, consistency of character, and literary merit, but who was constrained either by his editor or by his own judgement to refrain from shocking the conventionalised taste of the *Graphic*'s reading public.[20] □

Although now superseded by the textual work of J.T. Laird, Mary Jacobus and Simon Gatrell, who appear later in this Guide, Mary Ellen Chase's study was the first to illustrate the kind of damage that Hardy had to do to his work in order to get it published in the magazines. She also demonstrates that, in spite of Hardy's statement in his Preface that he is printing the novel complete in its original version, he in fact revised it not only during its progress from serial to first edition but also in subsequent editions, to enhance its realism. *Tess of the d'Urbervilles* is revealed as being, from its early stages, a radically unstable text, which Hardy was continually revising and refining.

The response to *Tess* of the great Modernists, Virginia Woolf and D.H. Lawrence, is of particular interest. The extracts below come from Woolf's appreciation of Hardy, first published in the *Times Literary Supplement* (19 January 1928) on the occasion of Hardy's death (later printed as 'The Novels of Thomas Hardy' in *The Common Reader: Second Series*, 1932). In general terms Woolf endorses the traditional tragi-comic novelist of Wessex. She also implicitly contrasts her own novels about the nature of consciousness, personal relations and social life with Hardy's symbolic and idealised rendering of human nature in its tragic force, most strikingly in *Tess of the d'Urbervilles*:

■ . . . If we do not know his men and women in their relations to each other, we know them in their relations to time, death, and fate. If we do not see them in quick agitation against the lights and crowds of cities, we see them against the earth, the storm, and the seasons. We know their attitude towards some of the most tremendous problems that can confront mankind. They take on a more than mortal size in memory. We see them, not in detail but enlarged and dignified. We see Tess reading the baptismal service in her nightgown 'with a touch of dignity that was almost regal' (p. 99) . . . They have a force in them which cannot be defined, a force of love or of hate, a force which in the men is the cause of rebellion against life, and in the women implies an illimitable capacity for suffering, and it is this which dominates the character and makes it unnecessary that we should see the finer features that lie hid. This is the tragic power; and, if we are to place Hardy among his fellows, we must call him the greatest tragic writer among English novelists.[21] □

D. H. Lawrence's famous essay, 'Study of Thomas Hardy', is a notable landmark in Hardy criticism. Although written in 1914–15, it was not published until six years after Lawrence's death in *Phoenix: The Post-humous Papers of D. H. Lawrence* (1936). In this original and penetrating psychological interpretation of human sexuality, Hardy's characters are seen as striving for some form of self-definition against the forces of social convention. Lawrence's passionate rhetoric and idiosyncratic style render his meaning at first sight unclear. It is evident from his discussion of Tess as an 'aristocrat' that he includes within this term the traditional idea of her inherited d'Urberville nobility; but more important he also employs the term to signify archetypal characters who display deeply instinctual traits and the possession of a profound sense of selfhood. In Tess it is this latter attribute, instinctual rather than moral and involving a passivity that amounts to a weakness, that marks her as a victim, as Lawrence urges in the following extract:

■ . . . She is of an old line, and has the aristocratic quality of respect for the other being. She does not see the other person as an extension of herself, existing in a universe of which she is the centre and pivot. She knows that other people are outside her. Therein she is an aristocrat . . .

Tess is passive out of self-acceptance, a true aristocratic quality, amounting almost to self-indifference. She knows she is herself incontrovertibly, and she knows that other people are not herself. This is a very rare quality, even in a woman. And in a civilization so unequal, it is almost a weakness.

Tess never tries to alter or to change anybody, neither to alter nor to change nor to divert. What another person decides, that is his decision. She respects utterly the other's right to be. She is herself always.[22] □

Lawrence also identifies an aristocratic quality in the archetypal maleness of Alec d'Urberville, whose compulsion to pursue the female is driven by a deep psychological need to compensate for his essential incompleteness:

■ There seems to be in d'Urberville an inherent antagonism to any progression in himself. Yet he seeks with all his power for the source of stimulus in woman. He takes the deep impulse from the female. In this he is exceptional. No ordinary man could really have betrayed Tess. Even if she had had an illegitimate child to another man, to Angel Clare, for example, it would not have shattered her as did her connection with Alec d'Urberville. For Alec d'Urberville could reach some of the real sources of the female in a woman, and draw from them. And, as a woman instinctively knows, such men are rare. Therefore they have a power over a woman. They draw from the depth of her being. [23] □

But, Lawrence continues, Alec knows only sensual gratification and is unable to submit to the impulse he receives:

■ Which was why Tess was shattered by Alec d'Urberville, and why she murdered him in the end. The murder is badly done, altogether the book is botched, owing to the way of thinking in the author, owing to the weak yet obstinate theory of being. Nevertheless, the murder is true, the whole book is true, in its conception.[24] □

For Lawrence then, Tess and Alec are aristocrats in a spiritual and symbolic sense, as representatives of their essential natures of male and female:

■ And just as the aristocratic principle had isolated Tess, it had isolated Alec d'Urberville. For though Hardy consciously made the young betrayer a plebian and an imposter, unconsciously, with the supreme justice of the artist, he made him . . . a true aristocrat . . . [25] □

Angel Clare, on the other hand, is subjected to Lawrence's penetrating psychological analysis of his radical self-division. Unlike Alec d'Urberville, as a result of his Christian indoctrination, he has rejected the female dimension of his personality that reverences the flesh. His endeavour to engage with Tess reveals the split within him between the repressed Female Principle and what Lawrence calls the 'Male Principle, of Abstraction, of Good, of Public Good, of the Community'.[26]

It is because Lawrence is concerned with the unconscious motivation of character that Tess, Alec and Angel are for him beyond moral judgement.

Yet Tess is still perceived in traditional terms as a victim of their insistent claims upon her. In the following passage Lawrence traces the psychological process of her tragic undoing:

■ It is not Angel Clare's fault that he cannot come to Tess when he finds that she has, in his words, been defiled. It is the result of generations of ultra-Christian training, which had left in him an inherent aversion to the female, and to all in himself which pertained to the female. What he, in his Christian sense, conceived of as Woman, was only the servant and attendant and administering spirit to the male. He had no idea that there was such a thing as positive Woman, as the Female, another great living Principle counterbalancing his own male principle. He conceived of the world as consisting of the One, the Male Principle . . . . . .

And Tess, despising herself in the flesh, despising the deep Female she was, because Alec d'Urberville had betrayed her very source, loved Angel Clare, who also despised and hated the flesh. She did not hate d'Urberville. What a man did, he did, and if he did it to her, it was her look-out. She did not conceive of him as having any human duty towards her.

The same with Angel Clare as with Alec d'Urberville. She was very grateful to him for saving her from her despair of contamination, and from her bewildered isolation. But when he accused her, she could not plead or answer. For she had no right to his goodness. She stood alone.

The female was strong in her. She was herself. But she was out of place, utterly out of her element and her times. Hence her utter bewilderment. This is the reason why she was so overcome. She was outwearied from the start, in her spirit. For it is only by receiving from all our fellows that we are kept fresh and vital. Tess was herself, female, intrinsically a woman.

The female in her was indomitable, unchangeable, she was utterly constant to herself. But she was, by long breeding, intact from mankind. Though Alec d'Urberville was of no kin to her, yet, in the book, he has always a quality of kinship. It was as if only a kinsman, an aristocrat, could approach her. And this to her undoing. Angel Clare would never have reached her. She would have abandoned herself to him, but he would never have reached her. It needed a physical aristocrat. She would have lived with her husband, Clare, in a state of abandon to him, like a coma. Alec d'Urberville forced her to realise him, and to realise herself. He came close to her, as Clare could never have done. So she murdered him. For she was herself.[27] □

At the opposite pole to Lawrence's psychological reading were the early tentative steps in the investigation of Hardy's intellectual development, exemplified by William R. Rutland's *Thomas Hardy: A Study of His Writings and their Background* (1938). This was the first scholarly endeavour to attempt to trace the influence on Hardy of his reading in Greek and the Bible, and of the general climate of Victorian thought. Rutland's discussion of *Tess* follows Lionel Johnson's view that Hardy's indictment of society lacked consistency, but Rutland sees Hardy's complaint against the universe as the result of cumulative cultural influences:

■ The natural, almost inevitable, culmination of this spiritual development is the notorious sentence at the end of *Tess*: 'The President of the Immortals (in Aeschylean phrase) had ended his sport with Tess' (p. 384) . . .
. . . he did not, by those words, intend to signify what believers in a personal Deity signify by the word God. At the time when he wrote *Tess* he was no longer able to conceive the Prime Cause as a personal Deity . . . he was, when he wrote that famous sentence, doing much more than employ a mere figure of speech. He was deliberately reviling, under the name 'President of the Immortals' that which he afterwards came to call the Immanent Will . . . [28] □

William Rutland takes a traditional view of tragedy, appealing to Aristotelian criteria. But *Tess* falls short of these since its element of terror lies in the background rather than in the substance of the story; an element of conflict is lacking because right is on one side only; and Tess is a victim rather than the chief cause of her own catastrophe. So for Rutland (as for Lionel Johnson) *Tess of the d'Urbervilles* is a tragedy of pity:

■ . . . Were it altogether true that neither our pity nor our fear are purified by *Tess*, the book would, of course, not grip us as it does. *Jude the Obscure*, to one reader at least, comes under the condemnation of complete failure on this count. But in *Tess*, one of Aristotle's desiderata remains. We may remain unmoved by the President of the Immortals. But our pity is surely purified.[29] □

An important year in the process of Hardy stocktaking, 1940, was marked by the appearance of Carl J. Weber's biography, *Hardy of Wessex*, which sought to identify in Hardy's life incidents, places and people who contributed to the creation of his fictions. And in the same year the *Southern Review*, a journal founded and developed under the impetus of the New Criticism (see chapter three of this Guide) produced a 'Thomas Hardy Issue', whose essays submitted Hardy's texts to a more objective scrutiny than had been employed before.

Although Morton Dauwen Zabel's essay, 'Hardy in Defence of his Art: The Aesthetic of Incongruity', only glances at *Tess*, it should be mentioned as indicating how far the gradual revision of Hardy had come. A penetrating piece of criticism, Zabel's discussion sets out Hardy's essential aesthetic, whose incongruous elements of anti-realism are seen as arising from the dichotomies within his own character, a discordance that 'Hardy saw . . . as a primary rift or dichotomy in man which post-rationalist Europe had thrown into a new relief'.[30] Zabel argues forcefully that Hardy self-consciously developed a personal aesthetic out of the connection between pessimism and humanism but that 'what Schopenhauer arrived at by something resembling a counsel of desperation, Hardy arrived at by the humane insight and compassion of a great artist', as he moved 'from doubt and negation to humanistic hope'.[31] Summarising this, Zabel sees Hardy as essentially modern:

■ Hardy becomes in his poetics something very different from the victim of scientific determinism that the literal reading of his novels and key-phrases makes him . . . His force as a stylist, dramatist, and allegorist is clarified by his refusal to fall in with the restrictions of naturalism, or with an aesthetic based on the rigid and obvious congruities of physical fact . . . by those brilliant strokes of dramatic incident which illuminate and suddenly justify the wildness of his plots – the door closed against Mrs Yeobright, the tree-planting by Marty and Winterborne,[32] Tess's seeing the blood-stained paper as she stands ringing the bell of the empty house of Clare's parents. He now appears to us as a realist developing towards allegory – as an imaginative artist who brought the nineteenth century novel out of its slavery to fact and its dangerous reaction against popularity, and so prepared the way for some of the most original talents of a new time . . . the achievements of Joyce, Proust, Gide, and Kafka.[33] □

In another stimulating *Southern Review* essay, 'The Traditional Basis of Thomas Hardy's Fiction', Donald Davidson focuses on the issue of incongruity from a different point of view, drawing on a vein of Hardy criticism that includes, among other works, Ruth Firor's *Folkways in Thomas Hardy* (1931). Essentially Davidson regards Hardy's fiction as having little to do with nineteenth-century realism or naturalism. Its influences derive, he suggests, not from his studies in Greek drama, nor his encounter with 'Darwinian theory and modern social problems',[34] but from his early conception of the traditional art of story-telling in the Dorset of his boyhood. Davidson bases his essay on his belief that Hardy had an instinctive affinity with the old stories that was absolutely central in his art. Davidson also has a New Critical concern with the text's organic unity, and from this perspective Hardy's narratives, his settings and their mythology may be seen as contributing to a coherent whole:

■ My thesis is that the characteristic Hardy novel is conceived as a *told* (or *sung*) story, or at least not as a literary story; that it is an extension, in the form of a modern prose fiction, of a traditional ballad or an oral tale . . . The conscious side of his art manifests itself in two ways: first he 'works up' his core of traditional, or non-literary, narrative into a literary form; but, second, at the same time he labours to establish, in his 'Wessex', the kind of artistic climate and environment which will enable him to handle his traditional story with conviction – a world in which typical ballad heroes and heroines can flourish with a thoroughly rationalised 'mythology' to sustain them . . . [35] □

Tess is readily identified as the heroine of traditional ballads:

■ Tess of the d'Urbervilles, whatever else she may be, is once more the deserted maiden who finally murders her seducer with a knife in the effective ballad way. And she, with the love-stricken trio – Marian, Retty, and Izz – is a milkmaid; and milkmaids, in balladry, folk song, and folk tale, are somehow peculiarly subject to seduction. [36] □

For Davidson, Hardy's anti-realistic bias stems from a profound feeling for narrative, rather than from the influence of contemporary sensational fiction. Hardy keeps to the improbable, rather than indulging in the supernatural. And the oral tradition that lies behind his writing takes no account of such concepts as 'pessimism':

■ . . . In formal doctrine Hardy professed himself to be an 'evolutionary meliorist', or almost a conventional modern. But that had nothing to do with the stories that started up in his head. The charge of pessimism has about the same relevance as the charge of indelicacy which Hardy encountered when he first began to publish. An age of polite literature, which had lost touch with the oral arts – except so far as they might survive in chit-chat, gossip, and risqué stories – could not believe that an author who embodied in his serious stories the typical seductions, rapes, murders, and lusty love-makings of the old tradition intended anything but a breach of decorum . . . But Hardy did not know he was being rough, and had no more notion than a ballad-maker of turning out a story to be either pessimistic or optimistic . . .

To be sure, Hardy is a little to blame, since he does moralise at times. But the passage about the President of the Immortals in *Tess* . . . probably came to him like such ballad tags as 'Better they'd never been born' . . . [37] □

It is in Hardy's creation of changeless characters that Davidson finds confirmation of this habit of mind; traditional figures who find their parallels in epic, saga, romance and ballads, who live in passive accommodation to unchanging nature, the basis of Wessex life, but whose struggle with one or more modern characters comprises the story:

■ . . . In *Tess* there are two changeful and ruin-wreaking characters. In Alec Stoke-d'Urberville the changeful character takes on a vulgar form. He is an impostor, who has appropriated an old country name and bought his way into Wessex; and the Stoke-d'Urberville establishment, with its preposterous chicken culture, is a fake rural establishment. Angel Clare, on the other hand, is a rarified form of alien. He is willing, condescendingly, to accept Wessex, and dairy farming, and Tess, provided he can possess all this in an abstractly 'pure', or respectable form. The tragedy arrives when he cannot adjust (the sociological term is necessary) his delicate sensibility to a gross, but, in the natural order, an understandable biological fact. It is the changeful modern character in Angel that cannot abide Tess's delinquency. The changeless characters might have found fault, but would not have been shocked, would not have sulked, would not have been slow to pardon . . . [38] □

Davidson sees the strength of Hardy's humanism in *Tess*, as in his other Wessex fictions, as being rooted in his relationship with his own rural society and the values expressed in its traditional tales, rather than in his own preferred 'evolutionary meliorism' or the 'pessimism' foisted on him by critics. And it embodies a flight from nineteenth-century realism. Davidson summarises thus:

■ . . . The achievement is the more extraordinary when we consider that he worked (if I read his career rightly) against the dominant pattern of his day. He did what the modern critic (despite his concern about tradition) is always implying to be impossible. That is, Hardy accepted the assumptions of a society which in England was already being condemned to death, and he wrote in terms of those assumptions, almost as if Wessex, and perhaps Wessex only, would understand . . . [39] □

The *Southern Review* essays of Zabel and Davidson reveal a new perception of Hardy as a novelist transitional between the dominant narrative basis of traditional fiction and the anti-realistic, symbolist techniques of the moderns. Another indicator of the stage the evaluation of Hardy had reached in the early 1940s was the publication in 1943 of Lord David Cecil's influential book, *Hardy the Novelist*, which marks Hardy's status among academic critics, since in its earlier form it was a series of Clark Lectures given at Trinity College, Cambridge in 1942. It is a lucid study, responsive to the visual and poetic qualities in Hardy's fiction, but it is also a fairly conventional assessment of those strengths and weaknesses to which his earliest reviewers first drew attention. References to *Tess of the d'Urbervilles* scattered throughout the book are drawn together here.

Cecil points to the intensely visualising and symbolising nature of Hardy's imagination in the sleepwalking scene in *Tess*, which 'suggests that the superhuman force of Destiny is compelling her irresistibly towards her death and that Angel is a blind instrument in the hands of this Destiny'.[40] It is an imagination, argues Cecil, that creates 'simple, elemental characters, actuated by simple, elemental passions . . . And the fact that they are seen in relation to ultimate Destiny gives them a gigantic and universal character'.[41] Cecil goes on to develop this theme:

▣ Indeed, Hardy – and here he is very different from almost every other great novelist – does not put his chief stress on individual qualities. As I have said, he writes about man, not about men. Though his great characters are distinguished one from another clearly enough, their individual qualities are made subsidiary to their typical human qualities. And as their stories increase in tension, so do his characters tend to shed individual differences and to assume the impersonal majesty of a representative of all mankind. Giles [Winterborne in *The Woodlanders*] stands for all faithful lovers, Tess [Durbeyfield in *Tess of the d'Urbervilles*] for all betrayed women, Eustacia [Vye in *The Return of the Native*] for all passionate imprisoned spirits.[42] □

In this context Hardy's employment of 'Wessex' intensifies the novels because, 'Concentrated in this narrow, sequestered form of life, the basic facts of the human drama showed up at their strongest; undisturbed by other distractions, the basic human passions burned at their hottest.'[43] Like Virginia Woolf, Cecil also recognises the great tragedian's affinity with the Elizabethan drama, and regards his movement away from realism as being in pursuit of tragic intensity. But Hardy is denied the achievement of Shakespeare because of his pessimism: while Shakespeare's tragic theme is man's struggle with omnipotent fate, Hardy's characters inhabit a meaningless existential world:

■ . . . Hardy's characters may be the Elizabethan characters; but how different they look when we realise that the fierce passions animating them are ineffectual to influence their destiny, that their ideal beliefs and fantasies fleet but for a moment across a background of nothingness . . . . . . For Hardy's characters . . . death is only the same meaningless and haphazard extinction as must in the end overtake alike the greatest hero and the meanest insect. They confront it with outward fortitude or outward resignation, they may even welcome it as a release from the intolerable agony of living, but always they meet it with despair in their hearts. Shakespeare's tragic emotion is a blazing flame; Hardy's broods like a thundercloud.[44] □

Cecil's humanist appraisal attempts a balanced assessment of Hardy, whose greatness, as the nineteenth-century critics believed, is flawed by didacticism, stylistic lapses, and improbabilities in both characterisation and plotting. For instance, Cecil points out, Hardy does not try to make Alec d'Urberville's conversion probable by hinting at a psychological cause, and when for the purposes of the plot he turns villain again, Hardy offers no convincing explanation. Indeed:

■ . . . All through his books, the reader is liable to knock up against these crude pieces of machinery, tearing the delicate fabric of imaginative illusion in tatters.[45] □

This study is very much a wartime book, written in the context of upheaval and threat. It is concerned with the values of tradition and stability to be found in an idyllic English rural countryside, and in the great heroic literature of the English past; and thus in a narrow sense it fulfils a political, patriotic function, as Cecil's nostalgic conclusion suggests:

■ . . . We take our farewell gaze at the England of Shakespeare through the eyes of one who, in spite of all his imperfections, is the last English writer to be built on the grand Shakespearean scale.[46] □

A more sophisticated work is Harvey Curtis Webster's *On A Darkling Plain: The Art and Thought of Thomas Hardy*, published in 1947, which explores the development of Hardy's philosophy in the context of nineteenth-century thought; tracing his loss of religious faith and the influence of scientific rationalism, particularly the deterministic and evolutionary ideas that came from Darwin. Webster does not treat the fiction as exemplifying Hardy's view of life, but rather sees the novels as embodying his search for a coherent philosophy. He tracks a shift in Hardy's thinking from the strong early influence of determinism to the impact of radical ideas and urgent social issues in later novels such as *Tess of the d'Urbervilles*.

In *Tess*, Webster argues, Hardy's assault on social conventions is contained within a view of life that is essentially pessimistic:

■ Hardy's avowed intention in *Tess of the d'Urbervilles* . . . was to present a story in which the conventions would be so reversed that a seduced girl becomes the heroine. If this true sequence of events should offend some, he asks that they remember that it is better that an offence should come out of the truth than that the truth should not be told. From Hardy's defensive attitude in this Preface to the work, one assumes that he is about to attack society more wholeheartedly than he has done before – an assumption that the book as a whole confirms. But *Tess* nonetheless illustrates the 'pessimistic' view of the world that has frequently been assumed to be the philosophy of the Wessex novels.

The characters and the author stress the magnipotence of Fate. Izz, Marian, and Retty do not blame Tess for winning the man they love. 'Twas to be. Although she was at first inclined to believe herself mistress of her fate, Tess soon begins to admit the fatalistic convictions of the neighbouring field folk, who associate more with natural phenomena than with man . . . [47] □

Webster goes on to demonstrate, with considerable subtlety, the elements that comprise this pessimistic philosophy – the impact on the unreflective peasants of Tess's fate, Hardy's sympathy with their fatalising, the insignificance of humanity, the inexorability of universal change, the way the will to enjoy is thwarted by circumstance, the deterministic impact of heredity and sexual selection, the social and economic struggle, and the operation of blind chance. Discussion of these elements is developed in the following passages:

■ The most memorable of these specifications is, of course, the ironical sentence, '"Justice" was done, and the President of the Immortals (in Aeschylean phrase) had ended his sport with Tess' (p. 384). But this is really no more than a trope, [figure of speech] indicative of the way the fate of Tess impresses unreasoning humanity. Hardy's more seriously intended statements are frequently addressed against conceptions that are conventional rather than statements of a new force such as we know he had conceived of. Where, Hardy asks, was the providence of Tess's simple faith when she was seduced? What justice satisfactory to man can be found in the retribution that offers up Tess as a sacrifice for the sins of her ancestors? After he had described the utter dependence of the Durbeyfield children upon their improvident parents, he says:

> Some people would like to know whence the poet [Wordsworth] whose philosophy is in these days deemed as profound and trustworthy as his song is breezy and pure gets his authority for speaking of 'Nature's holy plan'. (p. 28)

More positively, Hardy speaks of his sympathy with the fatalism of the peasants, the unalterable truth of their 'It was to be' (p. 77). He agrees with Angel Clare's denomination of 'It' as unsympathetic (p. 158). He believes that even so fine a woman as Tess is of no more consequence than a fly before the universe, that she is caught like a 'bird in a springe' (p. 196). No character, not even Alec, is truly responsible for his fate . . . But he never denominates this harshness as active or conscious. He does not even give It a name in the novel. He merely states, 'So do flux and reflux – the rhythm of change – alternate and persist in everything under the sky' (p. 338). This rhythm of change, before which human beings must willy-nilly bow, operates as relentlessly as it has in earlier novels, in such a way that birth often seems something which may be palliated, never justified . . .

. . . Those characters who understand their situation feel with Tess, even in happy times, that all good fortune will be scourged out of them later in heaven's usual way. The gods are persistent ironists . . . So, when Tess is ready for love, she meets Alec rather than Angel. So, when Angel learns how he has misjudged Tess, it is too late, and Angel and Tess can be happy together for only a short time, for the eternal flux and reflux dictate that their inherent will to enjoy be counterbalanced by the circumstantial will against enjoyment.

One of the laws by which this circumstantial will operates is emphasised for the first time. Although Hardy's notions of heredity have previously seemed both vague and incredible, in *Tess* heredity is an important and credible factor in the heroine's development. From her mother Tess inherits her prettiness and her early womanly fulness. The race from which she is descended transmitted to her a slight incautiousness of character. The latter quality partially accounts for her seduction. The former qualities account for the seducer's interest. These inherited traits help to account for the unhappiness for which the general principles of sexual selection are even more responsible . . . . . .

In addition to the play of sexual selection and heredity, the harshness of the struggle for existence contributes to the tragic nature of the action. This is particularly obvious in the desperate poverty of the Durbeyfields and in Tess's pathetic attempt to make a living after Angel deserts her. But it was also the poverty of the Durbeyfields that made Tess go to the d'Urberville estate in the first place.

Chance, too, plays a significant part in bringing about Tess's seduction and subsequent misery . . . . . . Indeed, though Hardy himself tends to confuse the reader by shifting the blame back and forth between inevitable and evitable causes, it might even be contended that Tess's life would not have been tragic at all if it had not been for society's cruel conventions. After her seduction it is the social chasm which opens before her that hurts . . . it seems that society believes maidenhood the only thing in Nature denied recuperative powers; so Tess suffers. Had it not been for the world's opinion, her experiences would have been simply a liberal education, Hardy tells us. It is, more-over, society, or its sacred book, convention, that is largely responsible for Tess's unhappiness after she meets Angel . . . And it is this conven-tional standard of judgement, adhered to by Clare, that is responsible for Tess's later unhappiness. Natural law – sex and heredity – can be held responsible for Tess's seduction; but the consequence of her seduction would have been only to teach Tess better judgement if social law were not so harsh . . .

. . . Through the mouth of Angel Clare, now repentant, Hardy preaches a superior moral law to society . . . 'The beauty or ugliness of a character lay not only in its achievements, but in its aims and impulses; its true history lay, not among things done, but among things willed' (pp.328–9) . . . Because this is true, *Tess* is more than a 'pessimistic' novel. It is a fine contribution to the war against 'man's inhumanity to man' which so importantly characterised the last decade of Hardy's career as a novelist.[48] □

Perhaps the most surprising contribution to this phase of Hardy criticism is actually one of omission. The hugely influential critic F. R. Leavis, pointedly left Hardy out of his book, *The Great Tradition* (1948), in which he defines and celebrates the realism and humanism of, among others, George Eliot and Henry James. Leavis refers with evident approval to Henry James's gibe about *Tess*:

■ The good little Thomas Hardy has scored a great success with *Tess of the d'Urbervilles*, which is chock-full of faults and falsity, and yet has a singular beauty and charm.[49] □

Leavis refuses to see Hardy as 'representative of the "modern conscious-ness"',[50] and most damningly he states that compared with George Eliot, 'Hardy, decent as he is, [appears] as a provincial manufacturer of gauche and heavy fictions that sometimes have corresponding virtues'.[51] The underlying reason for this striking neglect of such a major novelist is unclear, especially since Hardy seems to embody the notions of reality and humanity, Englishness and the rural community that Leavis held dear.

With Albert Guerard's *Thomas Hardy* (1949) we come to a watershed in Hardy criticism. In an immensely stimulating study, Guerard seeks to overturn the whole trend of 'post-Victorian' criticism, which 'looked upon its everyday experience as placid, plausible, and reasonably decent . . . [and which] assumed that realism was the proper medium of fic-tion'.[52] Although Hardy was in the tradition of the 'old-fashioned storyteller', he was, says Guerard a 'sufficiently conscious artist con-sciously to rebel against drab and placid realism . . . his symbolic use of mischance and coincidence carry us no small distance toward the symbolic use of the absurd in our time'.[53]

And Guerard goes on to identify as a project Hardy's 'deliberate anti-realism'.[54] But because his book is organised thematically, his comments on *Tess of the d'Urbervilles* are dispersed. However, enough of them have been drawn together here to indicate his main interests in this novel, including Hardy's 'unrelaxed consciousness and resentment of class feeling',[55] and his anxiety about the gradual disappearance of the stable rural society:

■ . . . In *Tess of the d'Urbervilles* . . . Old Lady-Day is a tragic time; the roads are choked with the pitiful carts of the migrating farm labourers and the dispossessed artisan cottagers. Only the Talbothays dairy remains as a green oasis in a Wessex which has become sombre and bleak. We are left with the unmistakable impression that the farm labourer has lost not only his ancient memories and folk customs but also the reasonable comforts of life . . . [56] □

After supporting this view by reference to Hardy's correspondence with Rider Haggard, who was investigating the contemporary situation in the countryside, Guerard discusses the relation between Hardy's traditional social concerns and his modern interest in alienation and clashes of ideology:

■ Hardy thus looked on the problems of Dorset and Wessex as raw material for his vision and drama. . . A few very real though somewhat rudimentary problems recur in most of the novels and provide a formal subject matter: the contrast between rural simplicity and urban or aristocratic complexity and corruption, the pathos of regional and class deracination, the destructive effect of class feeling, the problem of marriage and mis-marriage, and the conflicting impulses toward spontaneity and tradition or convention. Only in *Tess* and *Jude* does Hardy face the characteristic nightmares of the late Victorian age: the problem of ethics without dogma and the problem of the restless and isolated modern ego . . . [57] □

This involved the employment of realism, and Guerard subtly tries to negotiate and define the nature of Hardy's realism. He was:

■ . . . at times an orthodox realist, stubbornly faithful to fact, to the unheightened universe which we daily touch and see, to the unregenerated thing. He was alternately attracted to the occult and to the homely; as a consequence, his attitude toward literal realism was ambiguous . . . [58] □

Guerard wrestles with the term anti-realist to describe Hardy, and finding it unsatisfactory tries 'symbolist'. He is not a historian of his world of Wessex, says Guerard, but an artist who 'distorted actuality to achieve a kind of truth'.[59] This occurs particularly in the later novels where, employing the heightening effects of symbolism:

■ ... Hardy's descriptions of process tend to be symbolic rather than documentary: so in *Tess* the threshing of the wheat-rick, with its vicious struggle between man and machine, and the slaughter of the last unprotected rats ... [60] □

Guerard deals effectively with the obvious anti-realistic devices in Hardy's fiction; the sensational, the melodramatic, the symbolic use of reappearance and coincidence, hints of the supernatural, and the fundamentally improbable; but he is especially acute in his discussion of how in *Tess*, one of his 'closest approaches to orthodox realism',[61] in which Hardy's focus is clearly on society, his realist and symbolist methods are dovetailed so as to achieve a movement beyond the realistic:

■ The idyll of Talbothays, which is certainly beyond praise, especially required tact. For the overall intention could hardly have been a balder one: to blend Tess's recovery of calm and the resurgence of her 'unexpended youth' with an environment which suggests more than any other both fertility and a changeless placidity – that of a great dairy. It is no exaggeration to say that Tess might have become, when subjected to such symbolism, a figure of bovine rather than natural simplicity. The further and tragic intention was to show her innocent and sensuous naturalism corrupted by Victorian nastiness; her purity, already violated by Alec's selfish egoism, must now be violated by prudery. What could have been more obvious than to import the half-emancipated son of a clergyman, the insufferable Angel Clare? To avoid an awkward and obvious symbolism here demanded a more careful building-up of the enfolding atmosphere than in any other of Hardy's novels ... ... The atmosphere of Talbothays, deliberately sustained over nearly a hundred pages, nowhere detaches itself from the human drama of Tess's reconstruction and Angel Clare's intrusion; nor does it ever submerge that drama. This atmosphere is a triumph of realistic art constructed from the simplest of everyday things. And like any triumph of art, it is something more than realism.[62] □

In its early stages, post-Victorian criticism endorses the status of *Tess of the d'Urbervilles* as a tragedy of extraordinary power, in which the author's emotions are implicated to an unusual degree. Later, different approaches are brought to bear on *Tess*, as critics examine Hardy's creative processes through biography, textual study, and analysis of the influence of nineteenth-century thought and culture. These new contextualisations reinforce the early reviewers' identification of this novel as a humanist realist text. However, under the impact of Modernism, and later of the New Criticism, Hardy's work, including *Tess of the d'Urbervilles*, undergoes significant critical revision. And by the end of the 1940s, claims are beginning to be made for him as a writer whose fiction anticipates that of the great Modernists.

In the 1950s, however, the subject of the next chapter, Hardy critics struck out in major new directions. The New Criticism had been gathering momentum and was to be developed further, while Marxist, and the less overtly ideological, historical criticisms were also making considerable strides. The linguistic and sociological complexity of *Tess of the d'Urbervilles* provided these postwar critics with an ideal text on which to test their highly influential methodologies.

CHAPTER THREE

New Directions: The 1950s

IN THE more optimistic climate of the first postwar decade, although many of the emphases of post-Victorian humanism were still in evidence, a number of things conspired to encourage new directions in Hardy criticism. One of the impulses at work was the continuing rise of English studies in the universities, both in Britain and America, and the secure establishment of English as an academic discipline. In Britain it was pioneered principally by F.R. Leavis and in America by a number of critics, including John Crowe Ransom, whose book, *The New Criticism*, published in 1941, had given rise to a movement which appropriated that title, and which continued to be influential throughout the 1950s and 1960s.

In the postwar climate, New Criticism possessed the attraction of being ahistorical, though its underlying stance was liberal humanist. It was partly a reaction against the impressionism of much of the nineteenth- and early-twentieth-century criticism; against historicism and the concept of intentionality; and also against rival critical methodologies, such as psychoanalytical criticism and Marxist criticism. New Criticism was a programme based on a close reading of individual literary texts, which avoided reliance on other disciplines such as history and philosophy. Originally based on the reading of poetry, its emphasis on the autonomy of the work, on the generation of meaning through language and the internal structure of the text, and on organic unity, proved understandably difficult to transfer to the analysis of fiction. However, an impetus had already been given to this area of New Critical activity by Henry James and by Modernists such as Joseph Conrad, D.H. Lawrence and James Joyce, who employed a broadly similar aesthetic and who attempted, in differing degrees and with varied success, to achieve greater psychological truth by banishing the intrusive authorial voice and dramatising the novel's action.

A second major new direction, Marxist criticism, involved a sociological and historical approach to the study of fiction. Marxist criticism embraces a variety of methodologies. Originally, following Marx and

Engels, critics argued that literary texts are permeated with ideology, and reproduce that of the ruling class, whose values and ideas they naturalise. More sophisticated developments took up another strand in Marxist thinking, the view of literature as a source of knowledge about society, and discovered in bourgeois realist texts the representation of a complete society, including its structure, inequalities, oppressions and the class struggle. Humanist Marxists read fictions for their ideological content and meaning. Their approach is concerned, in broad terms, with investigating the social history of the class struggle, and it involves the author's own understanding of his society.

The first significant exploration of Hardy's fiction employing the New Critical methodology was that of John Holloway in his book, *The Victorian Sage* (1953), an approach he confirmed later in a volume of essays, *The Charted Mirror* (1960), which included a comparison of *Tess of the d'Urbervilles* with Henry James's *The Awkward Age*. Holloway's sages include Carlyle, Disraeli, George Eliot, Newman, Arnold and Hardy and his project, as he announces in his Introduction, is to explore the relation between form and meaning, not in terms of the rhetoric of persuasion, but in the 'whole weave of a book'.[1] Holloway describes his critical procedure in the following terms:

■ . . . [The sage] **gives expression to his outlook imaginatively. What he has to say is not a matter just of 'content' or narrow paraphrasable meaning, but is transfused by the whole texture of his writing as it constitutes an experience for the reader . . . and the chapters which follow examine how, in a series of particular cases, the parts of this texture contribute to the impression mediated by the whole.**[2] □

And as a New Critic, Holloway is especially concerned with 'figurative language'[3] as a mode of expression.

Holloway's comments on *Tess of the d'Urbervilles* form only part of his chapter on Hardy, but they characterise his critical position and methods. He follows earlier critics in recognising *Tess* as embodying Hardy's pessimism and determinism, while his faith in the old agricultural order, his disdain for the *déraciné* (uprooted from the customary environment) individual, and his belief in the goodness of nature are shared by contemporary critics such as Arnold Kettle and Douglas Brown. However, unlike them, Holloway resolutely excludes any extra-textual reading, including of course one based on the 'real' history of Dorset.

In the first extract below, he extrapolates from the text Hardy's complex apprehension of nature:

■ *First,* **Nature is an organic living whole, and its constituent parts, even the inanimate parts, have a life and personality of their own.**

Second, it is unified on a great scale through both time and space.

Third, it is exceedingly complex and varied, full of unexpected details of many different kinds – details that are sometimes even quaint or bizarre.

Fourth, for all that, these heterogeneous things are integrated, however obscurely, into a system of rigid and undeviating law . . . [4] □

Clearly, for Holloway, nature fulfils his pursuit of organic unity in the text, particularly, as the following passages illustrate, in a landscape suffused with a humanistic love of a specifically national countryside, and in which the simultaneous function of geographical fact as 'figurative language' contributes to 'the whole weave of the book':

■ . . . For him, the life of Nature is such that the smaller unity lies always under the impress of the larger. Nothing is cosily self-contained, nothing can be seen in isolation. Hardy's view always quickly expands until it depicts something of a whole landscape, of the varied integration of a region. For him the proper expression of Nature's active principle tends always to lie in geography, in an organisation that runs on mile after mile through a massive and abiding English countryside . . . and one thing which exemplifies the unity of Hardy's work is how he uses rivers to evoke a sense of life, a sense of landscape, and a distinctive emotional quality. Tess leaves her home in the Vale of Blackmoor to start life afresh in the Froom Valley. Hardy describes how she crosses the intervening upland to find herself on a summit overlooking the whole new landscape:

The world was drawn to a larger pattern here. The enclosures numbered fifty acres instead of ten, the farmsteads were more extended . . . These myriads of cows stretching under her eyes from the far east to the far west outnumbered any she had ever seen at one glance before . . . the birdseye perspective before her was not so luxuriantly beautiful, perhaps . . . yet it was more cheering . . . The river itself which nourished the grass and cows of these renowned dairies, flowed not like the streams in Blackmoor. Those were slow, silent, often turbid; flowing over beds of mud . . . The Froom waters were clear . . . rapid as the shadow of a cloud, with pebbly shallows that prattled to the sky all day. (pp. 108–9)[5] □

Holloway notes that:

■ . . . Another similar complex image occurs in *Tess*, when Hardy writes of 'the irregular chalk table-land or plateau, bosomed with semi-globular tumuli – as if Cybele the Many-breasted were supinely

51

extended there' (p. 273). This image, I think, achieves no less than four things. It suggests . . . that the whole landscape is living; it makes possible a more integrated sense of the spatial expanse; through personification it *states* that the chalk-land is alive; and it hints also at the age and permanence of the scene – it is, we are made to feel, like the landscapes which first suggested the notion of Cybele to their early inhabitants.[6] □

Tess is unified above all by what Holloway discerns as a determinism contingent not, as for earlier critics, on the biological dictates of heredity, or the operation of fate, but on nature. For Hardy, suggests Holloway, human society is no more nor less than an integral part of nature and subject to its law, a view which Roy Morrell was later to denounce in *Thomas Hardy: The Will and the Way* (1965) (see pp. 79–84 of this Guide) as a denial of human freedom:

■ . . . all the variety of Nature is integrated within a system of necessity and undeviating law . . . . . . Hardy has a corresponding picture of human society; and this proves to show the life of mankind as, sometimes at least, a microcosm of Nature as a whole. The correspondence is integral to Hardy's work, for the former, in his opinion, is properly no more than a part of the latter, and moulded by it totally and without intermission.

That human life, and indeed human consciousness, is wholly subject to the control of Nature is something which the people in Hardy's novels illustrate everywhere . . . [7] □

To illustrate the tyranny of nature's law, Holloway draws on Tess's experiences at Flintcomb-Ash. In sharp contrast to Arnold Kettle's Marxist approach, Holloway ignores the socio-agricultural dimension of Tess's work – her status and function as a farm labourer – in favour of images relating to the effects on her of the operation of nature. For Holloway, the texture of the language has critical priority over the socio-economic conditions of the plot. This is evident from the following passage:

■ But that Hardy shows people as merely situated within a wider and spreading landscape is not the full story. They are not simply in, but governed by and subdued to their environment. Tess has this quality always: 'On these lonely hills and dales her quiescent glide was of a piece with the element she moved in . . . became an integral part of the scene' (p. 91). When she works at Fintcomb-Ash, 'a figure which is part of the landscape' (p. 272), Hardy goes on to show how everything about her, as she stands there, is subject to the system and operation of nature. She is 'a fieldwoman pure and simple, in winter guise; a grey serge cape . . . a stuff skirt . . . buff leather gloves. Every thread of that old attire has become faded and thin under the stroke of rain-drops, the burn of sunbeams, and the stress of winds' . . . (p.272–3).[8] □

As one would expect from a New Critic, in tracing the unifying relation between form and meaning in the novel's elements of structure, character, and incident, John Holloway regards language as the dominant effect. The patterned sequence of determined events resides in natural images of sexual convergence and entrapment, and in a series of proleptic images foreshadowing future events. (This last instance is taken up sharply by Morrell in his critical quarrel with Holloway, who develops this central aspect of his argument below.)

■ . . . Another commonplace metaphor, the man–river comparison, is used by Hardy (as it was by George Eliot) to convey the same notion; Tess and Clare were 'converging, under an irresistible law, as surely as two streams in one vale' (p.133) . . . Again, like George Eliot, he has some apparently sentimental images that are not sentimental, because of the doctrines they imply covertly. Tess listens to Angel's harp 'like a fascinated bird' (p.127); later Hardy says that she 'had been caught during her days of immaturity like a bird in a springe' (p.196). This is no vague sentimentality, but an exact and insistent image to remind us that when Tess was seduced at night in the wood, her experience really was like that of an animal caught in a trap – as might have happened in the very same place . . . If Nature's life is half-human, human life for Hardy is half like that of birds and animals.

Some other comparisons reinforce this impression, and confirm that sense of the unexpected and bizarre which runs through Hardy's portrait of man as of Nature. Tess 'was yawning, and he saw the red interior of her mouth as if it had been a snake's' (p.172); 'Having been lying down in her clothes she was warm as a sunned cat' (p.172); she is 'like a plant in too burning a sun' (p.173) . . . But several of these metaphors do more than suggest a continuity between man and Nature, or an element of the bizarre in human life. Some of them – Tess like a cat . . . or . . . like a snake – are potent in signifying the ultimate result of the casual moment they describe. They are *proleptic* images; they hint at the whole determined sequence of things. Two comparisons in *Tess* bring this out with surprising clarity. Angel's interest in Tess is first established when he finds her and her three companion dairymaids in difficulties with the flooded highway, and 'clinging to the roadside bank like pigeons on a roof-slope' (p.146). Hardy, at this very point, reinforces the dove-symbol by a detail in the scene: as Angel approaches, his gaze is captured by the innumerable flies and butterflies caught and imprisoned in the girls' gauzy skirts, 'caged in the transparent tissue as in an aviary' (p. 146). (Hardy makes us see how in different ways both Angel and Tess are victims, each of the other.) Later in the novel the bird-sacrifice comes again. Tess in her misfortunes spends another night out in a wood, this time alone; she hears the pheasants that have been wounded by shot fall one by one from the branches, and in the morning she *breaks their necks* (p. 271) [Holloway's italics]. There is another piece of proleptic metaphor in *Tess*: Crick the dairyman is listening to Tess herself describe how she can day-dream her mind out of her body: he 'turned to her with his mouth full, his eyes charged with enquiry, and his great knife and fork . . . *planted erect on the table, like the beginning of a gallows'* (p. 124) [Holloway's italics]. On every reading after the first, this comparison is incandescent; surely it does more than any volume of generalities to fix in us Hardy's sense of the unalterable sequence of things.[9] □

John Holloway, like Albert Guerard before him, views the anti-realistic elements in Hardy in a positive light, but he sees them as incorporated into the complexity of nature:

■ The varied, the unexpected, the bizarre in human life has been often noticed in Hardy; it could scarcely have been overlooked. Much that in a cursory or light reading might please by its quaint charm is taken from the fanciful customs or superstitions of Wessex peasantry. But these fanciful incidents prove on more serious reading to have a deeper meaning. Hardy is not exploiting them as oddities pure and simple; each is odd if thought of by itself, but all together they are the kind of things which for him largely constitutes the day-to-day pattern of life. They are integral to Hardy's general picture, and they are analogous to that element of the bizarre which he traces outside human life in the complexity of nature. This well illustrates how the outlook of a writer is not the sum of his abstractions, but how he interprets them. The abstractions of George Eliot and Hardy about the general course of things are to some extent similar. But their picture of life is totally different. In one Necessity suggests a bracing drabness; in the other a sometimes dreamlike inconsequentiality.[10] □

In his examples from *Tess*, Holloway excludes those bizarre elements of reappearance and coincidence that Guerard attends to, in favour of moments that may be seen as symbolic and contributing to Hardy's system of necessity. Again, as the passage below demonstrates, patterns of language replace patterns of incident as the critical focus:

■ There are similar oddities in *Tess* – Tess herself pricking her finger on one of Alec's roses, the moonlight haloes that surround the heads of her fellow-workers as they walk home through the dew and darkness, the strange diabolical figure of the engine-man in the threshing-scene at Flintcomb-Ash. Each of these, again, is a symbol. There is, too, the sleep-walking scene where Angel lays Tess in the stone coffin by the abbey (which no one, perhaps, finds very satisfactory), and Tess's final sleep, before her capture, upon the stone of sacrifice at Stonehenge. It should perhaps be said, in justice to Hardy, that although this scene may fail, he did a good deal to make Tess, in her last days, a symbolic and archetypal figure – in the sleep-walking scene, in many details, several of which have been mentioned, and also when she swears on the stone not to be a temptation to Alec. He, indeed, thinks her vow is made on a wayside cross; but in fact it is on a prehistoric monolith or a memorial to a devil-worshipper who was executed there. These are only a few examples of the kind of scene which Hardy introduces frequently; the problem is to see how they are integrated with, and profoundly qualify, his whole picture of what human affairs are like.

Quite frequently, though for the most part only in a passing phrase, Hardy suggests that all these events make up one great system of necessity . . . When Tess is seduced, and when her family is evicted, Hardy reminds us that when her ancestors were landowners they were doubtless the oppressors often enough, and comments: 'So do flux and reflux – the rhythm of change – alternate and persist in everything under the sky' (p. 338).[11] □

Pursuing Hardy the sage, Holloway believes that the essential view of life he seeks to communicate is the value of living enmeshed in one's total natural environment:

■ . . . The single abstraction which does most to summarise Hardy's view is simple enough: *it is right to live naturally*. But this is the abstraction central to any number of moralities; Hardy glosses it by showing how to live naturally is to live in continuity with one's whole biological and geographical environment . . . [12] □

Although Holloway speaks of people being governed by their environment, he suggests that this is 'not passive submission . . . human choice can exert some influence at least on the course of things simply by working with and not against it'.[13] He argues that the characters who have been uprooted from their proper worlds have forfeit all that is valuable, but while Angel Clare acquires something of Hardy's sage-like wisdom about the fundamental world of nature, Alec d'Urberville does not. The following extracts trace this line of thought and John Holloway's conclusion:

■ . . . The great disaster for an individual is to be *déraciné*. Perhaps, if Tess has a weakness, it is what she has in common with the dreamers. At the vital moment in the novel when Angel first catches sight of her, she is telling how 'our souls can be made to go outside our bodies when we are alive' by staring at a bright star in the darkness. Hardy brings this 'fancy' up against the kindly dairyman's down-to-earth amazement; and Tess goes significantly on to say 'you will soon find that you are hundreds and hundreds o'miles away from your body, which you don't seem to want at all' (p. 124), reminding us for a moment of the price she will ultimately pay for her dream-world spirituality. But Hardy makes plain, on the other hand, where Tess is likely to be at her strongest: 'All the while she wondered if any strange good thing might come of her being in her ancestral land; and some spirit within her rose automatically as the sap in the twigs' (p. 104).

Angel, on the other hand, is a *déraciné* who partially and temporarily takes root again. His religious scruples and the narrow tradition of his family cut him off from the university *milieu* relatively natural to a man of his type, and his life begins at that point to become disorganised and aimless. At the dairy he lives as a solitary at first; but he slowly joins in the life of the group and comes to belong to it. He begins to like outdoor life, to see the variety and richness of simple human nature, to shake off the 'chronic melancholy' of sceptical civilization. He finds that the creed of his own family is narrow and abstract and ignores the complexities of the real world; and in commenting upon his fuller insight into life Hardy makes an important juxtaposition:

> He grew away from old associations, and saw something new in life and humanity. Secondarily he made close acquaintance with phenomena which he had before known but darkly – the seasons in their moods, morning and evening, night and noon . . . water and mists . . . and the voices of inanimate things. (p. 123)

Angel is acquiring the kind of wisdom that the sage can teach in part; but Hardy points also to its ultimate source.

That the bad is essentially the rootless insinuates itself sometimes into Hardy's scenes and descriptions. Tess, at work in the reaping field has 'the charm which is acquired by woman when she becomes part and parcel of outdoor nature, and is not merely an object set down therein' (p. 93). In contrast to this scene . . . is the *parvenu* Alec d'Urberville's mansion:

> . . . a country-house built for enjoyment pure and simple . . . which rose like a geranium bloom against the subdued colours around . . .

Everything on this snug property was bright, thriving, and well-kept. (p. 41)

And in the tragic scene of her confession to Angel, Tess is deliberately placed in an alien and hostile setting: she is surrounded by the portraits of her by now irrelevant ancestors, she is wearing Angel's family jewels. Hardy emphasizes how 'All material objects around announced their irresponsibility with terrible iteration' (p. 225).

Finally, it is true that the whole trend of one novel after another portrays this same scale of values. To adapt one's life to one's traditional situation is good, to uproot oneself for material ends is bad, to do so for romantic passion or an abstract ideal is if anything worse . . .[14] □

In America Dorothy Van Ghent brought together two main lines of critical enquiry, the New Critical concern with the language of the text, particularly its patterns of imagery and symbolism, and the formalist interest in analysing structure. First and foremost a teacher, Dorothy Van Ghent's important book, *The English Novel: Form and Function*, published like John Holloway's *The Victorian Sage* in 1953, was, according to its Introduction, developed as the result of a course on fiction that she taught at Kansas University between 1948 and 1951. The book is an ambitious project spanning eighteen texts from Cervantes's *Don Quixote* to Joyce's *A Portrait of the Artist as a Young Man*, and it is directed very consciously towards university teachers and students. The novels are studied sequentially, and to each analysis is added 'Problems for Study and Discussion'.

Van Ghent's work is a pioneering study, an extended exploration, as its title implies, of the essential nature of the novel's form and its function, working towards a conception of it inclusive enough to account for the individual characteristics of the broad range of examples she has chosen to examine. Her notion of coherence is established in her Introduction, where she describes the novel as:

■ . . . one complex pattern, or Gestalt ['form'], made up of component ones. In it inhere such a vast number of traits, all organised in subordinate systems that function under the governance of a single meaningful structure, that the nearest similitude for a novel is a 'world'.[15] □

And since the novel's ideas and moments of illumination are articulated by its patterns, one index of its quality is the overall unity of its form. Unlike John Holloway, Van Ghent does not prioritise symbolism over incident. For her, both cooperate as elements of pattern, since '[the novel] has to have integral structure'.[16] She is New Critical in her stress, not only on unity, but on the imperative of reading texts ahistorically. However, there is also an obvious humanist inflection in her emphasis on the novel's realistic 'concreteness',[17] and on the intimate correlation between its form and its function of revealing to the reader the author's profound insights – its 'ability to make us more aware of the meaning of our lives'.[18]

Dorothy Van Ghent's essay on *Tess of the d'Urbervilles* explores Hardy's use of symbolism as part of an analysis which views Tess's tragic heroism in terms of a mythology that links the 'spectacular destiny of the hero with the unspectacular common destiny'.[19] In this she anticipates later critics who examine *Tess* from a similar critical standpoint, most notably J. B. Bullen (see pp. 142–7 of this Guide). But while Bullen is concerned with Hardy's employment of solar mythology, Van Ghent reveals a mythology that is grounded realistically in the earth.

Like earlier critics then, Van Ghent is concerned with realism, with Wessex, and with tragedy. Like them she has to deal with Hardy's penchant for coincidence and the sensational, and also his 'philosophy'. But in negotiating each of these she is dramatically original, defining them in terms that serve her view of the text's essential unity and meaning. Hardy's 'philosophy' in *Tess of the d'Urbervilles* is expressed chiefly by that bogy of post-Jamesian practitioners and New Critics, the intrusive narrative voice, which runs counter to her aesthetic criteria and offers a peculiar challenge to her methodology. Her remedy, as she reveals below, is brutal surgery:

■ To turn to one of Hardy's great tragic novels is to put 'internal relations' in the novel to peculiar test, for there is perhaps no other novelist, of a stature equal to Hardy's, who so stubbornly and flagrantly foisted upon the novel elements resistant to aesthetic cohesion. We shall want to speak of these elements first, simply to clear away and free ourselves from the temptation to appraise Hardy by his 'philosophy' – that is, the temptation to mistake bits of philosophic adhesive tape, rather dampened and rumpled by time, for the deeply animated vision of experience which our novel, *Tess*, holds . . . [20] □

She goes on to give examples: Hardy's comment on Wordsworth's spurious authority for revering 'Nature's holy plan' (p. 28) in the light of the plight of the Durbeyfields; or sentiments in Wordsworth's 'Intimations of Immortality' in the context of the Durbeyfields' enforced migration; the infamous reference to the 'President of the Immortals' (p. 384); and the note of 'ameliorism' in the joined hands of Angel Clare and Liza-Lu at the end. These are all external and devitalising elements, which constitute another form of discourse that belongs to an 'intellectual battlefield alien from the novel's imaginative concretions',[21] or that is redundant to the meaning already established, or that foists onto the text a meaning which as a whole it simply will not bear. Shorn of these, *Tess* is able to work organically:

■ What philosophical vision honestly inheres in a novel inheres as the signifying form of a certain concrete body of experience; it is what the experience 'means' because it is what, structurally, the experience *is* . . . as a structural principle active within the particulars of the novel, local and inherent there through a maximum of organic dependencies, the philosophical vision has the unassailable truth of living form . . . . . . in the minor notation is the furthest reach of form . . . [22] □

It is essential to Van Ghent's argument that she is able to demonstrate this organic relation between local symbolism and the larger structure, and she achieves this most effectively in the following extract, which continues from her quotation from the scene in which the collision of Tess's cart with the mail-cart kills the Durbeyfields' horse, Prince (Chapter 4, pp. 36–7):

■ . . . With this accident are concatenated in fatal union Tess's going to 'claim kin' of the d'Urbervilles and all the other links in her tragedy down to the murder of Alec. The symbolism of the detail is naïve and forthright to the point of temerity: the accident occurs in darkness and Tess has fallen asleep – just as the whole system of mischances and cross-purposes in the novel is a function of psychic and cosmic blindness; she 'put her hand upon the hole' (p. 37) – and the gesture is as absurdly ineffectual as all her effort will be; the only result is that she becomes splashed with blood – as she will be at the end; the shaft pierces Prince's breast 'like a sword' (p. 37) – Alec is stabbed in the heart with a knife; with the arousal and twittering of the birds we are aware of the oblivious manifold of nature stretching infinite and detached beyond the isolated human figure; the iridescence of the coagulating blood is, in its incongruity with the dark human trouble, a note of the same indifferent cosmic chemistry that has brought about the accident; and the smallness of the hole in Prince's chest, that looked 'scarcely large enough to have let out all that had animated him' p. 37), is the minor remark of that irony by which Tess's great cruel trial appears as a vanishing incidental in the blind waste of time and space and biological repetition. Nevertheless, there is nothing in this event that has not the natural 'grain' of concrete fact; and what it signifies – of the complicity of doom with the most random occurrence, of the cross-purposing of purpose in a multiple world, of cosmic indifference and of moral desolation – is a local truth of a particular experience and irrefutable as the experience itself. [23] □

Here is the stark, proleptic symbolism detected by John Holloway, the symbolism of blood developed later by Tony Tanner (see pp. 84–9 of this Guide), and the gulf between self and world, but rooted in the actual and the concrete. Similarly, suggests Van Ghent, the 'submerged and debased fertility ritual' of the May-walking foreshadows Tess's victimisation by the power of sexual instinct:

■ . . . Owing its form entirely to the vision that shapes the whole of Tess's tragedy, the minor incident of the May-walking has the assurance of particularised reality and the truth of the naturally given.[24] □

She also discusses the realism and symbolism of the visiting winter birds at Flintcomb-Ash, before concluding this stage of her argument with a comment on Tess in the outskirts of the garden at Talbothays, listening to Angel Clare's harp. Since this is a scene to which several critics in this Guide make extensive reference, the relevant paragraphs are quoted below:

■ It was a typical summer evening in June, the atmosphere being in such delicate equilibrium and so transmissive that inanimate objects seemed endowed with two or three senses, if not five. There was no distinction between the near and the far, and an auditor felt close to everything within the horizon. The soundlessness impressed her as a positive entity rather than as the mere negation of noise. It was broken by the strumming of strings.

Tess had heard those notes in the attic above her head. Dim, flattened, constrained by their confinement, they had never appealed to her as now, when they wandered in the still air with a stark quality like that of nudity. To speak absolutely, both instrument and execution were poor; but the relative is all, and as she listened Tess, like a fascinated bird, could not leave the spot. Far from leaving she drew up towards the performer, keeping behind the hedge that he might not guess her presence.

The outskirt of the garden in which Tess found herself had been left uncultivated for some years, and was now damp and rank with juicy grass which sent up mists of pollen at a touch, and with tall blooming weeds emitting offensive smells – weeds whose red and yellow and purple hues formed a polychrome as dazzling as that of cultivated flowers. She went stealthily as a cat through this profusion of growth, gathering cuckoo-spittle on her skirts, cracking snails that were underfoot, staining her hands with thistle-milk and slug-slime, and rubbing off upon her naked arms sticky blights which, though snow-white on the appletree-trunks, made madder stains on her skin; thus she drew quite near to Clare, still unobserved of him.

Tess was conscious of neither time nor space. The exaltation which she had described as being producible at will by gazing at a star, came now without any determination of hers; she undulated upon the thin notes of the second-hand harp, and their harmonies passed like breezes through her, bringing tears into her eyes. The floating pollen seemed to be his notes made visible, and the dampness of the garden the weeping of the garden's sensibility. Though near nightfall, the rank-smelling weed-flowers glowed as if they would not close, for intentness, and the waves of colour mixed with the waves of sound. (pp.127–8) □

Dorothy Van Ghent is primarily interested in the scene's symbolism:

■ . . . The weeds, circumstantial as they are, have an astonishingly cunning and bold metaphorical function. They grow at Talbothays, in that healing procreative Idyll of milk and mist and passive biology, and they too are bountiful with life, but they stain and slime and blight; and it is in this part of Paradise (an 'outskirt of the garden' – there are even apple trees here) that the minister's son is hidden, who, in his conceited impotence, will violate Tess more nastily than her sensual seducer: who but Hardy would have dared to give him the name Angel, and a harp too? It is Hardy's incorruptible feeling for the actual that allows his symbolism its amazingly blunt privileges and that at the same time subdues it to and absorbs it into the concrete circumstances of experience, real as touch.[25] □

In a brilliant leap of critical intuition, Van Ghent discerns in the text an organic relation which permits Hardy's symbolising vision, by linking his realistic presentation of the earth to a mythical construction in which it is dramatised as an antagonist:

■ The dilemma of Tess is the dilemma of morally individualising consciousness in its earthy mixture. The subject is mythological, for it places the human protagonist in dramatic relationship with the non-human and orients his destiny among preternatural powers. The most primitive antagonist of consciousness is, on the simplest premise, the earth itself. It acts so in *Tess*, clogging action and defying conscious motive; or, in the long dream of Talbothays, conspiring with its ancient sensuality to provoke instinct; or, on the farm at Flintcomb-Ash, demoralising consciousness by its mere geological flintiness. But the earth is 'natural', while, dramatically visualised as antagonist, it transcends the natural. The integrity of the myth thus depends, paradoxically, upon naturalism; and it is because of that intimate dependence between the natural and the mythological, a dependence that is organic to the subject, that Hardy's vision is able to impregnate so deeply and shape so unobtrusively the naturalistic particulars of the story.[26] □

Van Ghent's premise is that 'the earth is *primarily not a metaphor but a real thing*',[27] that obstructs human purposes, and the extract below picks up her discussion at the point at which she elaborates this idea, in order to demonstrate the relation between realism and symbolism at the level of the language in which Hardy's vision inheres:

■ . . . The insidiously demoralising effect of Tess's desolate journeys on foot as she seeks dairy work and field work here and there after the collapse of her marriage, brutal months that are foreshortened to the plodding trip over the chalk uplands to Flintcomb-Ash, is, again, as directly as anything, an effect of the irreducible *thereness* of the territory she has to cover. There are other fatal elements in her ineffectual trip from the farm to Emminster to see Clare's parents, but fatal above all is the distance she must walk to see people who can have no foreknowledge of her coming and who are not at home when she gets there. Finally, with the uprooting and migration of the Durbeyfield family on Old Lady-Day, the simple fatality of the earth as earth, in its measurelessness and anonymousness, with people having to move over it with no place to go, is decisive in the final event of Tess's tragedy – her return to Alec, for Alec provides at least a place to go.

The dramatic motivation provided by natural earth is central to every aspect of the book. It controls the style: page by page *Tess* has a wrought density of texture that is fairly unique in Hardy; symbolic depth is communicated by the physical surface of things with unhampered transparency while the homeliest conviction of fact is preserved ('The upper half of each turnip had been eaten off by the livestock' p.277); and one is aware of style not as a specifically verbal quality but as a quality of observation and intuition that are here – very often – wonderfully identical with each other, a quality of lucidity. Again, it is because of the *actual* motivational impact of the earth that Hardy is able to use setting and atmosphere for a symbolism that, considered in itself, is so astonishingly blunt and rudimentary. The green Vale of Blackmoor, fertile, small, enclosed by hills, lying under a blue haze – the vale of birth, the cradle of innocence. The wide misty setting of Talbothays dairy, 'oozing fatness and warm ferments', where the 'rush of juices could almost be heard below the hiss of fertilization' (p.151) – the sensual dream, the lost Paradise. The starved uplands of Flintcomb-Ash, with their ironic mimicry of the organs of generation, 'myriads of loose white flints in bulbous, cusped, and phallic shapes' (p.277), and the dun consuming ruin of the swede field – the mockery of impotence, the exile. Finally, that immensely courageous use of set-

NEW DIRECTIONS: THE 1950s

ting, Stonehenge and the stone of sacrifice. Obvious as these symbolisms are, their deep stress is maintained by Hardy's naturalistic premise. The earth exists here as Final Cause, and its omnipresence affords constantly to Hardy the textures that excited his eye and care, but affords them wholly charged with dramatic, causational necessity; and the symbolic values of setting are constituted, in large part, by the responses required of the characters themselves in their relationship with the earth.[28] □

Dorothy Van Ghent bridges realism and coincidentalism by identifying the ultimate mystery of the earth as a unifying concept; and drives her argument for unity forward by seeing Hardy's country folk with their fatalism and magic as a bridge between the mysterious earth and the moral dilemma of Tess:

■ . . . The naturalistic premise of the book – the condition of earth in which life is placed – is the most obvious, fundamental, and inexorable of facts; but because it is the physically 'given', into which and beyond which there can be no penetration, it exists as mystery; it is thus, even as the basis of all natural manifestation, itself of the quality of the supernatural. On the earth, so conceived, coincidence and accident constitute order, the prime terrestrial order, for they too are the 'given', impenetrable by human *ratio*, accountable only as mystery. By constructing the *Tess*-universe on the solid ground (one might say even literally on the 'ground') of the earth as Final Cause, mysterious cause of causes, Hardy does not allow us to forget that what is most concrete in experience is also what is most inscrutable, that an overturned clod in a field or the posture of herons standing in a water mead or the shadows of cows thrown against a wall by evening sunlight are as essentially fathomless as the procreative yearning, and this in turn as fathomless as the sheerest accident in event. The accidentalism and coincidentalism in the narrative pattern of the book stand, thus, in perfectly orderly correlation with the grounding mystery of the physically concrete and the natural.

But Hardy has, with very great cunning, reinforced the *necessity* of this particular kind of narrative pattern by giving to it the background of the folk instinctivism, folk fatalism, and folk magic. If the narrative is conducted largely by coincidence, the broad folk background rationalises coincidence by constant recognition of the mysteriously 'given' as what 'was to be' – the folk's humble presumption of order in a rule of mishap. The folk are the earth's pseudopodia, another fauna; and because they are so deeply rooted in the elemental life of the earth – like a sensitive animal extension of the earth itself – they share the authority of the natural. (Whether Hardy's 'folk', in all the attributes he gives them, ever existed historically or not is scarcely pertinent; they exist here.) Their philosophy and their skills in living, even their gestures of tragic violence, are instinctive adaptations to 'the given'; and because they are indestructible, their attitudes towards events authoritatively urge a similar fatalism upon the reader, impelling him to an imaginative acceptance of the doom-wrought series of accidents in the foreground of the action.

We have said that the dilemma of Tess is the dilemma of moral consciousness in its intractable earthy mixture; schematically simplified, the signifying form of the *Tess*-universe is the tragic heroism and tragic ineffectuality of such consciousness in an antagonistic earth where events shape themselves by accident rather than by moral design; and the *mythological* dimension of this form lies precisely in the earth's antagonism – for what is persistently antagonistic appears to have its own intentions, in this case mysterious, supernatural, for it is only thus that earth can seem to have 'intentions'. The folk are the bridge between mere earth and moral individuality; of the earth as they are, separable conscious ego does not arise among them to weaken animal instinct and confuse response – it is the sports, the deracinated ones, like Tess and Clare and Alec, who are morally individualised and who are therefore able to suffer isolation, alienation, and abandonment, or to make others so suffer; the folk, while they remain folk, cannot be individually isolated, alienated, or lost, for they are amoral and their existence is colonial rather than personal . . . [29] □

Equally illuminating is Van Ghent's identification of symbolism as fundamentally a magical strategy, and her perception that Hardy's use of it is also essentially a kind of magic:

■ The folk magic is, after all, in its strategy of analogy, only a specialisation and formalisation of the novelist's use of the symbolism of natural detail, a symbolism of which we are constantly aware from beginning to end . . . When a thorn of Alec's roses pricks Tess's chin, the occurrence is read as an omen – and omens properly belong to the field of magic . . . And there is very little difference, functionally, between Hardy's use of this popular symbol as an *omen* and his symbolic use of natural particulars – the chattering of the birds at dawn after the death of Prince and the iridescence of the coagulated blood, the swollen udders of the cows at Talbothays and the heavy fertilising mists of the late summer mornings and evenings, the ravaged turnip field on Flintcomb-Ash and the visitation of the polar birds. All of these natural details are either predictive or interpretive or both, and prediction and interpretation of events through analogies are the profession of magic. When a piece of blood-stained butcher paper flies up in the road as Tess enters the gate of the vicarage at Emminster, the occurrence is natural while it is ominous; it is realistically observed, as part of the 'given', while it inculcates the magical point of view. Novelistic symbolism is magical strategy. In *Tess*, which is through and through symbolic, magic is not only an adaptive specialisation of the 'folk', but it also determines the reader's response to the most naturalistic detail. Thus, though the story is grounded deeply in a naturalistic premise, Hardy's use of one of the commonest tools of novelists – symbolism – enforces a magical view of life.[30] □

This view of life accommodates the supernatural, and Van Ghent points to the presentation of Alec d'Urberville late in the novel with his pitchfork among the flames of the planting-fires, the queerness of his stage clothes, and his final insane trick on Tess in the d'Urberville vaults. But he and Angel Clare are also seen as representing extremes of human behaviour, two forms of egoism between which Tess stands, with her combination of d'Urberville blood and Victorian education, 'incapacitated for life by her moral idealism, capacious of life through her sensualism'.[31] Thus the text draws together the heroine's spectacular destiny, and the destiny of ordinary lives:

■ . . . When, after Alec's evilly absurd trick, she bends down to whisper at the opening of the vaults, 'Why am I on the wrong side of this door!' (p. 351) her words construct all the hopelessness of her cultural impasse. But her stabbing of Alec is her heroic return through the 'door' into the folk fold, the fold of nature and instinct, the anonymous community. If both Alec and Angel are spiritually impotent in their separate ways, Tess is finally creative by the only measure of creativeness that this particular novelistic universe holds, the measure of the instinctive and the natural. Her gesture is the traditional gesture of the revenge of instinct, by which she joins an innumerable company of folk heroines who stabbed and were hanged – the spectacular but still anonymous and common gesture of common circumstances and common responses, which we, as habitual readers of newspaper crime headlines, find, unthinkingly, so shocking to our delicate notions of what is 'natural'. That she goes, in her wandering at the end, to Stonehenge, is an inevitable symbolic going – as all going and doing are symbolic – for it is here that the earthiness of her state is best recognised, by the monoliths of Stonehenge, and that the human dignity of her last gesture has the most austere recognition, by the ritual sacrifices that have been made on these stones.[32] □

A very different approach to Van Ghent's, and an invigorating one, is that of Arnold Kettle in his book, *An Introduction to the English Novel*

(1953), a critical study in two volumes, which examines a range of major texts from the early nineteenth century onward. Its sociological strategy, which belongs to an early generation of humanist Marxist critics, is an investigation of social history and a critique of mechanical materialism, which also employs more traditional critical strategies. For Kettle the tragedy of Tess is not an individual tragedy, dependent on her morality or actions, but one brought about by the impersonal march of economic forces in which she and her peasant society are caught up in the Dorset of the 1890s. *Tess of the d'Urbervilles* is, he says, a thesis novel. He thus derogates the text as psychological realism, finding it implausible, and offers his own rather schematic symbolic reading. Recognising the essay's limitations, Arnold Kettle modified his position in 1966 for his Introduction to the Standard Edition of *Tess of the d'Urbervilles*, and in 1982 in writing a course unit on *Tess* for the Open University, he revised the social history approach to the novel in favour of one based more squarely on the text. But Kettle's early essay is an important landmark in *Tess* criticism, and gains its strength from its particular focus and conviction. Here is its opening section:

■ The subject of *Tess of the d'Urbervilles* is stated clearly by Hardy to be the fate of a 'pure woman'; in fact it is the destruction of the English peasantry. More than any other nineteenth-century novel we have touched on it has the quality of a social document. It has even, for all its high-pitched emotional quality, the kind of impersonality that the expression suggests. Its subject is all-pervasive, affecting and determining the nature of every part. It is a novel with a thesis – a *roman à thèse* – and the thesis is true.

The thesis is that in the course of the nineteenth century the disintegration of the peasantry – a process which had its roots deep in the past – had reached its final and tragic stage. With the extension of capitalist farming (farming, that is to say, in which the landowner farms not for sustenance but for profit and in which the land-workers become wage-earners) the old yeoman class of small-holders or peasants, with their traditions of independence and their own native culture, was bound to disappear. The developing forces of history were too strong for them and their way of life. And because that way of life had been proud and deep-rooted its destruction was necessarily painful and tragic. *Tess* is the story and the symbol of the destruction.

Tess Durbeyfield is a peasant girl. Her parents belong to a class ranking above the farm labourers, a class:

. . . including the carpenter, the smith, the shoemaker, the huckster, together with nondescript workers other than farm-labourers; a set of people who owed a certain stability of aim and conduct to the fact of their being life-holders, like Tess's father, or copyholders, or, occasionally, small freeholders. (p.339)

Already by the opening of the novel the Durbeyfields have fallen on hard times, a plight by no means solely due to the lack of stability in the characters of John and Joan. A further twist is given to their difficulty in making ends meet by the accident in which their horse is killed. It is her sense of guilt over this accident that allows Tess to be persuaded by her mother into visiting the Trantridge d'Urbervilles to 'claim kin' with a more prosperous branch of the family. And from this visit (itself an attempt to solve the Durbeyfields' economic problems) the whole tragedy derives.

In these opening chapters of the novel there is an immediate and insistent emphasis on historical processes, so that from the start the characters are not seen merely as individuals. The discovery by John Durbeyfield of his ancestry is not just an introductory comic scene, a display of quaint 'character'. It states the basic theme of the novel – what the Durbeyfields have been and what they become. The landscape in the second chapter (it is far more effective description than the famous set-piece at the beginning of *The Return of the Native*) is described and given significance almost wholly in terms of history. The 'Club-walking' scene, again, is contrasted with the May Day dances of the past and early pagan rites are recalled. Tess is revealed as one of a group, typical ('not handsomer than some others', p.20), and in the comparison between her and her mother the differences brought about by historical changes are emphasised. Joan Durbeyfield lives in the peasant folk-lore of the past, Tess has been to a National school. 'When they were together the Jacobean and the Victorian ages were juxtaposed' (p.28).

The sacrifice of Tess to d'Urberville is symbolic of the historical process at work. D'Urberville is not, of course, a d'Urberville at all, but the son of the *nouveau riche* Stoke family, capitalists who have bought their way into the gentry, and Tess's cry when she sees the d'Urberville estate: 'I thought we were an old family; but this is all new!' (p.42) carries a world of irony.[33] □

In his arresting opening sentence Arnold Kettle makes a number of important assumptions. He discards the intentionalist fallacy announced by the author's stated aim, and shifts the emphasis immediately from the tragic heroine to her social class. He recognises what earlier critics have noted, Hardy's movement in his last novels to an overt concern with social issues; but for Kettle the Victorians' attitude to sexuality is a marginal matter compared with the larger historical process observed in *Tess*. As we saw, Dorothy Van Ghent read the May-walking scene symbolically as representing proleptically Tess's victimisation by sexual instinct. Kettle also reads it symbolically, but in his case as representing an aspect of historical process, the contrast between past and present, as he also reads Tess's transitional position between the worlds of the Jacobeans and the Victorians. Kettle seeks the unity of the novel – its 'moral fable' as he calls it later in the essay – in the novel's symbolism. This becomes clear as his discussion proceeds. When Joan Durbeyfield dresses Tess in her working clothes to go to Trantridge, Kettle says:

■ Again the moment is symbolic. Tess, prepared to become, since change she must, a worker, is handed over by her mother to the life and the mercies of the ruling class.[34] □

Alec d'Urberville here clearly represents the new rich, the alien, intrusive ruling class whose money has been made not in land in Dorset, but in trade in the north of England. In the extracts that follow, Kettle pursues his analysis of this social and economic victimisation of Tess:

■ From the moment of her seduction by d'Urberville, Tess's story becomes a hopeless struggle, against overwhelming odds, to maintain her self-respect. After the death of her child she becomes a wage-labourer at the dairy farm at Talbothays. The social degradation is mitigated by the kindness of the dairyman and his wife, but the work is only seasonal. Here however she meets and falls in love with Angel Clare and through marriage to him thinks to escape her fate. But Angel, the intellectual, turns out to be more cruel than d'Urberville, the sensualist. Angel, with all his emancipated ideas, is not merely a prig and a hypocrite but a snob as well. He understands nothing of the meaning of the decline of the d'Urbervilles and his attitude to Tess is one of self-righteous idealisation.

> . . . 'My position – is this,' he said abruptly. 'I thought – any man would have thought – that by giving up all ambition to win a wife with social standing, with fortune, with knowledge of the world, I should secure rustic innocence, as surely as I should secure pink cheeks . . .' (p.234)

And when his dream of rustic innocence is shattered he can only taunt Tess with:

> 'Don't, Tess; don't argue. Different societies, different manners. You almost make me say you are an unapprehending peasant woman, who have never been initiated into the proportions of social things.' (p.229)

Even at the moment of her deepest humiliation Tess is stung to the retort:

> 'Lots of families are as bad as mine in that. Retty's family were once large landowners, and so were Dairyman Billett's, and the Debbyhouses who now are carters were once the De Bayeux family. You find such as I everywhere; 'tis a feature of our county, and I can't help it.' (p.230)

It is important (I shall return to this point) to give these passages their full weight because they emphasise the kind of novel this is. Such passages, read as 'psychological drama', ring queer and unconvincing. Their function in the novel is to stress the social nature of Tess's destiny and its typicality.

After Angel has left her the social degradation of Tess continues. At the farm at Flintcomb-Ash she and the other girls (once again it is significant that Tess's fate is shared by Marian and Izz who have not, in the same way, 'sinned' morally) become fully proletarianised, working for wages in the hardest, most degrading conditions. The scene at the threshing is here particularly important, a symbol of the dehumanised relationships of the new capitalist farms. At Talbothays there had at least been some possibility of pride and interest in the labour as well as a certain kindliness in the common kitchen at which the dairyman's wife presided. Here there is nothing kind or satisfying and the emphasis on Marian's bottle is not casual, not just a matter of the individual 'character'.

The final blow to Tess's attempts to maintain her self-respect comes with the death of her father and the consequent expulsion of the Durbeyfields from their cottage . . .

It is the need to support her family, thus driven off the land, that finally forces Tess back to Alec d'Urberville. And when Angel, chastened and penitent, returns, the final sacrifice is inevitable. Tess kills d'Urberville. The policemen take her from the altar at Stonehenge and the black flag is run up on Winchester jail.[35] □

As Arnold Kettle's earlier reference to the unconvincing quality of some of the novel's episodes implies, he is uncomfortable attempting to read *Tess* as realism. He suggests that Hardy is in fact not fundamentally concerned with the credible presentation of character, but with its typical, representative quality and function. Kettle's reading of the novel as a 'thesis' and a 'moral fable' about social and historical trends focusses on the symbolic function of character and event as forming part of a historical pattern:

■ It is important for a number of reasons to emphasise that *Tess of the d'Urbervilles* is a moral fable, that it is the expression of a generalised human situation in history and neither (what it is generally assumed to be) a purely personal tragedy nor (what Hardy appears to have intended) a philosophic comment on Life in general and the fate of Woman in particular. If we read the novel as a personal tragedy, the individual history of Tess Durbeyfield, a great deal strikes us as extremely unsatisfactory.[36] □

And he develops this point a little later in his essay:

■ . . . *Tess* is not a novel of the kind of *Emma* or *Middlemarch*. It does not illuminate within a detailed framework particular problems of human conduct and feeling. Its sphere is the more generalised movement of human destiny . . . . . . Once we recognise that the subject of *Tess* is the destruction of the peasantry many of the more casual criticisms of the book are seen to be rather wide of the mark.[37] □

Kettle draws attention to the heavy presence of coincidence, and also to the psychological implausibility of Tess's behaviour, such as her acute sensitivity: 'Could she, for instance, have *afforded* – bearing in mind the conditions of Flintcomb-Ash – to be merely hurt and unprotesting when Angel's brothers take away her boots when they find them in the ditch?';[38] and: 'Again, in the broad realm of probability, is there really any adequate reason why Tess, at the end, should murder d'Urberville?'[39] And, Kettle continues, there is the problem of Alec's characterisation:

■ . . . Many readers are antagonised by his presentation as what amounts to the stock villain of Victorian melodrama, the florid, moustache-twirling bounder who refers to the heroine (whom he is about to seduce) as 'Well, my beauty . . . ' (p.43). Is this not a character who has stepped direct out of the tenth-rate theatre or 'She was poor but she was honest'? It seems to me that almost the whole point about d'Urberville is that he is indeed the archetypal Victorian villain. Far from being weakened by the associations of crude melodrama he in fact illuminates the whole type and we understand better *why* the character of which he is a symbol did dominate a certain grade of Victorian entertainment and was enthusiastically hissed by the audience. It is the very typicality of d'Urberville that serves the purposes of the novel.[40] □

Hardy's treatment of religion also interests Kettle, but only as an agent of the social process of Tess's destruction:

■ . . . Hardy is not attempting an estimate of the total validity of the Christian philosophy. His subject is the destruction of the peasant Tess. It is the place of religious influence in that destruction that is his concern. And in the pattern of the novel the Christian church is seen as at best a neutral observer, at worst an active abettor in the process of destruction. It is not, historically considered, an unreasonable comment.[41] □

Like many critics, Kettle wrestles with the problem of Hardy's 'philosophy' and its representation in the novel. In the passage that follows, his close reading makes clear the grounds of his distaste for Hardy's loading of the dice and he endeavours to read this scene, in which Tess and Abraham discuss the stars, as rooted in basic economic reality:

■ . . . It emerges in its least palatable form in passages of the book most obviously intended as fundamental philosophical comment. There is the famous episode, for instance, in which Tess, driving the cart to market, speaks to her little brother of the stars:

> 'Did you say the stars were worlds, Tess?'
> 'Yes.'
> 'All like ours?'
> 'I don't know; but I think so. They sometimes seem to be like the apples on our stubbard-tree. Most of them splendid and sound – a few blighted.'
> 'Which do we live on – a splendid one or a blighted one?'
> 'A blighted one.'
> "Tis very unlucky that we didn't pitch on a sound one, when there were so many more of 'em!'
> 'Yes.'
> 'Is it like that *really*, Tess?' said Abraham, turning to her much impressed, on reconsideration of this rare information. 'How would it have been if we had pitched on a sound one?'
> 'Well, father wouldn't have coughed and creeped about as he does, and wouldn't have got too tipsy to go on this journey; and mother wouldn't have been always washing, and never getting finished.'
> 'And you would have been a rich lady ready-made, and not have had to be made rich by marrying a gentleman.'
> 'O Aby, don't – don't talk of that any more!' (pp. 35–6)

We tend to reject such an episode on two grounds: in the first place we are not convinced that any peasant girl would talk like that, in the second the philosophy implied (and the whole organisation of the book makes us give it the weight of the author's full sympathy, if not assent) is not calculated to win our support. The world as a blighted apple is an image too facile too satisfy us, even though we may recognise the force of Tess's pessimism. I think it is important, however, to empha-sise that even in this passage the pessimism is given a very explicit basis in actual conditions. It is the kind of life her parents lead that drives Tess to her feelings of despair and it is the sentence about her mother never getting finished that in fact saves the scene. For here is no pretentious philosophy of fatality but a bitterly realistic recalling of the actual fate of millions of working women.[42] □

Kettle finds Hardy's consciously pessimistic 'Aeschylean' philosophy 'bogus'.[43] He feels that his belief in the Immanent Will distorts the novel: 'And yet *Tess* survives Hardy's philosophy. It survives because his imagi-native understanding of the disintegration of the peasantry is more powerful than the limiting tendencies of his conscious outlook.'[44] But Kettle does not join those who sneer. Instead, as we have seen, he re-focuses Hardy's pessimism: 'there was more basis to his pessimism – the pessimism of the Wessex peasant who sees his world and his values being destroyed – than can be laughed away with an easy gesture of contempt'.[45]

In spite of its 'queer cramped literary style',[46] much of the achieve-ment of *Tess* depends, for Kettle, on its realistic, detailed evocation of the rural scene as an integral part of the text. However, this impact is dimin-ished in scenes such as that of Tess's confession and Angel's obtuse response, when 'Hardy allows his own inadequate *ideas* to weaken his profound instinctive *understanding*'.[47] And Kettle continues:

■ It is not, of course, a fatal error (there are far graver difficulties in the book) but I quote it to illustrate the battle going on throughout *Tess* between Hardy's ideas and his understanding. It is the inadequacy of his ideas that gives much of the book its oddly thin and stilted quality and which leads, in particular, to the unsatisfactory manipulation of chance which, more than anything in the novel, arouses our suspi-cions as to its validity. For the loading of the dice is an admission not so much of cunning as of impotence, a desperate gesture which attempts through artificial stimulation to achieve a consummation oth-erwise unobtainable. Hardy's understanding, his deep instinctive comprehension of the fate of the Wessex peasants, told him what had to be said, but his conscious philosophy did not give him adequate means always to say it. Hence the unduly long arm of coincidence, hence the half-digested classical allusions, hence the psychological weaknesses. Whereas from the social understanding emerges the strength of the novel, the superb revelation of the relation of men to nature, the haunting evocation of the Wessex landscape not as back-cloth but as the living challenging material of human existence, and the profoundly moving story of the peasant Tess.[48] □

Arnold Kettle's forceful reading of social collapse in *Tess* is supported by Hardy's detailed presentation of rural social conditions, but Kettle offers a rather static account of social history, and a later historical critic, Raymond Williams (see pp. 104–9 of this Guide) suggests that contemporary rural society was more complex than is indicated by Kettle's phrase 'the destruction of the English peasantry'. Moreover, Kettle flattens the characters into schematic roles, denying for instance the incipient complexity of Alec d'Urberville and Angel Clare, as well of course as of Tess herself.

The other influential study of the 1950s is Douglas Brown's *Thomas Hardy* (1954). It remains an important contribution to Hardy criticism, partly because it is one of the limited number of studies to address Hardy's treatment of a historical rural society. Brown uses documentary evidence of the decline of agriculture during the period in order to reinforce his reading of Hardy's fiction – for instance the research of Rider Haggard, published in his *Rural England* (1902), to which Hardy had contributed a section on Dorset; and Hardy's own essay, 'The Dorsetshire Labourer' (1883), written in the depths of an agricultural depression. Brown records the effects of such important influences as free trade, poor harvests and the import of cheap food. His focus on the collapse of Hardy's agrarian society in the face of industrialisation, though historical in emphasis, contains echoes of Lord David Cecil's humanist nostalgia for a vanishing and idealised essentially English world under invasion by an urban culture. He also situates himself within the New Critical strategy by supporting his historical commentary with close textual analysis, and attending to the relations between metaphor and structure. Moreover, in his appreciation of Hardy's use of the ballad narrative he gestures towards the generic tradition represented by Donald Davidson.

Brown's perception of the pattern in Hardy's major fiction, which *Tess of the d'Urbervilles* shares, goes back, as he admits, to Lionel Johnson:

■ . . . His protagonists are strong-natured countrymen, disciplined by the necessities of agricultural life. He brings into relation with them men and women from outside the rural world, better educated, superior in status, yet inferior in human worth. The contact occasions a sense of invasion, of disturbance . . . and the theme of urban invasion declares itself more clearly as the presence of the country, its labour and its past, make themselves felt . . .

This pattern records Hardy's dismay at the predicament of the agricultural community in the south of England during the last part of the nineteenth century and at the precarious hold of the agricultural way of life. It records a profound activity of the memory, a deep-seated allegiance of the writer's personality, a degree of dependence upon an identified and reliable past . . . [49] □

Brown feels that Hardy's urgent personal involvement in the impending catastrophe for his rural world betrays his artistic instincts in *Tess of the d'Urbervilles*, a point which he returns to later in his essay:

■ . . . *The Woodlanders* and *Tess of the d'Urbervilles* have for their setting the years of the contemporary agricultural tragedy. In these, and particularly in the second, the artistic purity is sullied. The weaving of a ballad tale into the agricultural environment, together with the expression of Hardy's profound and vigorous feeling for the status of man in the natural order, no longer absorbs sufficiently the novelist's anxiety, his sense of imminent disaster . . .

It is true to say that *Tess* is a flawed work of art, but it is little to the purpose. The novel survives its faults magnificently. The simplicity and force of its conception have given it a legendary quality. Here is not merely the tragedy of a heroic girl, but the tragedy of a proud community baffled and defeated by processes beyond its understanding or control. The resonance of the tale makes itself felt over and over again. The superb opening, the death of Prince the horse, the lovely elegiac scene of the harvesting, the sequence in the dairy farm, the scene of the sleepwalking, the episodes of agricultural life at Flintcomb-Ash, the climax at Stonehenge, are powerful and original imaginative inventions. The rather tawdry theatricality of that climax, the deceptive offer of tragic symbolism, reveal themselves only on reflection. We scarcely try to understand – we feel that Hardy himself did not altogether measure this defeat, this calamity. But the insistent tenderness exacts concurrence, by a force like make-believe. The falsities, the intrusive commentaries, the sophisticated mannerisms in the prose, do only local damage.[50] □

Like Arnold Kettle, Douglas Brown is less concerned with the tragic experience of Tess as an individual than with her representative function. This is shaped by her dual roles as country girl and representative of an ancient family ruined by urban invaders. Brown's view involves a somewhat idealised view of rural traditions (Hardy himself suggests that no one can recall the original function of the May Day celebrations), and a highly schematic view of Hardy's characterisations of Tess, Alec d'Urberville and Angel Clare:

■ Hardy composed nothing finer than the opening of *Tess*, and the style of it is entirely his own. The whole invention is at once substantial with social and historical perceptions, and quick with metaphorical life. How effectively the May Dance evokes a country mirth springing from traditional ways and reliance upon natural processes! The three ominous visitors, one of them later to become an agent of destruction, suggest how the dance of vitality is jeopardised by the thrust of sophisticated urban life. Then the appearance of the spurious country squire adds to the sense of jeopardy. The masquerader, the economic intruder, the representative of processes at work destroying the bases of agricultural security, stands with the spiritual intruder. Alongside this image, there unfolds that of the old father's discovery of his ancient but unavailing ancestry: a disclosure of the community's past which helps to define what Tess represents in the ensuing tale, at the same time as it sharpens the intrusive and invading quality invested in Alec d'Urberville. We feel the lost independence and the helplessness of agricultural man in this decrepit figure, as also in old South, Durbeyfield's equivalent in the previous novel.[51] The art ordering the whole is marvellously secure of its purpose. The metaphorical terms reside so naturally within the ballad narrative. The preparation for such later scenes as Tess harvesting at Marlott, Tess in the early dawn at Talbothays, is perfect. For Tess is not only the pure woman, the ballad heroine, the country girl: she is the agricultural community in its moment of ruin . . . Here is the impulse behind the legend. It dramatises the defeat of Tess, the country girl and representative of an ancient country line, and her ruin by the economic and spiritual invaders of country life. It takes its origin in a past lively with traditional activity; it ends in Stonehenge, in passivity, the primitive place confirming a sense of doom which has gathered intensity all along. What has happened in the agricultural society is by now irrevocable. It is 1890, in south-west England.[52] □

Brown's close reading of the sleep-walking incident is particularly interesting. He locates the scene's symbolic power and peculiar impact in Hardy's own experience as a *déclassé*, *déraciné* figure; a famous novelist returned from the metropolis to his roots. The strong pyschological dimension of this scene, so important to later critics such as Rosemary Sumner (see pp. 116–21 of this Guide) is ignored in favour of an exclusively sociological reading, so that Tess's passivity here, like her society, is discovered to be a fundamental aspect of both their strengths. And Brown supports this sociological reading by reference to the impersonal drive of the narrative's ballad context:

■ The powerful, if faulty, sleepwalking scene records the passivity and the doom most poignantly. It balances precariously between sentimentality and tragedy, yet its impact transcends its place in the story. Hardy has constructed a perfect imaginative equivalent for the deepest perceptions which inform the novel as a whole. Old John South's paralysis and death had something of this fascinating quality, but here the enacted image proves more distressing. For the most part the narrative issues as if from the consciousness of Tess herself, impotent in the hold and motion of an alien force. She is awake and strong-willed, yet passive, stunned. You may feel that her strange passivity (she makes no effort to alter the course of events) is welded into her strength. She is the agricultural predicament in metaphor, engaging Hardy's deepest impulses of sympathy and allegiance. Clare is helpless too: a blind, unknowing force, carrying the country girl to burial. Hardy's sense of curt, impersonal powers (such as preside in the world of balladry) who order human destiny, here becomes a strength to his fiction. Clare, so the narrative implies, is the impassive instrument of some will, some purpose, stemming from the disastrous life of the cities, from the intellectual and spiritual awareness – and confusion – of the world outside the agricultural community, and doomed to destroy the worthiness, innocence, and vitality of country life, rather than intending their destruction. The invention, here, goes beyond nostalgia. But the image is painful; all the suffering with which Hardy felt the defeat of agricultural life by nullifying urban forces, has gone into it, and the private despair that was the novelist's own inheritance from his sojourn 'outside'.[53] □

Like Dorothy Van Ghent, Douglas Brown's concern with narrative form relates the local effect to the novel's larger patterns, but he sees its movements very much in terms of Hardy's preoccupation with the destruction of the rural world. The following passages display Brown's attention to narrative movement, balance and symbolism, supported by Hardy's realism and suffused by his distress:

■ The second movement whose power and beauty are sustained at length balances the account of life at Crick's dairy farm. It records the life of Flintcomb-Ash . . . [which] directly reflects the new farming, contrasting in every essential with Talbothays. It is as essential to the meaning of the novel as the historical analysis of the opening, or the violent uprooting of the family driven out of the agricultural community at the end. And it affords an apt environment for this bitter part of the narrative. Tess's second recovery is painfully gradual, described in grave and laboured prose. The end of the movement is very moving; it brings us close to Hardy's distinction as a tragic writer. His incipient nostalgia is controlled by a scrutiny of the natural environment and the daily toil of the agricultural 'home', a scrutiny almost fierce in its anxiety. There is deep distress in this contemplation of Tess and the girls and the little labouring society of which they are a part. There is the nagging rigour of this life, and there is the will to endure and to persist and to labour on regardlessly. The writing vibrates with both.

An epilogue to this movement of the second recovery balances the harvest scene at Marlott which was prologue to the first. Harvest tide has returned. But now the human threshers stand side by side with the invading threshing machine. The narrative quality suggests the sleepwalking scene again. The sleepwalker, impersonal agent of destruction, is now the machine. The sleepwalking scene gave a first impression of some mechanical force not to be baulked, once released. Now the impression grows clearer. The helpless Tess of the earlier scene is here the trapped, exhausted Tess whose task is to feed the machine. Her predicament gets a richer imagery from the group of labourers of 'an older day' who cannot resist, or accept, the new power, and who are bewildered and defeated . . .

Into this situation, reinforcing an aspect of its meaning, comes the invader, the son of the merchant from the North, 'dressed in a tweed suit of fashionable pattern, [who] twirled a gay walking-cane' (p. 317). Tess in Clare's arms as he sleepwalks, Tess in the clutch of the threshing machine, Tess before Alec d'Urberville – her predicament is the same.[54] □

Turning from Tess, who has resumed her position on the threshing machine, with its symbolism and narrative parallelism, Brown's analysis of the intensely sensuous language of the scene reveals Hardy's passionate engagement with his agricultural theme:

■ . . . The marvellous passages that follow have a sensuous force and a depth of feeling Hardy rarely equalled:

> . . . From the west a wrathful shine . . . had burst forth after the cloudy day flooding the tired and sticky faces of the threshers, and dyeing them with a coppery light . . .
> A panting ache ran through the rick. The man who fed was weary, and Tess could see that the red nape of his neck was encrusted with dirt and husks. (p. 322)

Wrathful takes its force from the mood of the contemplation. The *tired and sticky faces* seen as the shine breaks out suggest the weakening before the machine, and the *dyeing* of those faces reinforces that: they slip out of human expressions. *Coppery* both defines the observed tint, and reflects from the machine, holding the machine there beside their faces.[55] □

The essay concludes by drawing together Brown's central preoccupations: the disastrous collapse of the agricultural order under the impact of new economic conditions and the urban invader; Hardy's linking of Tess's story to social upheaval through her representative function; her symbolising the passivity and incomprehension of the rural society in the face of these impersonal forces; and the pervasive presence of Hardy's bitterness at the vanishing of his world:

■ Hardy sets the culminating family tragedy against the ominous background of the Lady-Day migration of so many village folk. The erasure of long local life by these contemporary migrations, Hardy perceived, was a grave social and spiritual loss. It is no accident of art that the story of Tess should end amid scenes of uprooting. The narrative of the Durbeyfields' own moving from home is full of disquiet. The migration of so many others, the dissolving social order, is not particularly dwelt upon; but the ironical reception of the forlorn family at Kingsbere, its ancient home, dramatises a personal bitterness of spirit. Only a place in the family vault, a home there, remains to the derelict inheritors. It is this homeless despair of a family which has lost its rights and independence in the village community, that gives Tess finally into the invader's power.

The sensation of moving unresistingly through a dream recurs in the passages that describe Tess impelled towards her doom and trapped for the last time. The hints of madness are indecisive enough to leave a nightmare quality around her experiences. The situation is blurred for her; the forces that have defeated her are beyond her comprehension.[56] □

Although still concerned with the recurrent issues of tragedy, realism, and Wessex, the criticism of the 1950s opens up more sophisticated ways of reading Tess of the d'Urbervilles. New Criticism explores the patterns created by its language, and discovers in the text a structure independent of the plot, which possesses an organic unity, determined in different ways by nature. In contrast, the sociological approach of Marxist and historical criticism attends to the novel's shaping incidents, and exposes the socio-economic conditions of a historical society subjected to urban invasion, and threatened by collapse.

These new directions of the 1950s were linked, however, by a concern with symbolic language, by an interest in form, and by a distrust of the elements of 'philosophy' articulated by the intrusive narrative voice. They also shared a humanistic concern with the value of the individual, and with the integrity of the organic society. These features pointed forward to the development of humanist formalism, the dominant critical force in the next two decades, which is discussed in the following chapter.

CHAPTER FOUR

The Dominance of Humanist Formalism: The 1960s and 1970s

DURING THE 1960s and 1970s there occurred an explosion of critical interest in Hardy, which gathered momentum in tandem with the development of humanist formalism. The liberal humanist ideology had been in evidence in the earliest reviews, with their emphasis on Tess's individual struggle with fate, on the strength of the human spirit, and on the naturalisation of the novel's world and its values. In the post-New Critical decades the humanist concepts – the value of the individual and the recognition of character as presenting a unified subject, the importance of maturity, the integrity of the organic (and preferably rural) society – came to be the dominant force in criticism. However, in the 1960s and 1970s critics brought fresh vigour to the humanist approach by developing critical strategies out of the New Critical formalism practised by, for instance, Dorothy Van Ghent, with its assertion of the unity of the text and the importance of its language as the origin of meaning.

The picture of *Tess of the d'Urbervilles* criticism during these two decades of humanist formalist ascendency is one of both continuity and change, with many stimulating variations of critical approach, and this chapter will examine the major strands: the continued interest in Hardy's use of mythology, exciting applications in the analysis of language and form, the renewed study of intellectual influences, the valuable development of genetic criticism, and fresh encounters with *Tess* as tragedy, together with new departures in the humanist Marxist analyses of *Tess*.

One of the most interesting works of these two decades is Roy Morrell's polemical study, published in 1965, *Thomas Hardy: The Will and the Way* (its title comes from the saying, 'Where there's a will there's a way'), an existential humanist approach that attacks both conservative critics and the New Critics. Its thesis is that, contrary to the – by the mid-1960s – almost consensual view that Hardy's outlook was pessimistic and fatalistic, Hardy in fact believed that humanity always retained, even in the direst situation, the capacity to will the future through choice and action. Morrell thus seeks to overturn a tradition in *Tess* criticism established by William R. Rutland, who located Hardy's own determinist views in his reading of nineteenth-century science and philosophy, and more immediately the approaches of Morrell's predecessors in the 1950s; Arnold Kettle, Douglas Brown and most obviously, John Holloway:

■ As far as Hardy is concerned, I shall deal mainly with the criticism of Dr John Holloway, since this is admirably representative of the two most typical lines of interpretation today: those which assume in Hardy, first, a narrow belief in pessimistic determinism, a denial of man's freedom, and, second, an abiding faith in the goodness of nature and of the old agricultural order . . . [1] □

Contrary to Kettle and Brown, Morrell argues that 'the novels and stories are much more intimately concerned with personal and human dilemmas than with the documenting of social conditions'.[2] And in asserting his own humanist approach, he is concerned to contradict John Holloway, whose 'distortions', though not large, 'all are in the same direction of denying a margin for the exercise of human intelligence or freedom, till finally we are led well out of sight of the truth'.[3] He also vehemently rejects the New Critical procedures exemplified by John Holloway. In Morrell's view, while a novel 'offers limitless opportunities for the selective or imagist methods of the New Critic',[4] these distort the relation between text and context and produce serious misreadings. Morrell's own formalist approach depends upon the structure of the plot rather than language. In his discussion of *Tess of the d'Urbervilles* in the following passage, he engages with John Holloway to demonstrate how New Critical readings serve to reinforce the critic's own ideological position and his own version of humanistic despair:

■ But Holloway continues to reduce Hardy's writings to pointlessness, to a denial of any meaning in human choice or human effort, and perhaps none of his arguments is more calculated to convince his fellow critics than his dubbing of certain images 'proleptic'. These images, he says, 'hint at a whole determined sequence of things'. Could they not hint, equally well, at the uncertainty of the future, at untoward *contingencies*? Could they not jolt man out of too placid an acceptance, and suggest that the worst might after all 'happen to us', if we let the 'sequence' drift? If the sequence is determined, we have no choice: but isn't this where Holloway begs the question? He reminds us of something he calls a proleptic image in *Tess*:

Crick the dairyman is listening to Tess herself describe how she can day-dream her mind out of her body: he 'turned to her with his mouth full, his eyes charged with enquiry, and his great knife and fork . . . *planted erect on the table, like the beginning of a gallows*' (p. 124). On every reading after the first, this comparison is incandescent; surely it does more than any volume of generalities to fix in us Hardy's sense of the unalterable sequence of things. [See p. 54 of this Guide.]

This won't do. It is Holloway, not Hardy, who is trying to 'fix in us' this 'sense of the unalterable sequence of things'; and he asks us to accept the interpretation (which is, to say the least, unproven) not instead of a 'volume of generalities' but instead of Hardy's novel. In the three hundred pages of that novel between the 'proleptic' image and the gallows (no wonder that the reader is not struck by it on first reading!) the whole rhythm and tension of our interest is controlled by the reprieves, the rallies, the second chances; by our sense of what might, even at a late stage, be done to prevent the disaster. Why do circumstances prompt Tess again and again to confess? Why does she find the letter before her marriage? Why are we told she would have been spared all her later sufferings had she persisted in her plan to visit Angel's parents? Why did Hardy show her as so nearly reaching that objective? Why, after Izz Huett's admission that no one could love Angel more than Tess does, is Angel shown as 'within a feather-weight's turn' (p. 265) of going back and searching her out, and taking her with him? Why does Angel tell Tess at the end that 'it might have prevented much misunderstanding and woe' (p. 376) had she told him of the sleepwalking? At these, and other points, the 'unalterable' sequence might have been altered. And any reader with an eye for images that 'fix' the sequence of things as 'unalterable' or 'determined', cuts himself off from the full experience of *Tess* and from all Hardy's other novels, where again and again the point of the narration is to indicate not only events, but also possibilities . . . [5] □

These instances of events that appear to reinforce the novel's tragic pattern, may instead be read as emphasising opportunities that the characters refuse to take up. They represent failures of will. For Morrell, the meaning of *Tess of the d'Urbervilles* is dependent not on language and the structure of imagery but on character as revealed in action, on incident or plot:

■ The New Critics will have nothing but bored contempt for my simplicity in supposing that mere incidents can weigh in an argument against *images* – the latter being regarded as in some way more essentially part of the book, part of its 'weave'.[6] □

Crucial to *Tess*, Morrell suggests, is the characters' failure to choose – to postpone, to drift, to wait on events – including Angel Clare, but principally Tess herself whose failure lies in 'choosing not to choose'.[7] Morrell argues that she lacks the moral courage to make the self-defining choices she is only too aware are essential, lacks the will to translate into actuality alternatives that are allowed to remain potential. For him the scene in the garden at Talbothays serves to reveal how she has lost touch with reality. Morrell develops this insight and its implications in the following extracts:

■ Postponement is a theme of the book. At the beginning the Durbeyfields are described as *'waiters* on Providence' (p. 41), and even Tess, conscious as she is of the weaknesses of her family and anxious to do something to help the budget and pay for the loss of the horse, makes only half-hearted attempts to get 'some light occupation in the immediate neighbourhood' (p. 48). It is because she fails to control circumstances in time, that circumstances push her eventually in the direction of Trantridge and Alec. Even then Hardy does not describe Tess as hopelessly trapped: she has paid one visit to the d'Urbervilles, and knows, or has misgivings about, what she is in for. But even if she has had only slight misgivings about Alec after her first visit, these become definite enough when Alec fetches her for the second journey and pesters her on the road. The seduction is not a sudden one; she knows what to expect; but does nothing with the reprieve.

So too with the confession: she knows what she must do, but fails to act in time. And when she turns back from Emminster Vicarage, it is with thoughts of summoning up courage for another attempt later; but the attempt is never made, though her meeting with Alec should have urged upon her the still greater necessity for it . . .

. . . One recalls Angel's negligence, too, in not writing to Tess. 'Too Late, Beloved', Hardy's first title for the book, clearly refers to these failures of Angel's; but at the moment we are more concerned with the tendency to drift, to postpone, to leave things to chance, on the part of Tess herself.

And here the threshing machine assumes a central position: a symbol of time's tyranny, time's pressure, amidst the comparatively easy-going seasonal rhythm of the countryside; and yet also a reprieve from Alec, the very temporariness of which is a reminder that she must do something. For all the time she knows Alec is waiting. And, ironically, the very shaking of the machine tires her out, shakes her resolution; although that same evening she also writes a long and desperate appeal to her husband.

That is all she does with her reprieve. When the other girls, less capable than Tess, leave Farmer Groby and secure better-paid and more congenial work, Tess – having had 'a vaguely shaped hope that something would happen to render another outdoor engagement unnecessary' (p.310) – is unemployed. Hardy's words are critical; but Tess herself had on several occasions in the past proved the value of encountering life's difficulties realistically, she had learnt to distrust 'd'Urberville air-castles' (p.103) and the Durbeyfield *Compleat Fortune Teller*; so to her too 'a vaguely shaped hope that something would happen' must have seemed an inadequate basis for inaction. Hardy goes on to point his moral by describing a Lady-Day encounter between the brightly painted waggon taking Marian and Izz to their new work and the unpainted 'creaking erection' (p.348) on which the Durbeyfield family and furniture with its typical 'muck and muddle' is in disorganised transit to Kingsbere, where Mrs Durbeyfield has failed to secure lodgings, so that they and their belongings have all to be dumped in the approach to the churchyard.

Less capable than Tess: there is the irony. It is Tess's capability, her physical strength and stoical endurance, of which indeed she has already given abundant proof at Flintcomb-Ash, that comes out most strongly in the threshing machine scene. Farmer Groby puts Tess to work on the machine perhaps because he has a grudge against her, but partly because she can best do it: 'she was one of those who best combined strength with quickness in untying, and both with staying power' (p.317). Moreover, she stays at the tiring and exacting work longer than she need in her desire to escape Alec. How is it that this same girl, almost heroic in her patience and endurance, turned back so weakly at Emminster, and despite Alec's molestations, made no second attempt? Hardy may be implying something here about Tess's nature which could not be said more openly in those times without losing the sympathy of too many readers; I mean a certain compliance and weakness that were essential accompaniments of her very warmth and passionate womanliness. But whether that is the case or not, he is clearly keen to suggest a curious mingling of strength and weakness in other parts of Tess's character, in her will; and to indicate how far Tess fell short of her considerable potentialities.[8] □

Roy Morrell then, offers a muted existential view of tragic experience in *Tess*, which involves not fate, nor society, but only human agencies and human weakness:

■ . . . All through the novel Hardy is writing of human weaknesses, and pleading for just that degree of greater effort and courage, of readier sympathy and tolerance and humanity. And after all these protests against the alterable in the human situation, it is hardly sensible to take the 'President of the Immortals' literally, thus *contradicting* its whole context. Instead, the phrase must *take its meaning from* its context: 'Some people, God help them, may still suppose', Hardy is saying, 'like Aeschylus long ago, or like Joan Durbeyfield, shifting the blame from her own shoulders, that Fate can be blamed for Tess's disaster. The reader may wish to believe this too: but surely I have shown where the real blame lies'.[9] □

Irving Howe in his book *Thomas Hardy* (1968), which remains a sound introduction to Hardy, also finds the concerns of Kettle, Brown and Van Ghent too narrow and he inflects the humanist treatment of character somewhat differently, stressing Tess's human individuality and her capacity to represent the resilience of human life. In this view the secondary characters, rural environment and formal attributes simply serve to heighten the reality of Tess herself. The passages that follow are characteristic of the mainstream liberal humanist approach that Howe's criticism represents:

■ . . . in *Tess* he stakes everything on his sensuous apprehension of a young woman's life, a girl who is at once a simple milkmaid and an archetype of feminine strength. Nothing finally matters in the novel nearly so much as Tess herself: not the other characters, not the philosophic underlay, not the social setting. In her violation, neglect and endurance, Tess comes to seem Hardy's most radical claim for the redemptive power of suffering; she stands, both in the economy of the book and as a figure rising beyond its pages and into common memory, for the unconditional authority of feeling.

Tess is one of the greatest examples we have in English literature of how a writer can take hold of a cultural stereotype and, through the sheer intensity of his affection, pare and purify it into something that is morally ennobling . . . [10] □

Howe thus advances the humanist ideal of the unified subject and the organic nature of the novel's form:

■ . . . Though subjected to endless indignities, assaults and defeats, Tess remains a figure of harmony – between her self and her role, between her nature and her culture. Hardy presents her neither from the outside nor the inside exclusively, neither through event nor analysis alone; she is apprehended in her organic completenesss, so that her objectivity and subjectivity become inseparable. A victim of civilization, she is also a gift of civilization.[11] □

A shrewd and penetrating essay, 'Colour and Movement in Hardy's *Tess of the d'Urbervilles*', by the stimulating critic Tony Tanner, was published in 1968 in the *Critical Quarterly* and has been frequently reprinted. Tanner is concerned with the profound, almost Sophoclean sense of tragedy in *Tess*, seeing it in universal terms as humanity's tragic inhabiting of a universe in destructive conflict with itself, which is focused in the experience of its heroine. This is manifested in the novel's form, composed of extensive patterns of imagery of colour and movement, which Tanner's close reading uncovers. Like Dorothy Van Ghent, he discovers 'the furthest reach of form' in the 'minor notation'.[12] The perhaps surprising starting point of Tanner's essay is Henry James, who disdained the crudity of Hardy's art. However, argues Tanner, compared with James, 'Hardy's art is more truly impersonal'.[13] And one way in which this impersonality is achieved is through Hardy's detached, scrupulous observation – the 'incomparable clarity of his eyes'.[14] An anonymity associated with folktale and ballads is also gained through a second aspect of the novel's form, Hardy's employment of the architectonic and the plastic: 'the overall architecture of the novel is blocked out with massive simplicity in a series of balancing phases – The Maiden, Maiden No More, the Rally, the Consequence; and so on'.[15] Hardy's indifference to the causative in his narrative, says Tanner, 'enhances the visibility of the most basic lineaments of the tale'.[16]

Tony Tanner begins his account of the universal nature of *Tess* by looking at Hardy's use of colour in its individualising and proleptic functions:

■ . . . For an artist as visually sensitive as Hardy, colour is of the first importance and significance, and there is one colour which literally catches the eye, and is meant to catch it, throughout the book. This colour is red, the colour of blood, which is associated with Tess from first to last. It dogs her, disturbs her, destroys her. She is full of it, she spills it, she loses it. Watching Tess's life we begin to see that her destiny is nothing more or less than the colour red. The first time we (and Angel) see Tess, in the May dance with the other girls, she stands out. How? They are all in white except that Tess 'wore a red ribbon in her hair, and was the only one of the white company who could boast of such pronounced adornment' (p. 20). Tess is marked, even from the happy valley of her birth and childhood. The others are a semi-anonymous mass; Tess already has that heightened legibility, that eye-taking prominence which suggests that she has in some mysterious way been singled out. And the red stands out because it is on a pure white background. In that simple scene and colour contrast is the embryo of the whole book and all that happens in it.[17] □

Tanner picks up the idea of the red ribbon as one of a series of omens – for instance, the red blood in the scene in which the horse Prince is killed. It represents the beginning of a pattern of crude economic cause and effect in the text, but Tess's attempt to staunch the blood is also a memorable, graphic image. Indeed, suggests Tanner, it is a powerful omen:

■ . . . It adumbrates the loss of her virginity, for she, too, will be brutally pierced on a darkened road far from home; and once the blood of her innocence has been released, she too, like the stoical Prince, will stay upright as long as she can until, all blood being out, she will sink down suddenly in a heap. Compressed in that one imponderable scene we can see her whole life.[18] □

The essay continues to record all the instances of the colour red in the text – the references to the red interior of Tess's mouth (for, says Tanner, 'it is part of the whole meaning of the book that there is as much red inside Tess as outside her'),[19] the red d'Urberville house, the roses and strawberries Alec forces on her, his phallic red cigar, the sign-writer's red paint, the red threshing machine, the stains on her skin in the garden, and even the meat-buyer's blood-stained paper which 'is not a clumsy symbol [but] one of a number of cumulative omens'.[20] These omens include Tess's drawing blood from Alec's mouth with a gauntlet, which anticipates the blood-stained ceiling with its appearance of an ace of hearts. And Tanner comments: 'In that shape of the heart, sex and death are merged in utmost legibility.'[21]

Tony Tanner then traces more briefly those other omens that cumulatively figure Tess's destiny, including the sun, altars and tombs, concluding with the scene at Stonehenge, in which these are drawn together:

■ . . . The sun and the redness which have marked Tess's life, now converge at the moment of her approaching death. Finally Tess takes her last rest on the altar of Stonehenge. She speaks to Angel – again, it is before dawn, that sunless part of the day when he can communicate with her.

> 'Did they sacrifice to God here?' asked she.
>   'No', said he.
>   'Who to?'
>   'I believe to the sun. That lofty stone set away by itself is in the direction of the sun, which will presently rise behind it.' (p. 380)

When the sun does rise it also reveals the policemen closing in, for it is society which demands a specific revenge upon Tess. But in the configuration of omens which, I think, is the major part of the book, Tess is indeed a victim, sacrificed to the sun. The heathen temple is fitting, since of course Tess is descended from Pagan d'Urberville, and Hardy makes no scruple about asserting that women 'retain in their souls far

more of the Pagan fantasy of their remote forefathers than of the systematized religion taught their race at a later date' (p. 109). This raises
an important point. Is Tess a victim of society, or of nature? Who wants
her blood, who is after her, the policemen, or the sun? Or are they in
some sadistic conspiracy so that we see nature and society converging
on Tess to destroy her? I will return to this question.[22] □

Tanner's discussion moves on to consider his second theme, movement.
Each of the novel's phases, Tanner points out, commences with a figure
moving. At the opening of the novel it is Jack Durbeyfield, Phase the
Second opens with Tess lugging a basket along the road, Phase the Third
begins with her leaving home for the second time at first in a trap and
then on foot. After her banishment by her husband she later walks to
Emminster Vicarage and she walks home when she is summoned back to
her family. Tanner concludes this section of his essay with a culminating
example, which reinforces his view of the schematic, repetitive quality of
Hardy's visualisation – brief, arresting glimpses of a figure in motion,
which imply her place in a larger world:

■ . . . Perhaps the ultimate reduction of Tess, the distillation of her
fate, is to be seen when she runs after Angel having murdered Alec.
Angel turns round, 'the tape-like surface of the road diminished in his
rear as far as he could see, and as he gazed a moving spot intruded on
the white vacuity of its perspective' (p. 371). This scene has been antici-
pated when Tess was working at Flintcomb-Ash:

 . . . the whole field was in colour a desolate drab; it was a
 complexion without features, as if a face from chin to brow should
 be only an expanse of skin. The sky wore, in another colour, the
 same likeness; a white vacuity of countenance with the lineaments
 gone. So these two upper and nether visages confronted each
 other, all day long . . . without anything standing between
 them but the two girls crawling over the surface of the former like
 flies. (p. 277)

In both cases we see Tess as a moving spot on a white vacuity. And
this extreme pictorial reduction seems to me to be right at the heart of
Hardy's vision.[23] □

At the core of Tony Tanner's illuminating essay is his view of *Tess of the
d'Urbervilles* as the expression of Hardy's profound tragic vision of
humanity's place in a fundamentally conflictual universe, in which the
ultimate mystery of experience is visualised symbolically:

■ This brings me to a problem I mentioned earlier. We see Tess suffering, apparently doomed to suffer; destroyed by two men, by society, by the sun outside her and the blood inside her. And we are tempted to ask, what is Hardy's vision of the *cause* of this tale of suffering. Throughout the book Hardy stresses that Tess is damned, and damns herself, according to man-made laws which are as arbitrary as they are cruel. He goes out of his way to show how Nature seems to disdain, ignore or make mockery of the laws which social beings impose on themselves. The fetish of chastity is a ludicrous aberration in a world which teems and spills with such promiscuous and far-flung fertility every year (not to say a brutal caricature of human justice in that what was damned in the woman was condoned in the man). So, if the book was an attempt to show an innocent girl who is destroyed by society though justified by Nature, Hardy could certainly have left the opposition as direct and as simple as that. Social laws hang Tess; and Nature admits no such laws. But it is an important part of the book that we feel Nature itself turning against Tess, so that we register something approaching a sadism of *both* the man-made *and* the natural directed against her. If she is tortured by the man-made threshing machine, she is also crushed by the forge of the sun; the cold negating metal in Angel is also to be found in the 'steely stars' (p. 333); the pangs of guilt which lacerate her are matched by the 'glass splinters' of rain (p. 278) which penetrate her at Flintcomb-Ash . . . This suggests a universe of radical opposition, working to destroy what it works to create, crushing to death what it coaxes into life. From this point of view society only appears as a functioning part of a larger process whereby the vertical returns to the horizontal, motion lapses into stillness and structure cedes to the unstructured. The policemen appear as the sun rises: Tess is a sacrifice to both, to all of them. Hardy's vision is tragic and penetrates far deeper than specific social anomalies. One is more inclined to think of Sophocles than, say, Zola, when reading Hardy. The vision is tragic because he shows an ordering of existence in which nature turns against itself, in which the sun blasts what it blesses, in which all the hopeful explorations of life turn out to have been a circuitous peregrination towards death. 'All things are born to be diminished' said Pericles at the time of Sophocles; and Hardy's comparable feeling that all things are tended to be obliterated, reveals a Sophoclean grasp of the bed-rock ironies of existence.

. . . Tess is gradually crucified on the oppugnant [antagonistically opposed] ironies of circumstance and existence itself, ironies which centre, I have suggested, in the fact of blood, that basic stuff which starts the human spot moving across the white vacuity. Blood, and the spilling of blood; which in one set of circumstances can mean sexual passion and the creation of life, and in another can mean murderous passion and death – two forms of 'red' energy intimately related – this is the substance of Tess's story. And why should it all happen to her? You can say, as some people in the book say fatalistically, 'It was to be' (p. 77). Or you can go through the book and try to work out how Hardy apportions the blame – a bit on Tess, a bit on society, a bit on religion, a bit on heredity, a bit on the Industrial Revolution, a bit on the men who abuse her, a bit on the sun and the stars, and so on. But Hardy does not work in this way. More than make us judge, Hardy makes us see; and in looking for some explanation of why all this should happen to Tess, our eyes finally settle on that red ribbon marking out the little girl in the white dress, which already foreshadows the red blood stain on the white ceiling. In her beginning is her end. It is the oldest of truths, but it takes a great writer to make us experience it again in all its awesome mystery. [24] □

The by now familiar stress on the centrality of language in fiction, particularly imagery, which Tony Tanner subjects to a rigorous examination in his essay on *Tess*, is developed further by David Lodge, in his book *Language of Fiction* (1966). He regards the novel like poetry, as being 'essentially an art of language', which demands 'that close and sensitive engagement with language which we naturally expect from the critic of poetry'.[25] Lodge's critical project is to relate his identification of patterns in the novel to his rigorous linguistic analysis of selected passages, and this formalist bias is also influenced by the contemporary interest in rhetorical strategies represented by Wayne Booth's seminal work, *The Rhetoric of Fiction*, which had appeared in 1961.

David Lodge is fascinated by the problem of Hardy's two narrative voices, 'the voice of the author as creator and maker, as one acquainted with the deepest interior processes of his characters' minds'[26] and the other, awkward voice of the pedant, to which Hardy's first reviewers drew almost unanimous attention. This problem of Hardy's two voices is seen as related to his use of the narrative point of view. Lodge subjects the language of the famous scene in the garden at Talbothays (see pp. 60–1 of this Guide) to close scrutiny, noting the interest in this nodal section of the novel displayed by John Holloway and Dorothy Van Ghent. (Lodge's own view of this scene is later placed in perspective by Ian Gregor, see pp. 96–102 of this Guide.) Lodge picks out the paragraph describing the garden as being crucial to the reader's understanding of Tess herself, and as revealing a facet of her character of which Angel Clare is ignorant, and therefore crucial to the reading of the whole text. Focusing on its language, Lodge develops his analysis with characteristic lucidity:

■ The paragraph describing the overgrown garden might be aptly described as an image of 'unconstrained nature'. It reminds us of the wild, exuberant, anarchic life that flourishes on the dark underside, as it were, of the cultivated fertility of the valley. Does it not reveal something similar about Tess – that she is a 'child of Nature' in a sense that extends far beneath the surface of conventional pastoral prettiness and innocence which that phrase denotes to Angel? Let us examine one item in the description in the light of this interpretation:

> . . . rubbing off upon her naked arms sticky blights which, though snow-white on the appletree-trunks, made madder stains on her skin . . . (p. 127)

There is clearly an antithesis here between *snow-white* and *madder*, which is given a cautionary or ironic note by the *though*: i.e., though the blights looked pretty and pure on the tree trunks, they produced a red stain on Tess's naked arms when she rubbed against them. *Snow-white* has associations with chastity and virginity. Red (the colour of some of the weed-flowers earlier in the passage) is the colour of passion, and of blood (with which Tess is ominously splashed at the death of the horse, Prince). And it is difficult to avoid seeing an Empsonian ambiguity[27] in the word *madder* – no doubt many readers have, like myself, taken it to be the comparative form of *mad* on first reading, not the name of a vegetable dye. Thus, although one cannot paraphrase meanings so delicately hinted, I submit that the force of this connection between Tess and the natural world is to suggest the 'mad' passionate, non-ethical quality of her sensibility.

This dimension of Tess's character makes her life a peculiarly vulnerable one. It lays her open to seduction by d'Urberville – it is important to realise that she is seduced, not raped; and Tess herself is frightened by the intensity of her passion for Angel.

> . . . Her idolatry of this man was such that she herself almost feared it to be ill-omened. She was conscious of the notion expressed by Friar Laurence: 'These violent delights have violent ends.'[28] It might be too desperate for human conditions, too rank, too wild, too deadly. (p. 212)

Yet this vulnerability is something we value in Tess. Ironically it is valued by Clare, without his understanding the reason. He is intrigued and impressed by a quality of imaginative thoughtfulness in her speech which he finds surprising in one so young. 'Not guessing the cause', comments Hardy, 'there was nothing to remind him that experience is as to intensity, and not as to duration. Tess's passing corporeal blight had been her mental harvest' (p. 129). The play on 'blight' and 'harvest' here, and the metaphorical application of 'rank' and 'wild' to Tess's passion in my previous quotation, give further encouragement for a reading of the weeds paragraph as a metaphorical expression of Tess's character. But I offer it tentatively, because it does not account for everything in the paragraph and its immediate context. The readings of Mr Liddell[29] and Miss Van Ghent [see p. 61 of this Guide] require us to see the paragraph as ironic, the irony being directed at Tess, who does not realise how she is being smirched and stained. Mr Holloway seems to take a similar view.[30] . . . The cat simile . . . however, shows Tess at ease in her surroundings. And the clause 'in which Tess *found* herself' (my italics) in the opening sentence suggests that she is aware of these surroundings. One's reading of the whole paragraph depends very importantly on whether we take the observing consciousness to be primarily Tess's or primarily the author's. But it is very difficult to decide . . . [31] □

In his subtle, extended, consecutive close reading of the four central paragraphs of the garden scene, Lodge discovers the dual voice of Hardy – the poor writing of the ponderous generalities, but also the concrete evocation. What Lodge also finds is a problem of narrative point of view, when Hardy is employing what narratological critics were later to call 'free indirect speech'. And he identifies stylistic muddle:

■ . . . Hardy presents us with such a confusion of linguistic clues. What an astonishing diversity of tone is displayed in the four paragraphs! The first shows Hardy in his most ponderous, generalising authorial style, with which Tess herself is incongruously saddled in the penultimate sentence. The second paragraph establishes her keen sensuous response to the music with the striking image of nudity, and the simile of the fascinated bird, but qualifies this effect by some slightly patronising reference to the absolute and the relative. The third paragraph assaults us with an astonishing *tour de force* of concretely realised sensation. And the final paragraph leads us into a world of romantic synaesthesia [one kind of sensation being felt and described in terms of others]. It is as if Hardy, bewildered by the rich possibilities of the scene, has confused himself and us by trying to follow out all of them at the same time.[32] □

Developing alongside the interest in language, developed by Tony Tanner and David Lodge, was the study of myth. This forms an important dimension of Dorothy Van Ghent's essay on *Tess*, and it is pursued systematically by Richard Carpenter in his *Thomas Hardy* (1964), where he develops the thesis that in seeing Tess as the victim of both society and the universe, Hardy fuses symbolism and realism to produce meanings both mythic and human. As the following extract shows, Carpenter detects in *Tess of the d'Urbervilles* a uniting of fertility myth and folklore archetype, which gives the novel a basically mythic structure centred on the elemental feminine character of Tess:

■ . . . Her unconscious sexual attractiveness – her lush figure and 'peony mouth' (p.20) – relates her to the archetypal fertility principle symbolised by the goddesses of myth from Ishtar [the Assyrian and Babylonian goddess of love and war] to Venus. In addition, her story is an archetypal folk tale of the wronged maiden who cannot escape from her past, who finally turns on her seducer to destroy him, and who loses her own life as a result.[33] □

However, when Tess is at Talbothays, Carpenter sees the figures of the earth goddess and the wronged maiden come together in the narrative pattern provided by the 'archetypal scapegoat':

■ . . . In her naturalness, in her unsophisticated simplicity, and in her innocence, as well as in her deep-bosomed figure, the peasant girl is at this point as complete an image of the archetypal earth goddess as modern literature can show. True it is that Hardy does not permit her to remain such for long. '"Call me Tess," she would say askance' (p.135), when Angel used the names of goddesses for her . . . Hardy does not want to allegorise, but he does wish to gain the advantage of mythical overtones to lend significance to his folk tale . . .
. . . We hear no more references to Tess as a goddess, but she becomes ever more clearly the victim of the world's inexorable vengeance, the archetypal scapegoat. Like other gods and goddesses, she is made to suffer for the mistakes and misdeeds of her world.[34] □

Richard Carpenter's book marked a stage in the increasingly sophisticated investigation of Hardy's use of myth. Jean R. Brooks's *Thomas Hardy: The Poetic Structure*, published in 1971, employs a fairly complex humanist approach, that reveals how the form of *Tess of the d'Urbervilles* is created by the tension between the personal ('Tess') and the impersonal ('d'Urberville') parts of Tess's being. But while the surface tale is about the defeat of her quest for happiness in a Darwinian universe, its underlying mythic pattern offers a humanist redemption. The brief extract below indicates the thrust of her discussion:

■ [There is] a rich layer of archetypal myth directing the course of Tess's life . . . The central events are described in Darwinian terms of struggle and adaptation, extinction and renewal of the species. But the discovery of Tess's ancestry initiates all the myths about the meaning of being human; myths that are explored in the rest of the novel through an intricate network of poetic cross-references . . . . . . The dramatic and poetic vision that links Tess to her inheritance as animal, woman, and human being has already suggested the three fundamental and interconnecting myths that she will be lived by. They are the fertility scapegoat, Paradise Lost, and that twentieth century response to the 'ache of modernism' (p. 129), the exile . . . [35] □

The close investigation of Hardy's language and his employment of myth is a comparatively recent feature of *Tess* criticism. However, a constant concern, from the earliest reviewers onwards, has been the nature of the novel's tragic experience, and this governs several formalist views of the text. Jeannette King, in *Tragedy in the Victorian Novel* (1978), examines the impact of classical tragedy and its theory on the form of fiction in George Eliot, Thomas Hardy and Henry James, and she finds in *Tess* a clearly defined Aristotelian tragedy of situation, informed by an Aeschlyean belief in education through suffering. This interpretation is challenged by Dale Kramer, in *Thomas Hardy: The Forms of Tragedy* (1975), who suggests that the application of Aristotelian criteria to Hardy has encouraged the post-New Critical emphasis on rhetoric and unity. While this has moved our search for the heart of the tragedy to the substance of the text, he also suggests that it has led to a decline in Hardy's reputation as a tragic writer. Kramer sees each novel as dominated by an aesthetic feature that creates its expression of unique tragic experience. In *The Return of the Native*, for instance, this organising principle is the conflict of value systems, and in *The Mayor of Casterbridge* it is the shaping force of history. In *Tess of the d'Urbervilles*, however, it is subjectivity, for in this novel Hardy is concerned with defending the integrity and absolute moral value of individual consciousness against judgements based on social considerations. *Tess* is thus a tragedy founded on character in a specific sense:

■ The emphasis upon subjectivity of experience locates the source of the tragic emotion in *Tess of the d'Urbervilles* within the human consciousness rather than within some sort of relationship between the individual and the environment, or between individuals, or between an individual and the moral order of his world.[36] □

Moreover, argues Kramer:

■ . . . Tragedy occurs because Tess's character is hard-pressed by her past, the circumstance of her present, and her rejection by society and Angel. Hardy intimates, however, that society's reasons for rejecting Tess are not necessarily entirely wrong or evil. Indeed, neither the regenerated Angel nor the unsparingly besieged Tess categorically and permanently denies the validity of conventional views of chastity. The problem, as Angel comes to see in Brazil, is precisely that society makes no provision for a special case like Tess's, whose justifications rely upon the unique self (p. 329).

Hardy establishes subjectivity as the basis of perceiving the novel's action through a variety of methods, whose effect is to turn the individual upon himself for judgements and to deny the usefulness and trustworthiness of external perceptions and moralities. One method is to state explicitly that the individual creates his own world, that this view of the world may be in accord neither with pre-conceptions based on conventions nor with other people's views . . . [37] □

An important aspect of Kramer's discussion is the way his close textual reading reveals the intense subjectivity of human experience, the world as 'only a psychological phenomenon' (p. 91), as Hardy put it, and the impossibility of applying conventional judgements to utterly private matters:

■ She might have seen that what bowed her head so profoundly – the thought of the world's concern at her situation – was founded on an illusion. She was not an existence, an experience, a passion, a structure of sensations, to anybody but herself. To all humankind besides Tess was only a passing thought . . . Most of the misery [at being an unwed mother] had been generated by her conventional aspect, and not by her innate sensations. (p. 96)

This passage, as clearly as any that can be used to elucidate Hardy's interest in consciousness, stresses the isolation of the individual, his separation from the consciousness of the people around him, his lack of importance to his peers and environment. Hardy, by deflating the social significance of the individual, is obviously shifting the idea of tragedy away from one that assumes the existence of an externally signifying figure to one that assumes each figure 'signifies' only to himself. The idea expresses the unique quality of tragedy in *Tess of the d'Urbervilles*, that is, within the pages of the novel Tess is tragic only to herself. To others, she is a puzzling daughter, a temptingly lovely girl and woman, an image of purity, a fallen woman . . . [38] □

A crux in Dale Kramer's discussion, as in the arguments of so many critics, is the scene in the garden at Talbothays (see pp. 60–1 of this Guide). For Kramer, following David Lodge, the close reading of this scene suggests the 'non-moral and corresponsive nature' of what is essentially a 'mystical experience':

■ . . . The romanticism in the simile of the pollen and the pathetic fallacy in the simile of the damp garden of the last paragraph indicate that the allusions are meant to project Tess's state of mind. She identifies intimately with her sensuous knowledge, and she genuinely 'becomes' the totality of her experiences of sense. More than any passage in the novel, indeed, more than any passage in Hardy's fiction that I can recall, here is a fully articulated evocation of a sensitivity too extreme to survive the shocks of a powerful order of material Nature and the grossness of the social world. And, thus, the entire basis for tragedy is condensed into, and expressed through, this one paragraph and its context.[39] □

And the same impression is given in other scenes, Kramer suggests:

■ . . . As in the harp-playing episode, Tess's self-elevation on her wedding day suggests an ability to create her own intensity, to cut herself off from a world founded on rational relationships. Although a weakness and a cause for her destruction, this ability also accounts for her tragic power in the novel. She affirms the will to live and the will to enjoy in the face of what would be social disgrace if her past were to become known, and she makes this affirmation in response to an inner dynamism that triumphs over her awareness that conventional society considers her sexual guilt irredeemable.[40] □

Kramer goes on to demonstrate that the context for this 'underlying concept of mysticism'[41] is substantiated by extensive reference to dreams, as well as the recurrent motif of appearance and reality. The 'supremacy of individual feeling'[42] is similarly emphasised by closely related techniques such as the relativity of individual perspectives of events, and tentative judgements – for instance Angel Clare's varying attitudes towards ancient families – also Hardy's manipulation of the narrative point of view to foreground the novel's 'basis in subjectivity and in relativity of truth';[43] and his attribution of apparent life to inanimate objects, connecting Tess with 'the source of naturalistic power in her universe'.[44] But in spite of Tess's inescapable bond with nature, Kramer concludes, she is still a responsible chooser and sufferer:

■ In any case the emphasis throughout the novel upon the subjective creation of significance in a sensitive and serious consciousness is the more important indication of the origin of the tragic response aroused by Hardy. However insignificant in an absolute sense the individual might be, in his own subjective existence he is of consummate importance. The destruction of the individual might indeed be microcosmic and symbolic; the novel contains adequate evidence for such a view. But more important in *Tess of the d'Urbervilles* than the symbolic value of the fatedness of the individual is the self-status of the individual. Entirely within himself he constitutes a world of moral vigour. A particular moral stance may be good only for the fleeting moment in which it is taken, but then the ongoing moment here is the only meaningful unit of time in relation to morality. The physical world has substantial dimensions and a variety of more or less permanent forms; but the temporal conditions of human life are immediateness and instability. As Hardy makes clear in referring to the indifference of the new inhabitants of the Durbeyfield home towards the most intense feelings and activities of the old inhabitants, the capability of creating tragedy resides only in the character who feels the tragedy. In the novel, the situations of the characters also allow the reader to feel tragedy precisely because Hardy in his portrayal of Tess creates within the reader an awareness of the extent of her psychic sufferings. Through the enhancement of the subjectivity by means of the tactics I have described, Hardy not only allows but also requires the reader to create for himself his individual view of Tess, her essential personality. There are no absolutes in Tess's personality: she is both pure and corrupted, she is both idealistic and sensual; and no one in the novel understands her. Because Hardy breaks down all dispositions toward Tess, she is made capable of sustaining, in irresolvable contradiction and ambiguity, the awareness of her that the individual reader gains through the interreaction of his consciousness with hers and with those of the people around her. The attraction of *Tess of the d'Urbervilles* as a tragedy is this absorptive feature, which permits the reader to participate in tragic vision on his own terms. Every aspect of the novel's form glides away from a prescribed significance; nothing human 'means' outside itself. The psychic state of subjectivity, at once aesthetic and moral, defines the nature of the tragedy that *Tess of the d'Urbervilles* fulfils.[45] □

Dale Kramer's subtle examination of the forms of tragedy in the novels is a major contribution to Hardy criticism, but the most significant and comprehensive humanist formalist study of Hardy during the 1960s and 1970s is Ian Gregor's *The Great Web: The Form of Hardy's Major Fiction* (1974). It is a culmination of earlier work on Hardy that had produced a number of essays, including 'The Novel as Moral Protest: *Tess of the d'Urbervilles*' in his book *The Moral and the Story* (1962).[46] *The Great Web*, Gregor tells us, is essentially an 'extended meditation' on the theme of his article in *Essays in Criticism*:[47] 'What Kind of Fiction did Hardy Write?' And its humanist concern is focused through the exploration of Hardy's idea of humanity as one great network:

■ When we come to reflect on the relationship that exists between the kind of fiction Hardy writes and the substance of that fiction, we find an interesting correspondence. On 4 March 1885 we find Hardy making an entry in his journal: 'The human race to be shown as one great net-work or tissue which quivers in every part when one point is shaken, like a spider's web if touched'.[48] I would suggest that in that image we have a ruling idea in Hardy's development as a novelist, an idea which at once determines the shape of the fiction and its substance.[49] □

Gregor offers a highly intelligent formalist reading of the major novels, based on close textual analysis. He breaks with the static, Jamesian idea of fictional form as a single structural whole, best understood by its author/critic, to propose a more flexible conception of form in Hardy's fiction, based on the story conceived of as an 'unfolding process'[50] for the reader, a movement through the novel, and a crucial process of revela-tion. The plot is thus 'mimetic of Hardy's metaphysic . . . an analogue both for the plots men make for themselves, and for the plots over which they seem to have no control'.[51] And in Gregor's reading of Hardy's fic-tion, the narrator is as important as the story. A 'dialectic of feeling . . . is operative between the narrator and his narrative',[52] into which the reader is inserted, with the understanding that the 'narrator's reading [is] only as sharp and as fitful as our own'.[53] And although Hardy's novels contain a number of strands of interest – ballad, social history, contemporary science and philosophy – the coherence and unity of the fiction does not lie in these, for Hardy called his novels a 'series of seemings' and this suggests a 'seeking for a truth whose form is always provisional, whose dynamic is the tension between the story-teller and the sage, the author and the reader, a tension which, for Hardy, was the essential condition for the imaginative vitality of the quest'.[54] Fiction, like a web, is a 'provi-sional design flung across the vacancy of miscellaneous experience'.[55]

Gregor encourages a new way of looking at Hardy's fiction. Near the beginning of his discussion of *Tess of the d'Urbervilles* he identifies the novel's 'distinctive rhythm' as being the continuous oscillation between the world and the individual character. In the narrative description of Tess in the Durbeyfield household (p. 26), he argues, although Tess is cul-turally divided by her employment of two languages, the emphasis is on the reality of the public, historical world. However, in the account of Tess's conversation with Dairyman Crick about her ability (again self-divisive) to enter into a trance-like state at will (p. 124), the stress is on the individual psyche. 'World' and 'character', history and the individual psyche, are 'held in tension, and the novel is to explore the intimacy of relationship between them'.[56] Indeed the opening of *Tess*, Gregor reminds us, is also divided. Marlott is not the world before the Fall; it is only a few hours from London, includes fertility rituals, middle-class intellectual visitors, dreams of aristocratic lineage, and harsh economic realities. Tess reflects this when her dreaminess before the accident with the mail coach is replaced by guilt for the death of Prince. And this structure of feeling is enlarged in her relationship with Alec d'Urbverville, which is deeply ambiguous, the result of which is conflict between Tess and her family. And then, after the death of Sorrow, the pendulum of feeling swings again. This is the novel's essential rhythm.

Gregor's concern with flux is traced through the changing image of herself in Tess's consciousness in the novel's six Phases, where she is embedded both in the novel's world and in its varied reflections upon the meaning of her life. Gregor regards the central sections of the novel as displaying a 'calculated ambivalence', particularly in the wooing of Tess by Angel, which critics either see as lyrical intensity or as a 'sardonic comment on the blindness of love'.[57] To illustrate this he refers to the garden at Talbothays, and focuses close attention on two consecutive paragraphs (see pp. 60–1 of this Guide):

■ . . . Where Lodge sees confusion I see a calculated ambivalence, and I see it emerging not from the individual paragraph, but in the relationship set up in the movement from one paragraph to the next . . .
. . . The movement between the two paragraphs dramatises the fatal dislocation that exists within Tess between the world as an obdurate reality, making 'madder stains on her skin', and her apprehension of that world, which so exaltedly 'dissolves time and space'. What is writ small in these paragraphs is writ large in her whole relationship with Angel Clare.[58] □

And, as Hardy insisted, Gregor points out, Angel Clare is similarly divided between the 'man of advanced ideas' and the man of convention. This fundamental oscillation continues in the movement from the dream world of Talbothays to the grinding hardship of Flintcomb-Ash, but Tess will not succumb and she 'shares the traveller's ambition to tell and in the telling seek to understand'[59] through her abortive visit to Angel's parents. This, argues Gregor, is the beginning of Tess's efforts to link her past and her present, and to gain a sense of self-acceptance. And it occurs in the context of the wider social world:

■ . . . And so in the last two phases of the novel, 'The Convert', and 'Fulfilment', she faces again situations involving, first Alec, and then Angel, but this time in a way which is wholly committed and self-aware – a sense which later Hardy, reading over his completed novel, felt he wished to describe as 'pure'.

Alec's world, the world of the Stoke-d'Urbervilles, is inseparable from nineteenth-century *laissez-faire* capitalism, it is the triumph of the individual bourgeois ethic, what is wanted can be bought. So it is now – and really for the first time – that Hardy introduces in a sustained and explicit way the agricultural and economic crisis that has overtaken

Wessex, and turned families like the Durbeyfields, into migratory 'labour'. The wider world is now forcing itself in upon Tess, and the last phases are to be dominated not by the individual consciousness and its correlative, landscape, but by money, changing methods of work, migration of families, 'a fashionable watering-place' (p. 363), and the law. Social institutions, economic processes, these are to give a fresh definition to Tess's consciousness, and in its turn, that conscious-ness is to put such processes under judgment.[60] □

In her confrontations with Alec d'Urberville, says Gregor, Tess draws on her past and inheritance, to emerge as both tragic heroine and a d'Urberville, but with conscious acceptance of her economic dependency. With Angel Clare she finds 'fulfilment' but it still includes the sense of movement. And Gregor proceeds to discuss Tess's fulfilment from the governing perspective of the novel's ending:

■ . . . From another point of view, it is Tess's own acceptance of her-self: 'It is as it should be . . . I am almost glad – yes, glad!' (p. 381). Here the appropriate comment is not Joan Durbeyfield's so much as Hamlet's: 'If it be now, 'tis not to come; if it be not to come, it will be now; if it be not now, yet it will come – the readiness is all'.[61] She has vindicated herself, she has fused for Angel the image he adored with the woman he rejected, she has revealed the endurance, the patience and the forgiveness of which the human spirit is capable: she is, gen-uinely, 'fulfilled'.

In the last, notorious paragraph of the novel all the resonances of the novel are heard:

'Justice' was done, and the President of the Immortals (in Aeschylean phrase) had ended his sport with Tess. And the d'Urberville knights and dames slept on in their tombs unknow-ing. The two speechless gazers bent themselves down to the earth, as if in prayer, and remained thus a long time, absolutely motion-less: the flag continued to wave silently. As soon as they had strength they arose, joined hands again, and went on. (p. 384)

How often the opening sentence of that paragraph has been quoted in isolation, and made to serve as 'the conclusion' to the novel, whereas Hardy, true to his practice, makes his conclusion multiply in emphasis. The first sentence is a sombre acknowledgement of forces in the world over which we would seem to have little or no control. It is followed by a sentence which shifts from metaphysics to history, proclaiming the serene indifference of the past to the present. These two sentences are followed by two others which indicate contrary possibilities. We see an intimation of human resilience in 'the speechless gazers' who seek in the earth itself, in the conditions of man's terrestrial existence, notwithstanding his mutability, hope and not despair. In the last sentence hope turns into strength, strength to affirm the human bond and to give direction to action, 'they . . . joined hands again, and went on'. It is a sentence which recalls, in its rhythm, the sadness – and the resolution – present in the final lines of *Paradise Lost*:

> They hand in hand, with wandering steps and slow,
> Through *Eden* took their solitary way.

It would be as foolish to isolate Hardy's last sentence and see the final emphasis of the novel to lie there as it would be to isolate the first. For him, it is the four sentences taken together which constitute a human truth, by catching in varying lights our condition, flux followed by reflux, the fall by the rally; it is this sense of continuous movement which suggests that the fiction which records it should be described as 'a series of seemings' . . . . . .

From the viewpoint which finds the 'ideas' in *Tess* an unfortunate intrusion and the strength of the novel to lie in the presentation of the main character, the description I have given of the final paragraph will read as one of evasion, if not actual confusion, on the part of the author. I want to suggest that that criticism proceeds from a very precise aesthetic, which seeks to find in the individual paragraph a harmony of attitudes, a homogeneity of feeling, and which also reflects wider assumptions about the autonomy of the individual work of art and the relationship of the artist to his work . . . The last paragraph of the novel exhibits in miniature a structure of feelings, writ large throughout the whole work – a structure which can be most easily characterised first in terms of the movement in a Hardy novel, and second in the way the author or narrator is present in his tale . . . [62] □

Like Dorothy Van Ghent and Tony Tanner, Ian Gregor points to the symbolic importance of journeying in the novel, but he differs from them in discovering the 'energy and sense of purpose that these journeys evoke in the mind of the reader', and in seeing Tess's final journey of pursuit as chiming with another oscillation of mood, which in turn is linked to movement:

■ 'All is trouble outside there: inside here content' (p. 376). Tess's reflection on her brief interlude in the deserted house with Angel comes close to describing, in more general terms, her mood at the end, and it enables her to find within herself the strength to see Angel's life continuing without her. Life has become so precious to her that,

paradoxically, she cannot think of confining it to her individual existence, and in her sister she sees an extension of that life, 'She has all
the best of me without the bad of me; and if she were to become yours
it would almost seem as if death had not divided us . . .' (p. 380). And
so in a delicate and gentle way, 'the rally' begins again. The movement
of the novel, the flux and reflux, is misread if this final emphasis is not
taken. That the pendulum should begin to swing is not an intrusion
on the author's part of an unassimilated belief in 'evolutionary meliorism', affixed to a narrative quite alien to that idea, it is implicit within
the whole oscillating structure of the novel. It is in fact Hardy's own
way of paying tribute to the kind of strength he sees in Tess, a strength
which seeks to go beyond the sufferings of one individual: her seeing
herself, neither as 'a soul at large', nor as a fly trapped between the
blank gaze of earth and heaven, but as a person who can, with full
consciousness of purpose and with no self-diminution, give herself to
forces outside her and say 'I am ready'. That 'readiness' is built into
the hope which Angel and Liza-Lu draw from the earth and which in
turn gives them their strength. And it is with the phrase 'and went on'
that the novel ends.[63] □

Towards the end of Ian Gregor's discussion of *Tess*, he revives Lionel
Johnson's objection to the intrusive narrator who is always commenting
on the story with his 'ideas'. And Gregor concludes by summarising the
relation between the narrator and the story:

■ . . . Whether we think of those ideas in terms of the images which I
have used in this study – the great web, the fall and the rally – or
choose some other description, we can see that, with that profound
sense of process which is integral to the fiction, the narrator himself
will undergo the shifting experiences of his tale in a way not markedly
different from that of the characters. There is common tissue between
his reflections and theirs, his plotting and theirs. And if the substance
of his narrative is as ambivalent as I have attempted to suggest it is,
there will be a constant challenge to any authorial commentary which
seeks to claim rights of privilege. It was Lawrence, who created a very
similar kind of fiction, who delivered the famous admonition, 'Never
trust the artist, trust the tale', a remark whose weight only becomes
clear in a context of this kind. Unquestionably there is an impulse in
Hardy, and perhaps a dominant one, that makes him want to view
Tess's story through the eyes of the President of the Immortals; but the
narrative cannot leave that unchallenged, it demands a contrary voice,
and the author is too honest to deny it. The plurality of meaning in this
kind of fiction is always manifest.

To leave the matter in these abstract terms would be to falsify it, it is too instinctual for that. What harmonises the dialectic within the novel, what gives direction to its movement, is not just a reconciliation of contraries within the mind of the author, it is the feeling which encompasses both 'character' and 'idea'. And in Hardy that feeling is an overwhelming compassion, which virtually never fails him . . . it is Tess herself who releases in Hardy a feeling that we can only describe as love – a love prompted, at least, by the fact that Hardy finds woman expressive, in the purest form, of the human capacity for endurance and the steadfast refusal to be overcome. But, as I have tried to show . . . to think of Tess as 'a character', who can be extracted either from the world she inhabits or from the reflections which her life gives rise to, is to impoverish the whole fiction and to misunderstand the reasons for its imaginative power. In her, Hardy has invested his whole imaginative capital. What is history, what is fiction, what is an idea, what is character? – these distinctions hardly seem to make sense any more to the author as we see him pondering his title page, amend-ing 'faithfully depicted' to 'faithfully presented', inserting a subtitle, 'A Pure Woman', looking again at the title and finding in Shakespeare an epigraph which will finally obliterate the gap between the teller and his tale, and make the creator one with his creation:

> . . . Poor wounded name! My bosom as a bed
> Shall lodge thee.[64] □

The humanism that governs Ian Gregor's masterly investigation of the complexities of narrative form is inflected very differently in David J. De Laura's important essay, '"The Ache of Modernism" in Hardy's Later Novels', published in *ELH* in 1967. This is in the tradition of critics such as William R. Rutland and Harvey Curtis Webster, who trace the influence on Hardy's fiction of the climate of contemporary humanistic thought. David De Laura's article encompasses *The Return of the Native*, *Tess of the d'Urbervilles* and *Jude the Obscure*, but its title is taken from the scene in *Tess* when Tess is telling Angel Clare of her terrors: 'feelings which might almost have been called those of the age – the ache of modernism' (p. 129). It is a focused, probing exploration of the topic, which so far as *Tess* is concerned, omits matters of tragedy, society, or narrative form and con-centrates on the figure of Angel Clare, using him as a means of revealing how the novel is conceptualised. De Laura argues that a primary influence on Hardy's representation of scientific rationalism in *Tess* was Matthew Arnold, whose early poetry had defined, says De Laura, the 'emotional price of modernism: the sense of psychic dislocation and alienation, of wandering in an unmapped no man's land "between two worlds"', but who had 'fatally compromised himself'[65] by retaining, though agnostic, an emotional and moral reliance on the traditions of Christianity.

De Laura identifies three interrelated themes in *Tess*: Hardy's interest in Arnold's 'Hellenism' (the pursuit of a natural and pagan way of life modelled on Ancient Greece), the modern sense of anxiety and rottenness, and Hardy's attack on Christianity and 'neo-Christianity' (Arnold's own position). These are brought together in De Laura's discussion of Angel Clare as embodying Hardy's critique of Matthew Arnold:

■ . . . This is the position of Angel Clare, that 'sample product of the last five-and-twenty years' (p.258), a disciple of Mill and Arnold, whose sin, like that of the later Arnold, is precisely his imperfect modernism, his slavery in the ethical sphere to 'custom and conventionality'. *Tess*, especially, becomes a demand for greater honesty in confronting (to use Arnold's own youthful phrase) 'the modern situation in its true *blankness* and *barrenness*, and *unpoetrylessness*' . . . [66] □

So far as Arnoldian paganism is concerned, says De Laura, Hardy's heart simply is not in it. Angel's idealism is undermined by the contribution of his upbringing and his moral nature:

■ . . . It is even hard to believe in Angel Clare's 'Hellenic Paganism'. We hear briefly of his 'aesthetic, sensuous, Pagan pleasure in natural life and lush womanhood' (p.161) in Var Vale, his belief (borrowed from Arnold among others)[67] that 'it might have resulted far better for mankind if Greece had been the source of the religion of modern civilization, and not Palestine' (p.161), and his new experience of 'Life', 'the great passionate pulse of existence, unwarped, uncontorted, untrammelled by those creeds which futilely attempt to check what wisdom would be content to regulate' (p.161). But even this sally is sharply checked by Hardy's insistence on Angel's unexamined moral idealism, and on its origin in his ineffectual, disembodied temperament . . . [68] □

De Laura continues:

■ . . . This divison between intellectual commitment and high ethical resolve on the one hand (a mid-Victorian heritage), and the experience of paralysis of will and emotion in the late-nineteenth-century situation on the other, is the structure of the actual 'modern' dilemma faced by Hardy's latter-day heroes . . . [69] □

And in Hardy's presentation of the modern, David De Laura identifies a fundamentally existentialist imagination at work:

■ . . . The 'ache of modernism' which Angel detects in Tess is a nameless fear of 'life in general' (p. 128), or at least of the 'fierce and cruel' (p. 128) in life. In fact, the 'gloomy spectres' (p. 195) and 'shapes of darkness' (p. 195) which haunt Tess – 'doubt, fear, moodiness, care, shame' (p. 195) – seem closer to the 'fear and trembling' of the modern existentialist imagination than to the sunlit 'culture' of high-Victorian rationalism. Although we were told that Angel is somehow free 'from the chronic melancholy which is taking hold of the civilized races with the decline of belief in a beneficent power' (p. 123), even he, like Jude, looked 'upon it as a mishap to be alive' (p. 129) . . . [70] □

David De Laura's persuasive essay clearly offers a radically different perspective of Hardy's imagination from that of another important humanist voice, Raymond Williams, who explores Hardy's unique identity as a famous writer situated in a rural society that was experiencing rapid change. Williams was later to define himself as a Marxist critic, but at this stage in his development he is in the line of humanist criticism that opposes wholesale industrialisation and urbanisation. However, he does not view organic rural society in terms of the humanist-realist pastoral idyll of Victorian critics, nor even recent versions such as those of Lord David Cecil and Douglas Brown. Nor does he wish to endorse liberal humanist pessimism about the state and direction of English culture. Williams's interest lies in the text's complex ideological content and meaning; what it reveals about the history of social class, and Hardy's own relation to his society embodied in its language.

In his penetrating essay on Hardy in the *Critical Quarterly* in 1964 (later reprinted with some modification as a chapter in his influential book, *The English Novel from Dickens to Lawrence*, 1970), Williams takes issue with the simplifications of the Marxist, Arnold Kettle's view of 'the destruction of the English peasantry'. Williams argues that the term 'peasant' is inaccurate since peasants as such no longer existed in late-Victorian Dorset. He points out that, in fact, rural society comprised several different occupations:

■ . . . landowners, tenant farmers, dealers, craftsmen and labourers, and that social structure – the actual material, in a social sense, of the novels – is radically different, in its variety, its shading, and many of its basic human attitudes from the structure of a peasantry . . . [71] □

Williams also seeks to disprove Douglas Brown's simplistic idea of the collapse of the agricultural world under the assault of the 'urban alien'. Williams regards the pressure for change arising within the structure of the country community as being commoner than the influence of urban society. And as Hardy's comments concerning Tess's social mobility in the following passages illustrate, he was in particular sympathy with a world with which he was himself (as famous author, intimate of London society, son of a local mason, and dweller near Dorchester) so ambiguously connected:

▓ . . . It is common to reduce Hardy's fiction to the impact of an urban alien on the 'timeless pattern' of English rural life. Yet though this is sometimes there the more common pattern is the relation between the changing nature of country living, determined as much by its own pressures as by pressures from 'outside', and one or more characters who have become in some degree separated from it yet who remain by some tie of family inescapably involved. It is here that the social values are dramatised in a very complex way and it is here that most of the problems of Hardy's actual writing seem to arise.

One small and one larger point may illustrate this argument, in a preliminary way. Nearly everyone seems to treat Tess as simply the passionate peasant girl seduced from outside, and it is then surprising to read, quite early in the novel one of the clearest statements of what has become a classical experience of mobility:

Mrs Durbeyfield habitually spoke the dialect: her daughter, who had passed the Sixth Standard in the National school under a London-trained mistress, spoke two languages; the dialect at home, more or less; ordinary English abroad and to persons of quality. (p.26)[72] □

An important part of Williams's critical project is to tease out, in his style, the complexity of Hardy's 'real identity', as among other things an auto-didact and countryman – he is seen as 'both the educated observer and the passionate participant, in a period of general and radical change'.[73] Here, Williams sees as a complex experiment what earlier critics regarded as flaws in *Tess*. Williams develops this view by means of the following illustrations:

▓ . . . It would be easy to relate Hardy's problem of style to the two languages of Tess: the consciously educated and the unconsciously customary. But this comparison, though suggestive, is inadequate, for the truth is that to communicate Hardy's experience neither language would serve, since neither in the end was sufficiently articulate: the educated dumb in intensity and limited in humanity; the customary thwarted by ignorance and complacent in habit. The marks of a sur-render to each mode are certainly present in Hardy but the main body of his mature writing is a more difficult and complicated experiment. For example:

The season developed and matured. Another year's instalment of flowers, leaves, nightingales, thrushes, finches, and such ephemeral creatures, took up their positions where only a year ago others had stood in their place, when these were nothing more than germs and inorganic particles. Rays from the sunrise drew forth the buds and stretched them into long stalks, lifted up sap in noiseless streams, opened petals, and sucked out scents in invisible jets and breathings.

Dairyman Crick's household of maids and men lived on comfortably, placidly, even merrily. Their position was perhaps the happiest of all positions in the social scale, being above the line at which neediness ends, and below the line at which the *convenances* begin to cramp natural feeling, and the stress of threadbare modishness makes too little of enough.

Thus passed the leafy time, when arborescence seems to be the one thing aimed at out-of-doors; Tess and Clare unconsciously studied each other, ever balanced on the edge of a passion, yet apparently keeping out of it. All the while they were converging, under an irresistible law, as surely as two streams in one vale. (p. 133)

This passage is neither the best nor the worst of Hardy. Rather it shows the many complicated pressures working within what had to seem a single intention. 'The leafy time when arborescence' is an example of mere inflation to an 'educated' style, but the use of *'convenances'*, which might appear merely fashionable, carries a precise feeling. 'Instalment' and 'ephemeral' are also uses of a precise kind, within a sentence which shows mainly the strength of what must be called an educated point of view. The consciousness of the natural process, in 'germs and inorganic particles' . . . is a necessary accompaniment, for Hardy's purpose, of the more direct and more enjoyed sights and scents of spring. It is loss not gain when Hardy reverts to the simpler and cruder abstraction of 'Dairyman Crick's household of maids and men', which might be superficially supposed to be the countryman speaking but is actually the voice of the detached observer at a low level of interest. The more fully Hardy uses the resources of the whole language, as a precise observer, the more adequate the writing is. There is more strength in 'unconsciously studied each other', which is at once educated and engaged, than in the 'two streams in one vale', which shares with the gesture of 'irresistible law' a synthetic quality, here as of a man playing the countryman novelist.[74] □

'Hardy's special gift', suggests Williams, is his ability to encompass the 'native place and experience but also the education, the conscious enquiry'.[75] It is Hardy's unique place of vision that is the problem, he continues, citing this brief example from the text:

◼ If these two noticed Angel's growing social ineptness, he noticed their growing mental limitations. Felix seemed to him all Church; Cuthbert all College. His Diocesan Synods and Visitations were the mainsprings of the world to the one: Cambridge to the other. Each brother candidly recognized that there were a few unimportant scores of millions of outsiders in civilized society, persons who were neither university men nor churchmen; but they were to be tolerated rather than reckoned with and respected. (p.162)

This is what is sometimes called Hardy's bitterness, but in fact it is only sober and just observation. What Hardy sees and feels about the educated world of his day, locked in its deep social prejudices and in its consequent human alienation, is so clearly true that the only surprise is why critics now should still feel sufficiently identified with that world – the world which coarsely and brutally dismissed Jude and millions of other men – to be willing to perform the literary equivalent of that stalest of political tactics: the transfer of bitterness, of a merely class way of thinking, from those who exclude to those who protest. We did not after all have to wait for Lawrence to be shown the human nullity of that apparently articulate world. Hardy shows it convincingly again and again. But the isolation which then follows, while the observer holds to educated procedures but is unable to feel with the existing educated class, is severe. It is not the countryman awkward in his town clothes, but the more significant tension – of course with its awkwardness and its spurts of bitterness and nostalgia – of the man caught by his personal history in the general structure and crisis of the relations between education and class, relations which in practice are between intelligence and fellow-feeling.[76] ☐

Raymond Williams then turns his attack on those critics who through their critical agenda or sentimentality, or both, regard Hardy's fiction as presenting the disruption of a simple, static pastoral:

◼ Every attempt has of course been made to reduce the social crisis in which Hardy lived to the more negotiable and detachable forms of the disturbance of a timeless order. But there was of course nothing timeless about nineteenth-century rural England . . .

We then miss most of what Hardy has to show us if we impose on the actual relationships he describes a pastoral convention of the countryman as an age-old figure, or a vision of a prospering countryside being disintegrated by Corn Law repeal or the railways or agricultural machinery . . . ☐

Williams notes that Hardy himself points out how Dorset was less affected than most areas of England by the repeal of the Corn Laws and the cheap imports of grain. And as Hardy shows so graphically in *Tess of the d'Urbervilles*, where the railway facilitates the supply of milk to London, the forces at work are within the society itself, rather than external ones. This is amplified in the extract below:

■ . . . the social forces within his fiction are deeply based in the rural economy itself: in a system of rent and trade; in the hazards of owner-ship and tenancy; in the differing conditions of labour on good and bad land and in socially different villages (as in the contrast between Talbothays and Flintcomb-Ash); in what happens to people and to families in the interaction between general forces and personal his-tories – that complex area of ruin or survival, exposure or continuity. This is his actual society, and we cannot suppress it in favour of an external view of a seamless abstracted country 'way of life'.[78] □

In contrast with Arnold Kettle's Tess, Williams's Tess is therefore a more historically realistic and socially defined figure:

■ . . . Tess is not a peasant girl seduced by the squire; she is the daughter of a lifeholder and small dealer who is seduced by the son of a retired manufacturer . . . The Lady-Day migrations, the hiring fairs, the intellectually arrogant parson, the casual gentleman farmer, the landowner spending her substance elsewhere: all these are as much parts of the country 'way of life' as the dedicated craftsman, the group of labourers and the dances on the green. It is not only that Hardy sees the realities of labouring work, as in Marty South's hands on the spars and Tess in the swede field. It is also that he sees the harshness of economic processes, in inheritance, capital, rent and trade, within the continuity of the natural processes and persistently cutting across them. The social process created in this interaction is one of class and separation, as well as of chronic insecurity, as this capitalist farming and dealing takes its course . . . [79] □

It is part of Williams's argument that late-Victorian Dorset – the Wessex of *Tess of the d'Urbervilles* – must be seen in a proper historical perspective. It was, as Hardy himself insisted, a modern place that had been in the throes of continual change particularly since the eighteenth century. And Williams continues:

■ . . . The profound disturbances that Hardy records cannot then be seen in the sentimental terms of a pastoral: the contrast between coun-try and town. The exposed and separated individuals, whom Hardy puts at the centre of his fiction, are only the most developed cases of a general exposure and separation. Yet they are never merely illustrations of this change in a way of life. Each has a dominant personal history, which in psychological terms bears a direct relation to the social character of the change.[80] □

Unlike Kettle, whose argument depends on seeing Tess, Alec d'Urberville and Angel Clare as symbolic figures, representative of the workings of historical forces, Williams's humanistic leaning towards realism recognises (though it is not the burden of his essay) the importance of the fictional integrity and psychological truth of the individual character; *Tess of the d'Urbervilles* emerges from his discussion as a realist text rather than as a moral fable.

Merryn Williams's book, *Thomas Hardy and Rural England*, which appeared in 1972, is similarly concerned with Hardy as a historian of rural society, who reproduced in his fiction its class structures and conflictual patterns. Like Raymond Williams, she seeks to reveal the social complexity of Hardy's presentation of historical Wessex. She reveals Hardy's understanding of the role of labour in the rural economy and his acceptance of new mechanised agricultural methods. Williams also recognises Hardy's personal preoccupation with social class in *Tess of the d'Urbervilles*, though she disagrees sharply with Douglas Brown's assumption that the aristocracy has an authentic value and somehow legitimises Hardy's world as 'an integral part of the old-style agricultural community'.[81] This, she suggests, is a common error:

▨ The most common of these misreadings derives from the title – that the novel centres on the significance of Tess's d'Urberville blood. It is assumed that her tragedy consists in her family's loss of its ancestral inheritance; that her being a real d'Urberville and Alec a fake one symbolises the ruin and betrayal of the old aristocracy by a new urban class bent on exploiting the land . . . [82] □

Merryn Williams is interested in defining functions within the contemporary class structure and argues that in fact Hardy's attitude to the aristocracy was profoundly unromantic:

▨ Alec has thus taken over the role of his namesakes, the brutal aristocrats who exploited and raped girls in the same social position as Tess. What matters is not the name but the function; the real class relationship of exploiter and victim. Alec is the modern aristocrat, enriched by trade rather than land but behaving in the same way as his historical predecessors and inheriting their title with everything else . . . [83] □

In spite of the wealth of critical books and articles on *Tess of the d'Urbervilles* that had appeared by the mid-1970s, the text itself had received surprisingly little attention since Mary Ellen Chase's book in 1927, until J.T. Laird's important work of scholarship, *The Shaping of 'Tess of the d'Urbervilles'* was published in 1975. This fascinating study belongs to the school of genetic criticism that developed after 1970, partly as a reaction against the structuralists' abandonment of the role of the author in the production of the text. Genetic criticism concerns itself with the evolution of the text from its manuscript stages through to its final printed versions. It relies on the idea of authorial intention – the author working towards a final, definitive text – and it seeks to deduce this intention from textual revisions. It thus embraces the 'biography' of individual texts, the psychology of artistic creativity, the processes of writing itself, together with stylistic matters, and it also takes into account the historical context of publication. Laird studies *Tess* from its earliest stages in manuscript (from 1888) and its subsequent publishing history through several editions up to the quasi-definitive Macmillan 'Wessex' edition of 1912. Laird attends to Hardy's changes in plot, themes, imagery and characterisation over this period, and claims that this knowledge of the text's history enables us to understand it in its definitive state.

Mary Ellen Chase had noted the duplicity of Hardy's comment in *The Life of Thomas Hardy* about the restoration of material that had been part of the text before he bowdlerised it for the *Graphic* serial (see p. 33 of this Guide). And Laird confirms that a number of the alterations and sensational additions made to the manuscript version for the *Graphic* were not removed. Indeed some were subsequently developed further when the novel was published in volume form – for instance, the crucial d'Urberville motif, which bears the themes of heredity and mutability. In particular Laird reveals how in the first edition Hardy added passages relating to the melodramatic ancestral portraits that so affect Tess and Angel at the beginning of their honeymoon, in order considerably to increase their symbolic and ironic value as omens.

Some of Hardy's alterations had to do with problems of characterisation. Laird shows Hardy's uncertainty over the nature of Angel Clare, especially his inconsistency and ambiguous sexual motivation. More central are his changes to the characterisation of Tess. At the beginning, Laird suggests, Hardy's attitude was 'for the most part, one of moral neutrality'.[84] Far from neutral is Hardy's extraordinary comment in the baptismal scene (published separately in the *Fortnightly Review* and introduced into the first volume edition) on Tess's voice which the narrator says 'will never be forgotten by those who knew her' (p. 99). And of course there is his famous addition of the subtitle and epigraph for the first edition. A further influence on the development of the heroine's character, according to Laird, is Hardy's personal response to the disparagement of Tess by reviewers such as Mowbray Morris. Hardy included a Preface to the 1892 edition (the fifth) vigorously defending Tess from their attacks on 'the acts of a woman in her last days of desperation, when all her doings lie outside her normal character'.[85]

Laird also shows how, in the 1892 edition, Hardy gives a much franker treatment to the sexuality implicit in the seduction scene, as the following passage reveals:

▣ The relative frankness of the 1892 edition has already been noted in relation to the description of the actions of the villain at the beginning of the seduction scene, which was considerably bowdlerised in the first edition. For it is the 1892 edition which publishes for the first time the details italicised in the following extract: *'He knelt, and bent lower, till her breath warmed his face, and in a moment his cheek was in contact with hers.* She was sleeping soundly, *and upon her eyelashes there lingered tears'* (p. 77) . . . [86] □

And while Hardy enhances the sense of physical force involved in the relationship, with several amendments and interpolations, he also makes it clear, says Laird, that Tess remains Alec's mistress for a time. Of course this necessitated subsequent alterations. The following extracts chart this process and indicate just how unstable a text *Tess of the d'Urbervilles* was:

▣ The fact that the heroine had stayed on at 'The Slopes' as Alec's mistress for some time after her seduction is also brought out more specifically in the 1892 edition. This is seen in the following italicised insertion . . . :

> She had never wholly cared for him, she did not at all care for him now. She had dreaded him, winced before him, succumbed to a *cruel advantage he took of her helplessness; then, temporarily blinded by his flash manners, had been stirred to confused surrender awhile: had suddenly despised and disliked him, and had run away.* That was all. Hate him she did not quite; but he was dust and ashes to her, and even for her name's sake she scarcely wished to marry him. (p. 87)

In the earlier part of this insertion the words 'cruel advantage he took of her helplessness' refer to the seduction itself. The words 'cruel advantage', in particular, suggest the harshness of Alec's nature and behaviour and reinforce the implications of force and compulsion conveyed by an earlier-noted amendment in the first edition – 'She had been *made to break* a . . . social law'. (p. 91)

The implications of force are conveyed most strongly in a passage which constitutes the most significant single amendment in the 1892 edition. This is the interpolation in Chapter 14, during which the field woman comments to a companion, as she watches Tess moodily kissing her baby in the cornfield near Marlott . . . :

> 'A little more than persuading had to do wi' the coming o't, I reckon. There were they that heard a sobbing one night last year in The Chase; and it mid ha' gone hard wi' a certain party if folks had come along.'
> 'Well, a little more, or a little less . . . ' (p.95)

It is this passage, more than any other in the novel, which conveys to the reader the notion that the defloration of Tess should be termed an act of rape rather than a seduction. Its introduction, without doubt, serves to win for the heroine additional sympathy and respect, and, in so doing, underlines the concept of her essential purity, which, as we have seen, is already vigorously propounded in the Preface.

The insertion of the above passage in Chapter 14 necessitated the removal of a number of passages in Chapter 11. One such passage was the following, whose removal was dictated primarily by the needs of consistency; for, clearly, the field woman's second sentence ('There were they that heard a sobbing one night last year in The Chase') would have conflicted with the authorial statement in the first edition version of Chapter 11 . . . :

> Already at that hour some sons of the forest were stirring and striking lights in not very distant cottages; good and sincere hearts among them, patterns of honesty and devotion and chivalry. And powerful horses were stamping in their stalls, ready to be let out into the morning air. But no dart or thread of intelligence inspired these men to harness and mount, or gave them by any means the least inkling that their sister was in the hands of the spoiler; and they did not come that way. (I. p.141)

The other passages which needed to be removed from the text were those describing how the villain forced the heroine to drink a quantity of intoxicating liquor, before leaving her temporarily in the fog-bound Chase, while he ascertained their whereabouts. Once again, consistency was the main reason for the removal; for it was essential in the 1892 edition that there should not remain any suggestion that the heroine had been rendered either complaisant or unconscious by the effects of alcohol . . . [87] □

One of the main thrusts of these revisions was clearly to strengthen both the concept and the overall impression for the reader of Tess's 'purity'.

The following year this problem was addressed somewhat differently by another genetic critic, Mary Jacobus, in her essay, 'Tess's Purity', in *Essays in Criticism*, 1976 (later reprinted as 'Tess: The Making of a Pure Woman' in *Tearing the Veil: Essays on Femininity*, edited by Susan Lipshitz in 1978). This feminist materialist perspective is based on a scholarly investigation of significant changes that Hardy made to the novel while still at the manuscript stage. She argues that Hardy's alterations made to the characterisation, not only of Tess but also of Alec d'Urberville and Angel Clare, were dictated by the fundamental need to get Tess's story past the periodical censors and into print. Her essay is an excellent example of how critical judgements arise from a genetic investigation of the author's intentions, which in Hardy's case are in conflict with the historical conditions of publication. Its conclusions about the publishing industry's censorship of images of women afford an insight into Victorian society's control of their sexuality.

Mary Jacobus sets out clearly the problems surrounding a 'purified' Tess:

■ . . . To invoke purity in connection with a career that includes not simply seduction, but collapse into kept woman and murderess, taxes the linguistic resources of the most permissive conventional moralist . . . On the other hand, to regard Tess as unimplicated is to deny her the right of participation in her own life. Robbed of responsibility, she is deprived of tragic status – reduced throughout to the victim she does indeed become. Worst of all, she is stripped of the sexual autonomy and the capacity for independent being and doing which are among the most striking features of Hardy's conception.[88] □

Jacobus develops the view, on the basis of her reading of the manuscripts, that Tess's purity is 'a literary construct, "stuck on" in retrospect like the subtitle to meet objections that the novel had encountered even before its publication in 1891'.[89] And she goes on to discuss its implications:

■ The form of Hardy's compromise is implicit in his defiant subtitle. But its effects were much more far-reaching. Hardy's own account misleadingly suggests that his solution was a cynical and temporary bowdlerisation for the purposes of serial publication only. In reality he also made lasting modifications to his original conception in an attempt to argue a case whose terms were dictated by the conventional moralists themselves. The attempt profoundly shaped the novel we read today, producing alterations in structure, plot, and characterisation which undermined his fictional argument as well as strengthening it – or rather, since Hardy himself said of *Tess* that 'a novel is an impression, not an argument' (1892 Preface), substantially distorted its final impression . . . [90] □

And in particular Jacobus identifies as a source of historical understanding the changes Hardy made in purifying Tess in response to the objections of Mowbray Morris, the editor of *Macmillan's Magazine*, who rejected the novel on the grounds of Tess's sensuality and sexual power:

▪ . . . It is in the light of such reactions that Hardy's purification of Tess must be seen. The changes he made tell us not only about the strains which underlie one of his greatest novels, but about late Victorian attitudes to female sexuality.[91] □

Mary Jacobus goes on to make the case that in the Ur-'Tess' (the earliest version of the text) Tess is an ordinary girl who learns through experience, through her journeying and education into life, but in the revised manuscript she is made exceptional from the start, more refined and dignified, and the antiquarian parson's revelation about her ancestry throws the emphasis upon fate. All of which runs counter to the 'humane and egalitarian impulse at the heart of the novel'[92] and the underlying ideas of personal growth. Jacobus proceeds to describe Hardy's progressive blackening of the characters of Alec d'Urberville and Angel Clare, and the effect the purification of Tess has on her relationship with Angel:

▪ . . . Theirs had been a tragedy of mutual incomprehension, almost, a collision of cultures as well as morals. The gulf between them is nowhere clearer than in Tess's original preparedness, before their marriage, to accept 'another kind of union with him, for his own sake, had he urged it upon her; that he might have retreated if discontented with her on learning her story (f.253*)[93] . . . But such a thought is not allowed to cross the mind of a purified Tess; instead, the later version encumbers her with the naïve and exonerating belief – displayed only after the confession (i.e. in the post-1889 phase of composition) – that Angel could divorce her if he wished. This high-minded heroine is not the same as the Tess of earlier scenes, torn between her desire to be honest with Angel and an understandable longing for happiness at all costs. With purification comes inauthenticity and a new straining for effect in a novel previously marked by its realism . . . [94] □

And Mary Jacobus concludes that the post-1889 period of composition does not vitiate the novel's earlier realism; that Hardy's commitment to Tess is as a human being with a right to be, irrespective of the issue of 'purity':

▪ Though he chose to compromise in order to make his case and gain a hearing, he never falsified the issues. For all its blackening and whitewashing, the final version of *Tess of the d'Urbervilles* is justified not only by its power to move and disturb, but by its essential truth.[95] □

J.T. Laird's claim that studying the author's creative process, unlike 'impressionistic approaches', enables the reader to gain a 'surer and deeper understanding of the meaning of the definitive text'[96] is questionable. Indeed, we might conclude that these many revisions reveal how provisional and unstable the text and its meanings are. However, both studies illuminate the sociology of writing and publishing in the late nineteenth century, while that of Mary Jacobus shows how valuable critical interpretation may be based on the painstaking work of textual scholarship.

Humanist formalism embraces a wide range of stimulating essays on *Tess of the d'Urbervilles*. New Critical strategies reveal the universal nature of Tess's tragedy. Close reading of the text also exposes its narrative ambiguity. Alternatively, the whole New Critical project is called into question by an existential humanist reading of the novel, an approach which to some extent overlaps with analysis of the intensely subjective nature of tragic experience in *Tess*. In contrast, more conventional studies of the heroine as an archetypal figure examine the novel's mythological structure. Also from an earlier critical tradition is the illuminating study of Hardy in the context of contemporary humanistic thought; while a modern historical inflection of humanism offers considerable insight into the complexity of Hardy's class position as a writer. However, at the centre of critical writing on *Tess of the d'Urbervilles* during these decades is the analysis of Hardy's vision of humanity as a great web. From this critical perspective, the novel's form is seen as a provisional design, aimed at encompassing experience, and including, as the story unfolds, the involvement of both its narrator and reader. The critical understanding of *Tess* provided by humanist formalism is both extended and modified by the valuable work of genetic critics, who reinstate the author as the originator of the text, recover his creative 'biography', and reveal the constraints of Victorian social and publishing conventions under which this novel first appeared.

Although humanist formalism remained the governing critical ideology during the 1960s and 1970s, the 1980s marked a watershed in Hardy criticism. The old liberal certainties were swept away by the tidal wave of literary theory from Europe that had finally reached Britain and America. The new decade witnessed the widespread employment of unfamilar concepts and political strategies, such as structuralism, post-structuralism, deconstruction, and feminism. Because *Tess of the d'Urbervilles*, in particular, attracted the attention of critics strongly influenced by literary theory, the 1980s, the following chapter will suggest, was an unusually exciting period in which to study this text.

CHAPTER FIVE

Post-modern Departures: The 1980s

THE 1980s did not quite mark the disappearance of the humanist-formalist criticism that had dominated the preceding two decades, but the critical landscape changed dramatically as new ways of thinking entered universities in Britain and America. The radical theorisation of literary study begun in France in the 1960s eventually made its major impact in the 1980s, through theorists such as Jacques Lacan, Michel Foucault, Louis Althusser, Jacques Derrida and Julia Kristeva among others. As psychoanalytic and Marxist theory revived alongside structuralism, post-structuralism, deconstruction and feminism, traditional liberal humanist notions of the integrated individual, truth, reason, freedom and the aesthetic concept of formal unity, were all called into question. This chapter will consider examples of psychoanalytic, deconstructive, Marxist and feminist criticism of *Tess of the d'Urbervilles*. But in the welter of newness older approaches persisted tenaciously in fresh and engaging forms, including work on Hardy and the visual arts and on what Simon Gatrell calls textual biography (see pp. 147–51 of this Guide).

The sense of *Tess of the d'Urbervilles* as a text to be fought over had been evident since its early reviews. Later critics engaged each other over its elements of anti-realism and anti-humanism, some of them employing critical strategies to incorporate these within a liberal humanist paradigm. Some tried to hijack *Tess* for a more quietly political agenda, discovering in Hardy's Wessex values that are quintessentially English. In the 1980s, however, the battleground was very different. It was theoretical. And it was liberating. The benchmark for Hardy criticism was no longer the humanist realism of George Eliot, with whom Hardy had been so frequently compared, nor the economical fictional aesthetic of Henry James, which haunts the writing of so many formalist critics. Everything was possible.

One of the first of those to break free was the psychoanalytic critic, Rosemary Sumner, in *Thomas Hardy: Psychological Novelist* (1981). Sumner adduces in support of her approach Hardy's *Literary Notebooks*, which reveal an interest in psychological theory, particularly in the writings of

Fourier and Comte.[1] Her thesis is that in *Tess of the d'Urbervilles* Hardy's explicit concern with sexual relationships anticipates D.H. Lawrence's theme of harmony between body and spirit. She rejects Ian Gregor's view of Tess's fractured consciousness (see pp. 96–102 of this Guide), finding in her that psychological wholeness that D.H. Lawrence pursued (see pp. 34–6 of this Guide). However, in Angel Clare this harmony has become unbalanced, and so he looms large in Sumner's investigation. Indeed, she suggests, it is Hardy's ability to tap the subconscious in his writing, simultaneously to explore and create character, that explains why his stories often turned out differently from what his editors had been led to expect.

For Sumner, Hardy's treatment of character in *Tess* foreshadows aspects of psychology later formulated theoretically by Freud and Jung, which she sees as illuminating important areas of the novel. Quoting Sir William Watson's original recognition of Angel Clare's complexity in his *Academy* review (see pp. 18–20 of this Guide), she explores how his personality contains unresolved emotional conflict between rigid asceticism on the one hand and spontaneous sensuality on the other. His impulsive embracing of Tess is accompanied by inhibiting fears of loss of emotional control. Sumner finds this basic dichotomy similar to the idea Freud put forward in *The Ego and the Id* (1923), which introduced into psychoanalysis the concept of the ego (the conscious and unconscious strategy for mediating the demands of external reality), the id (the repressed unconscious) and the superego (the conscience). Freud was concerned with uncovering repressed material and making it subject to the control of the ego. Sumner shows in the extract below how precisely this perception is at work in Hardy's exploration of Angel Clare:

■ . . . Angel is shown from the beginning to be the kind of personality which has a demanding superego . . . while at the same time having powerful instinctive drives . . . Having decided that he may allow himself to think of Tess as a possible future wife, Angel, his superego temporarily placated, is able to respond to her in a markedly sensuous, physical way, impulsively embracing her at a moment 'when the most spiritual beauty bespeaks itself flesh; and sex takes the outside place in the presentation' (p. 172). He holds her 'still more greedily close' (p. 173), sucks the cream off her fingers, and 'passionately [clasps] her, in forgetfulness of his curdy hands' (p. 178) . . . Angel loves Tess's 'soul, her heart, her substance' (p. 167). Hardy creates an impression of Angel transformed by love into a sensuous, impulsive being . . . capable of feeling intensely . . . but he soon qualifies this impression: 'he was in truth more spiritual than animal; he had himself well in hand, and was singularly free from grossness . . . it was a fastidious emotion which could guard the loved one against his very self' (p. 193) . . . [2] □

Sumner also argues that in significant ways Angel Clare's character anticipates Jungian concepts of the 'animus' and 'anima', the contra-sexual components of the female and male psyches. She explains their function in Angel's relationship with Tess in the following extract:

▨ One factor in Angel's makeup, which makes his response to Tess's confession inevitably one of rejection, is his strongly idealising con-ception of her . . . Hardy says that he loved her 'ideally and fancifully' (p. 202), that to him, 'She was no longer the milkmaid, but a visionary essence of woman – a whole sex condensed into one typical form. He called her Artemis, Demeter' (pp. 134–5) . . . we see the close resem-blance to Jung. She is his anima: 'A collective image of woman exists in a man's unconscious, with the help of which he apprehends the nature of woman'.[3] According to Jung, so long as men are unconscious of their 'anima', they project this image on to various women they are attracted to, with disastrous results since they are projecting their own picture on to some one who is very different: 'Every mother and every beloved is forced to become the carrier and embodiment of this omnipresent and ageless image which corresponds to the deepest reality in man'.[4] Jung stresses the importance of recognising that the 'anima' is subjective. Only by doing this does it become possible for a man to love a woman objectively and not for the qualities he super-imposes on her. Neither Hardy nor Jung thought this happened very often . . . Jung sums up: 'Since the image is unconscious, it is always unconsciously projected on to the person of the beloved, and is one of the chief reasons for passionate attraction or aversion'.[5]

The reasons Angel gives for rejecting Tess are quite explicit; they are a direct admission that he has been idealising her in very much the way Jung describes and that the image of untouched purity which he had been superimposing on her had been shattered: 'You were one person: now you are another . . . the woman I have been loving is not you' (p. 226). 'She was another woman than the one who had excited his desire' (p. 240).

Hardy raises the possibility of an eventual reconciliation in Jungian terms: 'With these natures corporeal presence is something less appealing than corporeal absence; the latter creating an ideal presence that conveniently drops the defects of the real' (p. 240) . . . What it does show is that Hardy was exploring the same aspects of human nature as the psychological writers of the twentieth century. Whether or not we accept Jung's theory of the 'anima', we have to admit that Angel is an excellent illustration of the theory which was central to Jung's thought and plays a very important part in Hardy's.[6] □

Sumner finds a fascinating parallel to Angel's characterisation of Tess in 'Gradiva', a short story by the Danish novelist Jensen, which attracted Freud's attention. Its hero not only confers a classical name on his love, as does Angel, but suffers from the delusion that she once lived in Pompeii. She understands and enables him to confront the reality of her true presence by interpeting his dreams. What Angel shares with this hero is his deluded view of the object of his passion, his attempt to abstract it from reality, and his possessiveness. Drawing on this parallel and on Freud's theory that dreams permit access to the unconscious, Sumner offers a revisionary reading of the critically contentious sleepwalking scene (see Cecil, pp. 40–2; and Brown, pp. 73–8 of this Guide):

■ [Freud] states that 'the dreamer knows in his unconscious thoughts all that he has forgotten in his conscious ones, and that in the former he judges correctly what in the latter he understood in a delusion'.[7] This corresponds to Angel's expression of his love for Tess when he is sleepwalking; the love, rigorously repressed in his waking thoughts, is allowed to emerge in the dream; but in the dream he sees her as dead because at this stage, even in a dream, he cannot contemplate the possibility of accepting her as she really is. The dream 'censor' is at work, allowing through only as much reality as he can bear. He can contemplate the idea that his idealised symbol of rustic innocence is dead, but not that his ideal could be replaced by a real, living woman. The whole conception of Angel up to this point tallies with Freud's commentary on 'Gradiva': 'Every disorder analogous to Hanold's [the hero] delusion, what in scientific terms we are in the habit of calling "psychoneuroses", has as its precondition the repression of a portion of the instinctual life, or, as we can safely say, of the sexual instinct'.[8] Hardy expresses very similar ideas in scattered analytical passages: asleep he uttered only 'words of endearment, withheld so severely in his waking hours' (p. 242); awake 'he had himself well in hand', (p. 193), 'his small compressed mouth indexing his powers of self-control' (pp. 231–2).[9] □

Rosemary Sumner also points to the significant contrasts between 'Gradiva' and *Tess*. Unlike the girl in Jensen's story, Tess will not tell Angel about his unconscious sleepwalking because her self-abnegation will not allow her to take advantage of him 'while reason slept' (p. 246). However, Tess is aware of his malady and tells him 'It is in your own mind, what you are angry at, Angel; it is not in me' (p. 229). So, concludes Sumner, the reader has 'an anguished sense of missed possibilities here'.[10]

Sumner continues:

■ . . . In these ways the sleepwalking episode effectively deepens our insight into Angel. Most critics have felt this scene to be one of the weakest in *Tess*, largely on the grounds of implausibility; but it corresponds to the findings of psychoanalysis and it throws important and revealing light on the two characters. The fact that the whole event is told from Tess's point of view heightens the tension and focuses our attention on the external and physical, but the underlying psychological truth prevents it from becoming merely a melodramatic episode.

Hardy makes Angel's rejection of Tess psychologically convincing by relating it to his idealisation of her. First, he shows him neurotically withdrawing from reality by refusing to admit that she is the woman he loved. Then the fact that he despises her begins to emerge, but again this new emotion is closely related to his previous attitude to her; though he disguised it from himself, he has in fact treated her in a slightly contemptuous, patronising way throughout their relationship . . . Angel's love has clearly been of the narcissistic, self-regarding kind; Freud refers to 'the narcissistic rejection of women by men, which is so mixed up with despising them'.[11] This kind of male love, according to Freud, also displays 'marked sexual overvaluation'.[12] Hardy shows clearly these opposing tendencies, to contempt and to overvaluation, in Angel's development . . . [13] □

The essay then goes on to outline Freud's explanation of the mechanism of narcissism, which involves an illusion, in the case of repressed sexuality, that the object is loved for its spiritual value, whereas in fact these merits depend on 'sensual charm'. Narcissistic libido overflows and the love object is idealised as 'an unattained ego idea of our own'. We try to procure its perfections 'as a means of satisfying our narcissism'.[14] And Sumner finds that 'Many aspects of Angel's personality correspond quite closely to this. The repressed sexual impulses, the idealisation and falsification in valuing Tess for the one attribute which she has lost are all there in Hardy's account of him'.[15]

To his psychological analysis of Angel Clare, Sumner points out, Hardy adds the interesting, rather evasive comment: '"Some might risk the odd paradox that with more animalism he would have been the nobler man. We do not say it" (p. 240) . . . However the point is made, and it is a point which was to become central to Freud's theories.'[16] Angel's repression, she suggests, quoting Freud, was forced on him by his culture's 'restrictions on sexual life'.[17]

The burden of Sumner's psychoanalytic analysis reveals parallels with Freud, whose 'comments and suggested remedies are remarkably similar', and who also urged 'toleration and sympathy'[18] against the grain of contemporary opinion (though she notes that Freud's endorsement of pre-nuptial female virginity makes him significantly less liberal than Hardy). Of course, in the end, as Rosemary Sumner emphasises, Angel Clare is a character not a case study, and it is as a novelist not a psychoanalyst that Hardy is to be judged:

▨ Hardy's essential quality as a novelist emerges if we recognise the sensitivity of his treatment of Angel here. The main theme is, of course, Tess's suffering and undeviating love and loyalty in which he makes us feel intimately involved; but for a full apprehension of Hardy's art, we must be aware of the minor theme too and capable of entering into Angel's experience, even though this demands of us an emotional response which is in direct contradiction to the feelings evoked by our sympathy for Tess. Hardy is on the one hand challenging the conventional views of his contemporary readers, in asking them to accept Tess's 'purity', and on the other, suggesting that this acceptance does not justify condemnation of Angel who, for psychological and social reasons, cannot grasp this idea. This breadth of sympathy is particularly striking in this novel, since the whole story is a plea for a change in just those attitudes held by Angel.[19] □

Although in many respects a liberating influence, psychoanalytic criticism still relied on the assumption that the text possesses a relatively stable meaning. It is the study of *Tess of the d'Urbervilles* by the American critic, J. Hillis Miller, which perhaps exemplifies most strongly the divide between the liberal humanist and formalist–symbolist landscape of the 1960s and 1970s, and the uncharted theoretical territory of the 1980s. His essay '*Tess of the d'Urbervilles*: Repetition as Immanent Design', which forms a chapter of his book, *Fiction and Repetition: Seven English Novels* (1982), is particularly significant. Miller's earlier book, *Thomas Hardy: Distance and Desire* (1970), in which comments on *Tess* are widely scattered, had adopted a structuralist approach, pursuing in Hardy's fiction the hidden structure that will permit the critic an inclusive perspective – the complex relation between detachment and involvement. However, by the time he came to write *Fiction and Repetition*, Miller had become a post-structuralist, influenced by the French philosopher Jacques Derrida and deconstruction,[20] a movement that was strong in America, especially in the Yale school of criticism to which Miller belonged.[21] This was a complete break with traditional modes of reading, whether represented by the nineteenth-century and early-twentieth-century critics' need for biographical and historical contextualisation, or by the formalists' assumption that the text's plurality of structures and meanings is somehow related to an originating author. Together with the disappearance of the author went the end of the illusion, still offered by structuralism, of subject-centred discourse. For Derrida, writing always carries meanings that evade the confines of the text. An endless deferral of meanings is produced by the text, which challenges the conception of it as a stable structure. Derrida's strategy of reading in its 'margins' became an influential method of analysis. The identification of a key word or repeated words in marginal areas of the text produces doubleness and contradiction, undermining the text's intelligibility. The pursuit of coherence and unity is thus illusory and readers are free to produce their own meanings. The basic concepts of deconstruction – difference, repetition and marginality – inform J. Hillis Miller's approach to *Tess of the d'Urbervilles*, as the following extract from the beginning of his essay makes clear:

■ The narrative fabric of *Tess of the d'Urbervilles* is woven of manifold repetitions – verbal, thematic, and narrative. At the same time it is a story about repetition. This might be expressed by saying that the story of Tess poses a question: Why is it that Tess is 'destined' to live a life which both exists in itself as the repetition of the same event in different forms and at the same time repeats the previous experience of others in history and in legend? What compels her to repeat both her own earlier life and the lives of others? What compels her to become a model which will be repeated later by others? The question on the methodological level might be phrased by asking not why literary works tend to contain various forms of repetition, which goes without saying, but what concept of repetition, in this particular case, will allow the reader to understand the way repetitions work here to generate meaning. Another way to put this question is to ask what, for *Tess of the d'Urbervilles*, is the appropriate concept of difference. Are the differences between one example of a motif and another in a given case accidental or essential?

I shall concentrate on the interpretation of a single important passage in the novel, the one describing Alec's violation of Tess. This passage is one in which many forms of repetition are both operative and overtly named. I have called what happens to Tess her 'violation'. To call it either a rape or a seduction would beg the fundamental questions which the book raises, the questions of the meaning of Tess's experience and of its causes [Miller quotes from the four concluding paragraphs of Chapter 11, p. 77].

I have said that this passage describes Tess's violation. Yet, as almost all commentators on the scene have noted, the event is in fact not described at all, or at any rate it is not described directly. It exists in the text only as a blank space, like Tess's 'beautiful feminine tissue . . . practically blank as snow as yet' (p. 77). It exists in the gap between paragraphs in which the event has not yet occurred and those which see it as already part of the irrevocable past. It exists in the novel as a metaphor . . . Even so, the effacement of the actual moment of Tess's loss of virginity, its vanishing from the text of the finished novel, is significant and functional. It is matched by the similar failure to describe directly all the crucial acts of violence which echo Tess's violation before and after its occurrence: the killing of the horse, Prince, when Tess falls asleep at the reins, the murder of Alec, the execution of Tess. Death and sexuality are two fundamental human realities, events which it seems ought to be present or actual when they happen, if any events are present and actual. In *Tess* they happen only offstage, beyond the margin of the narration, as they do in Greek tragedy. They exist in the novel in displaced expressions, like that gigantic ace of hearts on the ceiling which is the sign that Alec has been murdered, or like the distant raising of the black flag which is the sign that Tess has been hanged.

The sign in the novel of Tess's violation, the metaphor which is its indirect presence in Hardy's language, has a deeper significance than those of the more straightforward ace of hearts or black flag. Tess's rape or seduction exists in the novel in a metaphor of drawing. It is the marking out of a pattern on Tess's flesh. 'Analytical philosophy', says the narrator, cannot explain 'why it was that upon this beautiful feminine tissue . . . there should have been traced such a coarse pattern as it was doomed to receive' (p. 77). This metaphor belongs to a chain of figures of speech in the novel, a chain that includes the tracing of a pattern, the making of a mark, the carving of a line or sign, and the act of writing.[22] □

The text insistently raises in the reader the question of Tess's suffering because of its origin in Hardy's own profound though obscure emotional identification with her, which makes the novel painfully moving; Miller suggests that it is in these marginal elements 'such as the use of the figure of writing to describe Tess's deflowering'[23] that the novel's fundamental emotional rhythms are communicated. A crucial point in his discussion occurs when he teases out the meaning of the figure of the tracing of a pattern on Tess:

■ The metaphor of the tracing of a pattern has a multiple significance. It assimilates the real event to the act of writing about it. It defines both the novel and the events it presents as repetitions, as the outlining again of a pattern which already somewhere exists. Tess's violation exists, both when it 'first' happens and in the narrator's telling, as the re-enactment of an event which has already occurred. The physical act itself is the making of a mark, the outlining of a sign. This deprives the event of any purely present existence and makes it a design referring backward and forward to a long chain of similar events throughout history. Tess's violation repeats the violence her mailed ancestors did to the peasant girls of their time. In another place in the novel, Tess tells Angel Clare she does not want to learn about history, and gives expression to a vision of time as a repetitive series. Tess does not want to know history because, as she says:

'. . . what's the use of learning that I am one of a long row only – finding out that there is set down in some old book somebody just like me, and to know that I shall only act her part; making me sad, that's all. The best is not to remember that your nature and your past doings have been just like thousands' and thousands', and that your coming life and doings 'll be like thousands' and thousands'.' (p. 130)

Sex, physical violence, and writing all involve a paradoxical act of cutting, piercing, or in some way altering some physical object. The paradox lies in the fact that the fissure at the same time establishes a continuity. It makes the thing marked a repetition and gives it in one way or another the power of reproducing itself in the future. The word 'paradox', in fact, is not, strictly speaking, appropriate here, since it presupposes a prior logical coherence which the paradox violates, going against what is normally taught or said. The dividing fissure which at the same time joins, in this case, is prior to logic, in the sense, for example, of the logical coherence of a plot with beginning, middle, and end. Any example of the division which joins is already a repetition, however far back one goes to seek the first one. This chapter attempts to identify this alogic or this alternative logic of plot and to justify giving it the Hardyan name of repetition as *immanent* [inherent] design. Such a plot will be without beginning and end in the Aristotelian sense, and the elements in the 'middle' will not be organised according to determined causal sequence. The acts of sexual conjunction, of physical violence, and of writing create gaps or breaks, as, for example, 'An immeasurable social chasm was to divide our heroine's personality thereafter from that previous self of hers' (p. 77).[24] □

These three acts Hillis Miller discerns as converging in the 'multiple implications of the metaphor of grafting used to describe the relation of Tess and Alec',[25] which he proceeds to trace in both its overt and covert manifestations in the text, based on the etymology of the word 'graft'. The violence of this relationship is also imaged by the sun, the 'fecundating male source' and 'dangerous energy able to pierce and destroy',[26] which prompts the reader's understanding of the 'chain of red things' in the novel.[27] Miller also pursues the metaphor of the novel as a mark on

Hardy's mind, which is reinscribed in the text and repeated in its title, subtitle, epigraph and four prefaces, which reaffirm Tess's life. Thus, argues Miller, 'each passage is a node, a point of intersection or focus, on which converge lines leading from many other passages in the novel and ultimately including them all'.[28] At this point in his discussion, Hillis Miller moves towards the central statement of his deconstructionist approach:

▧ . . . It is possible to distinguish chains of connection which are material elements in the text, like the red things; or metaphors, like the figures of grafting or of writing; or covert, often etymological, associations, like the connection of grafting with writing or cutting; or thematic elements, like sexuality or murder; or conceptual elements, like the question of cause or the theory of history; or quasi-mythological elements, like the association of Tess with the harvest or the personification of the sun as a benign god. None of these chains has priority over the others as the true explanation of the meaning of the novel. Each is a permutation of the others rather than a distinct realm of discourse, as the myth of the paternal sun is a version of the dangerous power of the all-too-human Alec d'Urberville, not its explanatory archetype.

Taken together, the elements form a system of mutually defining motifs, each of which exists as its relation to the others. The reader must execute a lateral dance of interpretation to explicate any given passage, without ever reaching, in this sideways movement, a passage which is chief, original, or originating; a sovereign principle of explanation. The meaning, rather, is suspended within the interaction among the elements. It is immanent rather than transcendent. This does not mean that one interpretation is as good as another but that the meaning must be formulated not as a hierarchy, with some ur-explanation at the top, truest of the true, but as an interplay among a definable and limited set of possibilities, all of which have force, but all of which may not logically have force at once. This does not exempt the reader from seeking answers to the question of why Tess is compelled to repeat herself and others and to suffer through those repetitions. The answers, rather, must lie in the sequence itself.[29] □

In Hillis Miller's reading of the passage that he has selected as his central example, Tess's violation, with its convergent chains of meaning, also points to the way the component items of the chain are altered significantly, for 'The relation among the links in a chain of meanings in *Tess of the d'Urbervilles* is always repetition with a difference, and the difference is as important as the repetition'.[30] In a detailed examination of the question, raised by Tess's violation, of what causes her life to assume a symmetrical pattern, Miller adduces and deconstructs five possible answers – the location of her violation in the Chase, which echoes the death of the legendary white hart; the general fecundity of nature; the retributive doctrines of orthodox theology; the idea of order suggested by analytical philosophy; and fate. Although Tess's life repeats what happens to her in the Chase, it does so in terms that deny explanation of this event. The reader, Miller concludes, is drawn into the pursuit of an explanation for Tess's tragic experience by Hardy's insistent questioning of the reason for Tess's suffering, only to retreat baffled by the plethora of conflicting and mutually contradictory explanations available in a text that is overdetermined (has a multiplicity of determinants):[31]

■ In one way or another most analyses of prose fiction, including most interpretations of *Tess of the d'Urbervilles*, are based on the presupposition that a novel is a centred structure which may be interpreted if that centre can be identified. This centre will be outside the play of elements in the work and will explain and organise them into a fixed pattern of meaning deriving from this centre. Hardy's insistent asking of the question 'Why does Tess suffer so?' has led critics to assume that their main task is to find the explanatory cause. The reader tends to assume that Hardy's world is in one way or another deterministic. Readers have, moreover, tended to assume that this cause will be single. It will be some one force, original and originating. The various causes proposed have been social, psychological, genetic, material, mythical, metaphysical, or coincidental. Each such interpretation describes the text as a process of totalisation from the point of departure of some central principle that makes things happen as they happen. Tess has been described as the victim of social changes in nineteenth-century England, or of her own personality, or of her inherited nature, or of physical or biological forces, or of Alec and Angel as different embodiments of man's inhumanity to woman. She has been explained in terms of mythical prototypes, as a Victorian fertility goddess, or as the helpless embodiment of the Immanent Will, or as a victim of unhappy coincidence, sheer hazard, or happenstance, or as the puppet of Hardy's deliberate or unconscious manipulations.

The novel provides evidence to support any or all of these interpretations. *Tess of the d'Urbervilles*, like Hardy's work in general, is overdetermined. The reader is faced with an embarrassment of riches. The problem is not that there are no explanations proposed in the text, but that there are too many. A large group of incompatible causes or explanations are present in the novel. It would seem that they cannot all be correct. My following through of some threads in the intricate web of Hardy's text has converged toward the conclusion that it is wrong in principle to assume that there must be some single accounting cause. For Hardy, the design has no source. It happens. It does not come into existence in any one version of the design which serves as a model for the others. There is no 'original version', only an endless sequence of them, rows and rows written down as it were 'in some old book' (p. 130), always recorded from some previously existing exemplar.[32] ☐

If J. Hillis Miller's deconstructive analysis denies the reader the possibility of a comprehensive interpretation of *Tess of the d'Urbervilles*, and an originating author for the text, feminist critics reinstated the idea of the author and his language as a focus of their investigation. The late 1960s and the 1970s saw the emergence of the women's movement as a political and cultural force. It led to the development of women's studies courses in universities, and feminist theory and criticism has become a dynamic area with a variety of methodologies. Some draw, for instance, on cultural criticism in the Marxist tradition, while for others the impetus comes from post-structuralism. Some of them coincide and overlap, while others compete for the centre ground.

Tess of the d'Urbervilles attracted the interest of a number of feminist critics in the 1980s, most notably Kathleen Blake, Laura Claridge, Janet Freeman and Kaja Silverman, who explored, among other aspects of the novel, the problematic concept of 'a pure woman', and the ways in which Tess is the object of the male gaze. However, the most influential feminist study of *Tess* was Penny Boumelha's chapter in *Thomas Hardy and Women: Sexual Ideology and Narrative Form* (1982). Her approach combines new historicist attention to the cultural ideologies that produced the text, a structuralist reading of the sign 'woman' that it creates, and a deconstruction of its gaps and discontinuities. Boumelha writes with critical rigour, and her reading reveals a radical Hardy.

Penny Boumelha's argument is that Hardy's aim in *Tess of the d'Urbervilles* was to employ an 'androgynous mode of narration, which has as its project to present woman, "pure woman", as known from within and without, explicated and rendered transparent'.[33] However, it breaks down because of the narrator's erotic fascination with Tess and the fact that she cannot be securely 'placed'. This strain is implied by Hardy's focusing in Tess different 'types' of women he has previously drawn upon in his fiction, women who are victims of their intense sexuality, or who are on the verge of marriage. Tess's complex class position is also a complicating factor. Furthermore, Hardy seeks to ensure that the narrative is structured solely by Tess. Boumelha points out that in the writing of *Tess* (with its prefaces and 'Candour in English Fiction'), Hardy's professional reticence was eroded, so that while his treatment of the sexual New Woman was not new, his polemicism was. The contemporary reception of the novel was thus partly conditioned by the passion of Hardy's defence of a woman whose career in several respects – including the 'fact that sexual and marital relationships are presented in such direct relation to economic pressures and to work'[34] – was deeply controversial.

Penny Boumelha develops the consequences of Hardy's 'project', deconstructing in the process the text's gender-based binary opposition, and rewriting Hillis Miller's preoccupation with textual repetition in different, feminist terms:

■ *Tess* presses the problem of . . . Hardy's urge towards narrative androgyny to the point where a break becomes necessary . . . In short, she is not merely spoken by the narrator, but also spoken *for*. To realise Tess as consciousness, with all that that entails of representation and display, inevitably renders her all the more the object of gaze and of knowledge for reader and narrator . . . And so it is that all the passionate commitment to exhibiting Tess as the subject of her own experience evokes an unusually overt maleness in the narrative voice. The narrator's erotic fantasies of penetration and engulfment enact a pursuit, violation and persecution of Tess in parallel with those she suffers at the hands of her two lovers. Time and again the narrator seeks to enter Tess, through her eyes – 'his [eyes] plumbed the deepness of the ever-varying pupils, with their radiating fibrils of blue, and black, and grey, and violet' (p. 172) – through her mouth – 'he saw the red interior of her mouth as if it had been a snake's' (p. 172) – and through her flesh – 'as the day wears on its feminine smoothness becomes scarified by the stubble, and bleeds' (p. 94). The phallic imagery of pricking, piercing and penetration which has repeatedly been noted,[35] serves not only to create an image-chain linking Tess's experiences from the death of Prince to her final penetrative act of retaliation, but also to satisfy the narrator's fascination with the interiority of her sexuality, and his desire to take possession of her. Similarly, the repeated evocations of a recumbent or somnolent Tess awakening to violence, and the continual interweaving of red and white, blood and flesh, sex and death, provide structuring images for the violence Tess suffers, but also repeat that violence . . .

But this narrative appropriation is resisted by the very thing that the narrator seeks above all to capture in Tess: her sexuality, which remains unknowable and unrepresentable. There is a sense here in which James's comment that 'The pretence of "sexuality" is only equalled by the absence of it'[36] could be justified. It is as if Tess's sexuality resides quite literally *within* her body, and must be wrested from her by violence. The most telling passage in this respect is Angel Clare's early morning sight of Tess:

She had not heard him enter, and hardly realised his presence there. She was yawning, and he saw the red interior of her mouth as if it had been a snake's. She had stretched one arm so high above her coiled-up cable of hair that he could see its satin delicacy above the sunburn; her face was flushed with sleep, and her eyelids hung heavy over their pupils. The brim-fulness of her nature breathed from her. It was a moment when a woman's soul is more incarnate than at any other time; when the most spiritual beauty bespeaks itself flesh; and sex takes the outside place in the presentation. (p. 172)

. . . Here, as elsewhere, and particularly at moments of such erotic response, consciousness is all but edited out. Tess is asleep, or in reverie, at almost every crucial turn of the plot: at Prince's death, at the time of her seduction by Alec, when the sleep-walking Angel buries his image of her, at his return to find her at the Herons, and when the police take her at Stonehenge. Important moments of speech are absent, too – her wedding-night account of her past life, for example, or the 'merciless polemical syllogism' (p. 311), learnt from Angel, with which she transforms Alec from evangelical preacher to sexual suitor once more. Tess is most herself – that is, most woman – at points where she is dumb and semi-conscious. The tragedy of Tess Durbeyfield . . . turns upon an ideological basis, projecting a polarity of sex and intellect, body and mind, upon an equally fixed polarity of gender. In this schema, sex and nature are assigned to the female, intellect and culture to the male . . . [37] □

Boumelha attends to the historical and social components of the relation of Angel Clare and Tess – his conflictual class, religious and moral anxieties – and to her experience of economic oppression, and of sexual double standards. Tess's tragedy is seen as hingeing on the way she is 'constructed as an instance of the natural', structured by the 'ideological elision of woman, sex and nature'.[38] Boumelha takes up this point in the following extracts:

■ . . . In *Tess*, the tragic claims of an ironised intellect are subordinated to those of sexuality. The intellectual drama of the male is not itself tragic, but functions rather as a component of the sexual tragedy of Tess. *Tess of the d'Urbervilles*, as one contemporary reviewer remarked, is 'peculiarly the Woman's Tragedy' [the anonymous contributor to the *Pall Mall Gazette*, see pp. 14–15 of this Guide]. If Tess can be said to have a tragic 'flaw', it is her sexuality, which is, in this novel, her 'nature' as a woman. Her sexuality is above all provocative: she is a temptress to the convert Alec, an Eve to Angel Clare. Such are her sexual attractions that she is obliged to travesty herself into '"a mommet of a maid"' in order to protect herself from 'aggressive admiration' (p.272). Her sexuality is constructed above all through the erotic response of the narrator . . .

Set against this provocative sexual quality is a lack of calculation, essential if Tess is not to become a posing and self-dramatising *femme fatale* in the style of Felice Charmond [a character in *The Woodlanders*]. She never declares herself as either virginal or sexually available, and yet her experience is bounded by the power that both these images exercise. Hardy tries to preserve a narrow balance between her awareness of this sexual force (for if she remains wholly unaware, she is merely a passive and stupid victim) and her refusal deliberately to exploit it (for that would involve her too actively as a temptress). The problem becomes acute at the point of her break from Angel:

> Tess's feminine hope – shall we confess it? – had been so obstinately recuperative as to revive in her surreptitious visions of a domiciliary intimacy continued long enough to break down his coldness even against his judgement. Though unsophisticated in the usual sense she was not incomplete; and it would have denoted deficiency of womanhood if she had not instinctively known what an argument lies in propinquity. Nothing else would serve her, she knew, if this failed. It was wrong to hope in what was of the nature of strategy, she said to herself: yet that sort of hope she could not extinguish. (p.239)

The archness of that parenthetical 'shall we confess it' and the elaborately distancing abstract and Latinate vocabulary testify to the difficulty of negotiating this area of a consciousness that must not become too conscious. The shared pronoun ('shall *we* confess it') hovers awkwardly between implying a suddenly female narrator and pulling the implied male reader into a conspiratorial secret (woman and their little ways) that remains concealed from Tess. He is obliged to fall back on the old standby of instinct (and, on the next page, intuition) for an explanation of a knowledge that Tess must have, in order not to be deficient in womanhood, and must not have, in order to avoid falling into anything 'of the nature of strategy'. 'Purity' is, in a sense, enforced upon Tess by the difficulty of representing for her a self-aware mode of sexuality.

. . . Tess . . . is trapped by a sexuality which seems at times almost irrelevant to her own experience and sense of her own identity. She is doomed by her 'exceptional physical nature' (p.240) and by the inevitability of an erotic response from men. That response binds her to male images and fantasies: to the pink cheeks and rustic innocence of Angel's patronising pastoralism (p.234), and to the proud indifference that Alec finds so piquantly challenging. Her sexuality, provocative without intent, seems inherently guilty by virtue of the reactions it arouses in others: 'And there was revived in her the wretched sentiment which had often come to her before, that in inhabiting the fleshly tabernacle with which Nature had endowed her, she was somehow doing wrong' (p. 301). Liza-Lu, the 'spiritualized image of Tess' (p. 383), is spiritualised by the execution of Tess, expunging the wrong-doing and expiating the guilt of her woman's sexuality. Liza-Lu and Angel Clare give an openly fantasy ending to the novel, in a de-eroticised relationship that nevertheless contravenes socially constituted moral law far more clearly than any of Tess's, since a man's marriage with his sister-in-law remained not only illegal but also tainted with the stigma of incest until after the passing of the controversial Deceased Wife's Sister Act (after several previous failed attempts) in 1907. The echo of *Paradise Lost* in the last sentence of *Tess* has often been remarked, but it is notable that the novel in fact offers a curiously inverted image of Milton's fallen world. The post-lapsarian world of *Tess* is attenuated (Liza-Lu is only 'half girl, half woman', and both she and Clare seem to have 'shrunk' facially (p. 383)) by expulsion from sexuality, and not by the loss of pre-sexual innocence. In Tess are imaged both a Paradise of sexuality (abundant, fecund, succulent) and the guilt of knowledge that inheres within it.[39] □

Far from being unified through its concentration on its heroine, Boumelha's *Tess* is a fractured, heteroglossic (multivocal)[40] text; not a single discourse, but many. Close attention reveals a number of discontinuities and gaps in the narrative, the editing out of crucial episodes such as Tess's seduction, her wedding night confession, her return to Alec d'Urberville, and her murder of him, which indicate how the narrator's voice fails to encompass Tess's sexuality. And there are abrupt movements from Tess's consciousness to a distanced placement of her in a scene. Boumelha proceeds to uncover other elements of discontinuity that threaten Hardy's aims:

■ . . . Equally, the narrator's analytic omniscience is threatened both by his erotic commitment to Tess, and by the elusiveness of her sexuality. The novel's ideological project, the circumscribing of the consciousness and experience of its heroine by a scientifically dispassionate mode of narration, is undermined by the instability of its 'placing' of Tess through genre and point of view. Structured primarily as tragedy, the novel draws also on a number of other genres and modes of writing: on realism, certainly, but also on a melodrama that itself reaches into balladry, and, of course, on polemic.
The polemic itself also exhibits a series of radical discontinuities.

As many of the novel's more recent critics have remarked, what Van Ghent has dismissively called the 'bits of philosophic adhesive tape' do not in any sense link together into a consistent or logical argument, and it would be a frustrating and futile exercise to seek in the generalisations and interpretations of the narrator any 'position' on extra-marital sex, or on the question of 'natural' versus 'artificial' morality, that could confidently be ascribed to Hardy as an individual or posited as a structuring imperative of the text . . . [41] □

Then there are the disruptive effects of Hardy's textual revisions, the 'purity' that is 'stuck on' to Tess, as Mary Jacobus put it, and the various conflicting ideologies of nature that are focused in Tess's sexuality. Boumelha continues:

■ . . . Tess . . . acts as the site for the exploration of a number of ideologies of nature that find their focus in her sexuality. The Darwinist nature of amoral instinct and the 'inherent will to enjoy' (p. 278) runs close to a naturalist version of sexuality, which posits an organicist continuity between the human and the non-human . . . Yet, even as the 'naturalness' of the sexual instinct is proclaimed [among the women at the Talbothays dairy], it is simultaneously perceived as 'cruel' and 'oppressive' (p. 149), by virtue of its extinction of difference and its imperviousness to circumstance. Here, almost implicitly, there dwells a hint of the tragic potential of sexuality in this novel: individual consciousness, or consciousness of individuality ('She was not an existence, an experience, a passion, a structure of sensations, to anybody but herself' p. 96), in conflict with non-human biological process, instinct.[42] □

Added to this, suggests Boumelha, are Rousseauesque notions of the normative function of nature, a version of the pathetic fallacy (crediting nature with human emotions), notions of reality as both 'actual' and 'psychological', and ironic reference to the beneficent nature of Wordsworth. Finally, Boumelha sees *Tess of the d'Urbervilles* as representing Hardy's radical questioning of his own narrative strategies, which recognises the boundaries of possibility in his project of presenting Tess's experiences and at the same time gaining an understanding of her female identity. She concludes:

■ Clearly, then, the novel's narrative method in a sense enacts the relativism of its structuring argument. But there is more to the discontinuities than this. They also mark Hardy's increasing interrogation of his own modes of narration. The disjunctions in narrative voice, the contradictions of logic, the abrupt shifts of point of view, form what Bayley has called 'a stylisation . . . of the more natural hiatus between plot and person, description and emotion';[43] they disintegrate the stability of character as a cohering force, they threaten the dominance of the dispassionate and omniscient narrator, and so push to its limit the androgynous narrative mode that seeks to represent and explain the woman from within and without . . . [44] □

The decade closed with a further development in feminist criticism. Patricia Ingham's *Thomas Hardy: A Feminist Reading* (1989), is an analysis through language and gender of Hardy's endeavour to transcend convention in his construction of female sexuality in the character of Tess. Ingham sees in Hardy's writing a 'fault-line', which denotes that 'there is in relation to women a subtle subterranean shifting taking place'. Ingham's approach 'involves the idea that "the subject" of a novel (in this case . . . a female subject) is created by the language, which in turn is a product of ideologies'.[45] She deals with aspects of *Tess* in separate chapters, which are brought together here. Ingham begins by revealing how the evolution in *Tess* of the sign of the fallen woman, who achieves a 'new meaning' through a measure of autonomy, nevertheless lacks a 'descriptive language'.[46] Although everyone, including of course Tess, is aware of her sexuality:

■ . . . the males of the novel cannot, with the men's language at their disposal, define and place her. Clare believes he can: '"She is a dear, dear Tess", he thought to himself, as one deciding on the true construction of a difficult passage' (p. 215). From early on he, as well as Alec, imposes the signifying framework of men's language upon her. When Tess resists his wooing it is as though 'he had made up his mind that her negatives were, after all, only coyness and youth, startled by the novelty of the proposal' (p. 183) . . .
. . . When he finds she has failed in 'purity' he is astonished: 'She looked absolutely pure. Nature, in her fantastic trickery, had set such a seal of maidenhood upon Tess's countenance that he gazed at her with a stupified air' (p. 234). The only conclusion that the categories of his language allow him to draw is that if she is not 'pure' then she is a fallen woman: 'You were one person: now you are another' (p. 226).
This erasure of Tess's identity and its replacement by a Magdalen figure is one resisted by that other interested male, the narrator. He deliberately sets aside the generalised reading of the unmarried mother who is innately wretched . . . 'But for the world's opinion those experiences would have been simply a liberal education' (p. 103). But he cannot entirely shake off the language of men even, or perhaps particularly, in his defence. The last minute addition to the novel of the subtitle 'A Pure Woman', though peripheral, deflects attention from meanings that Tess herself conveys, by attempting to rehabilitate her

under the old womanly category: she may not look it but she is, he says. This subtitle . . . is again referred to when the narrator says of Clare: 'In considering what Tess was not he overlooked what she was, and forgot that the defective can be more than the entire' (p. 259). The antithesis of 'defective' and 'entire' is of course itself a conventional one, and, like 'pure' assesses Tess in inappropriate terms. In his most emotional defences of her this tainted terminology undermines the narrator's account by measuring her against the old norms . . .

. . . The narrator's attempts at interpretation evoke the ambiguities of a language in transition. The shifting signification of the fallen, as of the womanly woman, involves problems of perception for those who encounter her.[47] □

So far as plot is concerned, argues Patricia Ingham, this too puts Hardy in conflict with his own views, for his explicit hostility to patriarchy and his defence of women raises questions about the discontinuity of his narrative syntax:

■ In *Tess* the belated subtitle 'A Pure Woman' is itself already a direction to read the text as an over-writing of the traditional fallen-woman-atones stories . . . In fact the subtitle accepts in advance some of the conventional assumptions that usually underlie such a narrative. Generic 'woman' is up for moral assessment and it is in respect of sexual morality that it is felt appropriate, even essential, to assess her: is she pure or not pure? To that extent the text colludes with the familar pattern. What is destabilised, however, is the account of what it means for a woman to be sexually pure or blameless.[48] □

Ingham goes on to discuss the breakdown of the line between rape and seduction in Tess's relationship with Alec d'Urberville, and shows how the plot displays the limitations of the fallen woman as autonomous subject:

■ . . . There develops a subtext about Tess, sexuality and naturalness that urges the exclusion of purely sexual relationships from the sphere of moral judgement. By implication Tess in a less artificial world might have regarded such a relationship as an available option. This is paradoxical: it cannot be logically reconciled with the equally urgent assertion that she is the victim of exploitation . . .

What is also innovatory in the syntax of *Tess* is that her punitive death is not the direct consequence of her fall: she survives her child's death, Angel's desertion and Alec's reappearance. Between the fall that is not a fall and her death is inserted a new sequence in which . . . she lives through a period of autonomy before she dies [in which] Tess's acts of will represent the culmination of the whole sequence. The events involved figure the monstrousness of the only choice that is left to her, the only meaning she can express after the final shock of Angel's coming to claim her when she has already returned to Alec as his mistress. In stabbing Alec to release herself for Angel she feels free even from guilt. As the latter listens to her confession of murder, 'his horror at her impulse was mixed with amazement at the strength of her affection for himself; and at the strangeness of its quality, which had apparently extinguished her moral sense altogether' (p. 372).

But Tess has formulated Alec's death to herself as logical . . . :

'I thought as I ran along that you would be sure to forgive me now I have done that. It came to me as a shining light that I should get you back that way . . . I was unable to bear your not loving me. Say you do now, dear dear husband . . . now I have killed him!' (p. 372)

Her logic is mad, but for once she dominates him:

It was very terrible, if true: if a temporary hallucination, sad. But anyhow here was this deserted wife of his, this passionately fond woman, clinging to him without a suspicion that he would be anything to her but a protector. He saw that for him to be otherwise was not, in her mind, within the region of the possible. (p. 373)

And he submits to her account of the possible.

There is no doubt that in her refusal to escape she still leads Angel, although she is clear as to the consequences of her act. It is she who, ironically, suggests that after her death he should marry her sister, Liza-Lu, realising that this would constitute legal incest: 'People marry sister-laws continually about Marlott' (p. 380). When she stretches out on the oblong slab at Stonehenge she is choosing her place of surrender. The death on the gallows that supervenes reveals the hollowness of her autonomy, a pretence with which Angel has colluded, knowing that they were out of time. Significantly she now says to him, with an understanding that goes beyond madness: 'I have had enough; and now I shall not live for you to despise me' (pp. 380–1). Like all fallen women she dies; all she has really been able to choose is the particular form of her death. Murder and execution as the only available expression of autonomy speak for themselves as to the real limits of agency for the fallen woman. Plot, as so often in Hardy, figures a central statement.[49] □

The sexual politics of *Tess of the d'Urbervilles*, discussed by Boumelha and Ingham, was also scrutinised through its ideological relation with history by the Marxist critic George Wotton, in his *Thomas Hardy: Towards a*

Materialist Criticism (1985,) which includes useful discussion of critics' gendered views of Tess as a sexual object. This followed John Goode's stimulating work in his essay, 'Women and the Literary Text' in *The Rights and Wrongs of Women* (1976), edited by Juliet Mitchell and Ann Oakley. There Goode argues that Tess is objectified by the images projected onto her by the various male gazers, including the narrator, a process which involves the reader in the shared guilt, and which creates the novel's contradictory discourses. Goode's finest study of Hardy, *Thomas Hardy: The Offensive Truth*, appeared a decade or so later in 1988. In it he develops a powerful materialist[50] analysis of the novel as an object of production. As a materialist critic, Goode's aim is to seek to understand the text as the product of social factors, and as a historical process. His approach also incorporates the concept of the text as a process of signification rather than representation, and as an object of production in which the reader is invited to participate. Like Penny Boumelha, Goode also draws on the idea of the text as being heteroglossic, composed of interacting discourses, and on feminist ideology. He rejects the humanist-formalist analysis, which discards the novel's polemic, and naturalises Tess as in some sense real and available to the reader. Equally, he is unable to accept Hillis Miller's critical model of discontinuity, which issues in infinite repetition of forms. After all, he suggests, unity of some kind is implied by Hardy's project in the subtitle – pure/faithful. So he sees the discontinuity of the text as part of its 'polemical design in which the discontinuities are seen as properties of the ideological discourses the text articulates', discourses that are identified in textual politics as that of an 'ideological hierarchy' – centrally the 'correlation of two discourses, that of "nature" and that of "gender"' together with a third, 'that of the "social relations of production"'.[51] Goode's paradigms are rather abstract and schematic, and his argument is sometimes compressed. The following passage summarises his critical strategy:

■ ... The presence of these discourses is not in doubt. What I want to establish is that they open out into one another. Or rather as the look such discourses bestow on life is returned from the contradictions within them, their intended foreclosure is subverted, not endlessly, but ending on a question. For each discourse is manifest as a way of looking which is at the same time looking at looking. Although the ideological discourse of nature and the discourse of the social relations of production correspond to the opposed metonymies of the return and the gesture (as being aligned with the repeated 'rhythms' of life and the 'march' of history respectively) and the discovery of gender constructing the object of love as symptom with the metaphor of human making, so that it manifests itself finally on the sacrificial stone, the identifying signal is the gaze, either appropriated or at last returned.[52] □

In the sections of his chapter entitled 'Nature's Holy Plan' and 'An Almost Standard Woman', John Goode argues that patriarchy employs the discourse of 'nature' as an agent of female oppression, and in discussing the discourse of gender he picks up once more a theme of his earlier essay, the text's obsessive preoccupation with looking, and links it with the discourse of the social relations of production. Later in the essay, he analyses the scene at the railway station and describes the evolution of the discourse of gender from eye to voice, together with the implication of the reader in this process:

■ The gaze of wisdom is the double gaze, the gaze of sexual oppression is the appropriated gaze, the gaze of the social relations of production is reciprocated – the gaze in exchange. It appears most dramatically when Tess and Angel take the milk to the trains:

> The light of the engine flashed for a second upon Tess Durbeyfield's figure, motionless under the great holly-tree. No object could have looked more foreign to the gleaming cranks and wheels than this unsophisticated girl with the round bare arms, the rainy face and hair, the suspended attitude of a friendly leopard at pause, the print gown of no date or fashion, and the cotton bonnet drooping on her brow. (pp. 187–8)

Like the fly on the billard table, and the girl in the pink cotton jacket, this is an image of Tess which momentarily turns the novel inside out so that we gain a certain determined distancing from the experiential narrative. But it is very different from these. For our intimacy with Tess at this point is much greater since it is mediated through Angel's company, so that the change in perspective is not merely from her to an opposing gaze, but her visibility to the opposing gaze of something outside the novel (and therefore outside the illusion in which it holds us). Moreover it is not the eye of the painter who picks out a girl from a landscape, or of a god, but the eye of the gleaming cranks and wheels of a locomotive. This estrangement of Tess involves therefore the construction of the reader's eye in terms of a specific social and cultural medium. We have to transpose ourselves to an unspecified passenger seeing Tess as an image lit only by the form of transport in which we are carried. Our vision in other words does not liberate the viewer in the manner to which he is accustomed in the construction of images. 'Foreign' also discards any possibility of an absolute possessing assessment – she is not simple or beautiful but only different (and 'unsophisticated' doesn't give a positive purchase). The moment is further troubled by the simile 'the suspended attitude of a friendly leopard at pause'. Again it is redolent of a strange paradox – it is a moment which returns the gaze we try to hold it in.

In terms of the novel's structure, the function of this passage is to remind us of the social specificity of the story that is being told. And it is not the image taken away by the train that is developed (the reader is whisked away by it and has to be returned to the text); it is a moment whose meaning is *voiced* by the 'receptive Tess'. What follows is her observation of the immensity of the social gap specifically in relation to the Ruskin–Morris[53] critique of the division of labour: '"Londoners will drink it at their breakfasts tomorrow, won't they? . . . Strange people, that we have never seen"' (p. 188). Angel who, as we know, reduces social experience to cultural choices (the ache of modernism is something that may be learnt by rote) vaguely comments on the adulteration of milk (note that his response is on behalf of the consumer), but is totally unable to grasp the social relations which Tess is defining. As she insists and elaborates, *he* takes refuge in the humorous potential of her unsophistication ('particularly centurions' p. 188), and as she continues, he tries to silence her by reminding her of the private function of their presence at the station. We have seen this before as well when Angel, 'privateering' at the garlic picking, singles out Tess. But what is different here is that he is not artificially selecting Tess but suppressing the real social relationship by which she relates, and thinks of herself as relating, to the world as a whole. More specifically, since the relationship is defined in the reciprocal gaze (the train watching Tess watching the train), I mean *our* world, the world of the consuming reader who will not only drink milk without ever having seen a cow but consumes Tess's story without having to undergo it.[54] □

Goode goes on to explain the central importance of the reciprocal gaze:

▨ . . . But just as the privileging of the voice over the eyes is a token of the evolution of the discourse of gender, so this return of the gaze across the social divide indicates the whole strategy of the novel. For the discourse of the social relations of production is present at first as the one-way gaze of the anthropologist and sociologist, Parson Tringham's thoughtless genealogy, or 'the yellow melancholy of this one-candled spectacle' (p. 25). But the attack on nature's holy plan is an anger that arises from a securely distant cliché, 'All these young souls were passengers in the Durbeyfield ship' (p. 28). And, at its most dislocating, the 'picture' of the Durbeyfields merely switches from the flippant to the serious: thus the lurching of the drunken John Durbeyfield between his wife and his daughter 'produced a comical effect, frequent enough in families on nocturnal homegoings; and, like most comical effects, not quite so comic after all' (p. 33). We only get *into* this world with the controlled terms of Tess's selection from it. Her emergence, and her consequent availability to the less determined ideologies of wisdom and love is the condition of the reader's involvement. But what happens during the passage from Tess's acquiescence in Angel's courtship and his rejection of her is that her mind is developed and her voice *audibly repressed*, so that we can no longer revert to the comfortably distanced realism of the opening. And yet that is precisely and explicitly what Hardy does – he sends Tess back into the world of the social structure from which both Alec and Angel have temporarily, and violatingly, separated her.[55] ☐

Goode's discussion then traces Tess's re-entry into the novel both as an isolated woman and as a 'social phenomenon', an alienated 'working-class woman', paying for the 'desire of middle-class males'[56] at Flintcomb-Ash, and during the Lady-Day eviction of her family, a process which 'explicitly revalues the discourse of nature',[57] as Tess is seen as part of a historical process. At the same time as she becomes increasingly the object of a text whose interest is not her but the 'social process she represents', she emerges as 'a woman capable of telling her story in her own voice'.[58] Goode outlines this phase of his discussion:

■ . . . The disconversion of Alec, the letters to Angel, the complaints about being a victim, the comment that life is vanity – these are not isolated outbursts but aspects of a structured development of a voice which does not accept the socialisation which is inevitable. So that we are both presented with a picture of Tess's life and times, and made to hear the voice that the picture silences. Obviously the fact that she has to speak through *writing* has its own kind of resonance and this is confirmed by the fact that Hardy reprints the second letter at its arrival. The only *voice* she is allowed is the imitation of Angel but nothing stops her from making a text. And, of course, this is exactly what is happening in relation to the reader. For we no more hear Tess than we see her: what we have is a textualisation which offers us (in theory) the choice. Clearly we only make the choice that is made necessary by the event but what is important is that Tess is a heroine for the writing age. She is 'fulfilled' in the space between the social rubric and the offensive truth.

This dialectical movement is intensified and it means that the novel has no satisfying end. But it does not mean that it has no end. What the reader is forced to do is to take on the inexorable logic of the socialisation of Tess in the context of her increased articulateness . . .[59] ☐

Goode argues that in Tess's conversations with Alec and letters to Angel, her voiced wisdom based on her experience and opposition to Angel's values, gives her authority for the reader at the same time that she is being 'deleted by oppressive forces',[60] and all she 'learns' is what will happen to her. And, crucially, the reader is involved in this experience:

■ The action of the text *puts the reader through* the primary working-class experience: the truth does not make you free, it simply exposes your chains. There are other novels which show this. But I know of none that actually thrusts it on the reader. This is strengthened by the fact that [Tess's] two decisions – to go with Alec and to murder him, which each in their turn trap her into the system whose consequences they attempt to subvert – echo Angel's 'truth': 'Yet a consciousness that in a physical sense this man alone was her husband seemed to weigh on her more and more' (p. 345). We want to ascribe this to the ideology which her whole development has denied. But in the end it is what is left her. Prostitution is the ultimate capitalist relationship for the woman. Her whole economic being is the sale of her body – the violation of the threshing machine is clearly coherent with the occupation of her body. In this perspective the murder is not an escape from this closure . . . [61] □

John Goode offers a subtle extended reading of the moment of recognition between Tess and Angel after the murder – the 'returned gaze as question and dream'[62] – before their refuge in the abandoned house, and Angel's seeing Tess for the first time 'as subject of her own sentence'[63] during this 'utopian interval'.[64] Goode then returns, in the following extracts, to the relation between this achieved sense of herself and the tension between the private and the novel as social process:

■ . . . This question of a woman telling her story is precisely the question of the novel which is compelled by the silence of her oppression to tell it for her, and tell it as an amusement, since that is what novels are, for others. Moreover her process of selection – this is Tess's story and not anybody else's – is part of the condition of the novel too. But, as we are constantly reminded, the distance between Tess and the other girls is not always so very great. There are other stories. Other women's lives are just as tremulous . . . To write a novel is always to lift the single story out of the social picture and for precisely that reason it is bound by its very nature to lure the reader towards the private solution. In other words we ought to be feeling very strongly that Tess needn't have actually murdered Alec and that she and Angel could have worked it out. And maybe if they had been actual living human beings they could have worked at some kind of private solution to the contradictions with which they engage. But it is precisely this kind of confusion that . . . Hardy, motivating Tess at the end as *actress* (in both senses of the word) avoids. He opens out the book not in the sense of leaving it available but in a sense that pushes it back into life, into the general. So that if we do feel very strongly that Tess didn't need to murder Alec, we ought in the end to understand that to feel that way is irrelevant.

It is irrelevant because Tess has understood what constructs her and the murder makes possible a parenthesis within the sentence (in both senses) in which she is inscribed.[65] □

And Tess's promoting Angel's marriage with his deceased wife's sister Goode sees as her final act of challenge to the 'hegemony . . . of the customs of her country'.[66]

John Goode concludes on a personal note with an account of his own experience as a passionately political reader of this text:

■ I have read and reread *Tess of the d'Urbervilles* many times during twenty years, and I still find the end impossible to read. Throughout I have warned against naturalising Tess, but, of course, it is part of the strategy of the novel that we should do so. The novelist aims at an illusion. But this novelist aiming at it and succeeding only does so to punish us for our complacency. How many other English novels end with the execution of the female protagonist, who has already been raped? To have her die would enable us to say amen – terrible and sad but so be it. But she is hanged by the neck until she is dead. 'Justice' is in inverted commas, both because it is a legal term carried over into aesthetic discourse (hence the savagely ironic invocation of the Aeschylean phrase). We know what average human nature thinks of divine morality, and we know that Tess understands the meaning of sport: 'She had occasionally caught glimpses of these men in her girlhood . . . strangely accoutred, a bloodthirsty light in their eyes' (p. 271). Our ruling classes, like gods, administering justice as sport. But notice how it continues – gaze and speech again – 'The two speechless gazers bent themselves down to the earth, as if in prayer, and remained thus a long time absolutely motionless' (p. 384). But the flag, the only signifier of narrative left, continues like some distant friend to 'wave silently' (p. 384). Invocations of *Paradise Lost* are not adequate here (though they are relevant). Hardy is making us read about the response to the *hanging* of a loved one. As soon as they had strength they arose. Nothing, of course, is left to reciprocate their gaze. They are not silent, but speechless. The only language is the flag's. But it is also the novelist's. 'Justice' is torn between legal action and poetic fitness, but, as we know, Hardy sent *Tess* to Morris, and the original newspaper of the Social Democratic Federation was called *Justice*. Justice is more than the prevailing law. It is something that is fought for, a truth that is on the offensive.[67] □

Approaching Hardy from an entirely different perspective, several critics have been attracted to the aesthetic, visual quality of his writing, including Penelope Vigar (*The Novels of Thomas Hardy: Illusion and Reality,* 1974) and Joan Grundy (*Hardy and the Sister Arts,* 1979), who both discuss Hardy's painterly, impressionistic techniques. But it is the elegant, scholarly study of J.B. Bullen, *The Expressive Eye: Fiction and Perception in the Work of Thomas Hardy* (1986), which offers the fullest understanding of a creative process that gives visual embodiment to Hardy's religious and ethical ideas. Bullen reads Hardy within his artistic milieu, shows how his visual sensibility structured his novels in series of images, and reveals connections between the conscious and the unconscious in his writing that relate to psychology and mythology. Bullen summarises these succinctly:

■ . . . The visual symbolism of Hardy's fiction can only be clearly understood in conjunction with his taste in painting, his reading of Ruskin, his attitude to the psychology of perception, and his reinterpretations of other literary forms such as Nordic and Greek myths.[68] □

Bullen draws on Hardy's intimate knowledge of the work of J.M.W. Turner, and in particular Hardy's understanding of how, by painting the effect of light on objects (in effect painting light itself), Turner's expressionism communicates a deeper reality. Its literary equivalent, Bullen argues, may be found in the landscapes of *Tess of the d'Urbervilles*:

■ In Turner, Hardy had found a painter who revealed the inner meaning of landscape by painting not objects, but the effect of light on objects . . . Here, in Turner's depiction of 'light as modified by objects',[69] is surely the source of so many of the brilliant scenes in *Tess of the d'Urbervilles* in which the landscape dissolves in the glow of light and sunlight . . .

. . . As Tess descends for the first time into the valley what she sees is indeed what Hardy had perceived in Turner's water-colours – light as modified by objects. The cows that were 'spotted with white reflected the sunshine in dazzling brilliancy, and the polished brass knobs on their horns glittered with something of a military display' (p.111). The courting of Angel and Tess in the dawn light of the water-meadows is played out not so much on terra firma but amongst a multiplicity of lights and shadows. Hardy carefully defines the exact quality of that light, pointing out that 'The grey half-tones of daybreak are not the grey half-tones of the day's close, though the degree of their shade may be the same' (p.134). And the evening landscape in which they walk is shaped by the light of the setting sun. Tess and Angel move amongst 'the beams of the sun, almost as horizontal as the mead itself', and the light forms 'a pollen of radiance over the landscape' (pp.193–4).[70] □

There are numerous instances, as Bullen demonstrates, where Hardy reads the effects of the sun as it points up crucial stages in Tess's life, the rhythm of her relationship with Angel Clare, the seasonal changes, alterations in mood, journeys undertaken at night, and the threatening forces of darkness. Hardy had noted how Turner uses light to communicate the mysterious forces of life in his paintings, and he adopts a similar strategy in *Tess*, giving visual form to moral conflict by linking its characters to the contrast between the primitive and the modern. Bullen develops this idea in terms of pagan (and especially Greek) mythology:

> Light and darkness, sunlight and shadow, the illumination from fires and the illumination from the sky, are treated both literally and symbolically in this novel. On the one hand, they help to create a credible setting for the pastoral tragedy, and on the other, they generate what Brunetière termed the 'latent affinities' and 'mysterious identities' between 'external nature and ourselves'[71] – between character and environment. Hardy creates these affinities in part by employing the archetypal power of light and darkness to suggest joy and sorrow, life and death, but he also draws on a more specific set of meanings related to sun and sunlight, darkness and night. At almost every point in *Tess of the d'Urbervilles* the solar symbolism which Hardy uses has close connections with the mythical properties of light and darkness. He was familiar with the current nineteenth-century view that the source of all primitive legends, even primitive religions, was to be found in the path of the sun through the sky. In early mythology the real, objective sun merges with the divinities which it inspired. In *Tess of the d'Urbervilles* the sun, which plays such a prominent part in the action, is imaginatively linked with the main protagonists, and the connection between them is derived from the ancient, mytho-poetical power of solar illumination.[72] □

Bullen notes the preoccupations of Tony Tanner and J. Hillis Miller with Hardy's repetition of redness in *Tess*, and its association with the sun, and develops its moral and cultural implications in the text:

> . . . Redness is certainly allied to the creative and destructive power of the sun in the novel, but what is more important is that the sun is also an emblem for a complex set of religious and cultural values. The persistent and ubiquitous struggle between sunlight and shadow is the visual equivalent, or visible essence, of a moral conflict within the novel – a conflict between a religious impulse which is primitive, simple, and untrammelled by the demands of conventional orthodoxy and religious dogmas which are deeply entrenched in an ethical code.
> The sun is the source of life and light, and in its benevolent form

rises as a god in the August dawn – a 'golden-haired, beaming, mild-eyed' creature. It is 'god-like' in appearance, 'gazing down in the vigour and intentness of youth upon an earth that was brimming with interest for him' (p. 92). This same appearance 'explained the old-time heliolatries in a moment', and 'One could feel', says the narrator, 'that a saner religion had never prevailed under the sky' (p. 92). It is the sun which is the deity presiding over the 'aesthetic, sensuous, Pagan pleasure in natural life' (p. 161) of Talbothays; it presides, too, over the religion of Greece, which, Angel argues, would have had a better influence on mankind than the religion of Palestine (p. 161). The sun is the heart of 'the great passionate pulse of existence', and it is solar worship which stands in opposition to the 'geocentric view of things' of dogmatic Christianity, with its 'zenithal paradise' and 'nadiral hell' (p. 161).

It is amongst the pagan customs of the remote areas of the countryside that ancient sun-worship has survived. At Marlott in the 'Club-walking' episode – itself a survival of fertility rituals – each girl, we are told, was 'warmed without by the sun', while at the same time 'each had a private little sun for her soul to bask in' (p. 20). Chaseborough is deeply pagan in both appearance and customs. Here the rustic girl Car, with her Greek form 'beautiful as some Praxitelean creation' (p. 70), dances with the other country folk in an Ovidian revel – 'satyrs clasping nymphs – a multiplicity of Pans whirling a multiplicity of Syrinxes' (pp. 66–67), but it is amongst the 'impassioned, summer-steeped heathens' (p. 160) of Talbothays that solar worship is most prominent, and there it has become absorbed into the rites of primitive Christianity. It is largely the women of the community who unconsciously perpetuate the old forms of religion, because women, living in the companionship of 'outdoor Nature', 'retain in their souls far more of the Pagan fantasy of their remote forefathers than of the systematized religion taught their race at a later date' (p. 109). This is particularly true of Tess herself, and though she is pursued by the 'moral hobgoblins' of orthodoxy, she yields spontaneously to the influence of the sun.

It is under the influence of the sun that Angel and Tess fall in love. The 'rush of juices' and the 'hiss of fertilization' (p. 151) created in the organic world by the July sun carry over to the human world, and mutual affection comes 'like an excitation from the sky' (p. 153). Consequently, when Tess embraces Angel, she not only embraces a man, she also opens herself to the power of the sun, which lights up her whole being:

> . . . there they stood upon the red-brick floor of the entry [to the dairy house], the sun slanting in by the window upon his back, as

he held her tightly to his breast, upon her inclining face, upon the blue veins of her temple, upon her naked arm, and her neck, and into the depths of her hair. (p. 172)

The identification in Tess's mind between Angel and the sun transforms her love for him into a kind of sun-worship: she lifts her heart to him 'in devotion' (p. 193); he is a 'divine being' (p. 201); he is 'godlike in her eyes' (p. 183); he is her 'Apollo' (p. 373) . . . [73] □

Bullen points out that Hardy would also have known that Turner was himself a sun-worshipper, whilst the philologist, Max Müller, with whose work Hardy was familiar, traced all myths back to primitive responses to the diurnal movement of the sun. In *Tess*, notes Bullen, we find Müller's worshippers of Apollo, as well as Tess's weak version of Apollo:

■ . . . The sun-god rises 'in the vigour . . . of youth' (p. 92), wrestles with the powers of darkness, and dies on the day of Angel's and Tess's marriage, at a point in the novel which is simultaneously the 'end of the day' and the 'end of the sunny season'. In the novel, Apollo's acolytes are the 'impassioned . . . heathens in the Var Vale' (p. 160) who possess 'the bold grace of wild animals' (p. 175), and resemble in many respects the 'youthful race' described in Müller's work. The worshippers of Apollo, he says, are 'free to follow the call of their hearts, – unfettered by the rules and prejudices of a refined society, and controlled only by those laws which nature and the graces have engraved on every human heart'.[74] In Talbothays, Angel felt for the first time the 'great passionate pulse of existence, unwarped, uncontorted, untrammelled by those creeds which futilely attempt to check what wisdom would be content to regulate' (p. 161).

Tess's love comes to her as an impulse, and it comes in the moments between sleeping and waking – first in the Apollonian light of dawn at Talbothays, then when she rises from her afternoon nap like a 'sunned cat' (p. 172). Müller describes the connection of love and solar worship, when

such hearts [are] suddenly lighted up by love, – by a feeling of which they knew not either whence it came and whither it would carry them; an impulse they did not even know how to name . . . Was not love to them like an awakening from sleep?[75]

Both Tess and her primitive antecedents look for a name for that love, and like the Greeks who, in Müller's account, were pervaded by a 'glowing warmth, purifying their whole being like a fresh breeze, and illuminating the whole world around them with a new light', they identify their love with Apollo. 'There was but one name by which they could express love', Müller says, 'there was but one similitude for the roseate bloom that betrays the dawn of love', and his account of the creation of mythological language fits exactly with Tess's own experience: '"The sun has risen", they said, where we say "I love"; "the sun has set", they said, where we say, "I have loved"'.[76]

Angel Clare, of course, is not Apollo. He is the youngest son of Parson Clare of Emminster, and has voluntarily given up a university career in order to train himself as a farmer. Yet he carries in him enough of the attributes of his mythological counterpart to make it clear that Tess's likening him to Apollo is not simply a figment of her imagination. His harp-playing, his role as herdsman, his power to bring both light and destruction, are all reminiscent of the god of the Greeks. But in Angel the power of Apollo is weak. He is like a lesser god who finds himself in a country where, and at a time when, a new religion and a new morality hold sway; consequently, the positive virtues for which he stands are suddenly and brutally eclipsed.[77] □

Hardy may also have been influenced, suggests Bullen, by Walter Pater's 'Apollo in Picardy',[78] which was being worked on while Hardy was thinking about *Tess of the d'Urbervilles*. Pater's Apollyon is a powerful duality ('lyre and bow'):

■ Like Pater's Apollyon, Angel is both the Good Shepherd – or at least the good herdsman – who by his love and his light keeps in 'subjection' the 'wolves' (p. 195) that seek to devour Tess, and he is also the bringer of plagues, violence, and sudden death. Both Pater and Hardy exploit the duality of the Apollo legend, but Hardy, unlike Pater, extends that duality to the Christian myth.[79] □

This leads J. B. Bullen to identify the tragic issue at the heart of the novel:

■ Tess's tragedy lies in the fact that, as a child of nature, she has been born into that 'grotesque phase' of Christianity in which moral precept is more important than worship. Hardy's reading of J. C. Morison and T. H. Huxley[80] seems to have convinced him of the idea that the true religious spirit – whether pagan or Christian – is fundamentally independent of ethical systems, and that only at a later date in the evolution of society was worship tainted by its association with moral codes.[81] □

The essay goes on to explore the range of thought and imagery in *Tess*: the parallel sunrises at Talbothays and Stonehenge, the biblical and

Arcadian symbolism of Talbothays, the destructive functions of Artemis (Tess) and Apollo (Angel), together with the concluding echo of Turner's watercolour of Stonehenge. These prompt Bullen's summary of his fundamental insight; how Hardy

■ . . . gives concrete and visible expression to abstract ideas about the relationship between contrasting views of religious worship and the ethical implications of religious belief . . . Even more remarkable, perhaps, is the way in which Hardy synthesises ideas and images with unobtrusive consistency throughout the narrative . . . [82] □

This more traditional vein of Hardy scholarship is extended inventively by Simon Gatrell's *Hardy the Creator: A Textual Biography* (1988). His work (with Juliet Grindle) on the Clarendon edition of *Tess of the d'Urbervilles* (1983), afforded him an insight into Hardy's development as a writer through the revisions he made to its various editions, and Gatrell initiated a new critical methodology, which, as his title announces, he terms 'textual biography'.

Gatrell's essay, from a chapter entitled 'From *Tess* to *Jude*: 1892–1894', concentrates on the single volume edition of *Tess* that Hardy revised for publication in 1892. Until then, as Gatrell points out, 'the novel had still not become a stable text in his mind, and . . . concepts and characters . . . were still being worked out',[83] after his restoration of the separate episodes published elsewhere. Hardy's endeavour to establish the first book edition from the version serialised in the *Graphic*, and from the two episodes that he had published separately, meant that he would not have had the energy or time for a thorough revision of the text, even though the second half of the novel (following Tess's confession to Angel Clare) must have been written with the *Graphic* readership in view. So *Tess of the d'Urbervilles* was unfinished in Hardy's mind when he came to revise it for the 1892 edition, and in Gatrell's view we can see in the changes he made to it the shaping pressure of his thinking about his 'ideas', his own class position, his relation to his characters, and finally to his text. Gatrell shows, in the extracts below, how progressive changes at the level of the paragraph have their effect on the overall text:

■ It is one of the most noticeable features of *Tess* that the narratorial tone is not homogeneous, that it is split into two voices, which may, in a simplified way, be defined as detached and engaged. Quite a large number of changes in this edition are made in the distanced authorial narrative voice, as if Hardy was only beginning to realise in one or two areas exactly what it was that his novel meant to him personally and what he was saying through it to the world (what one might call the manifesto aspect of the novel). An example of this is the rewriting of a

147

paragraph in Chapter 5. It occurs at a place where the manuscript folio is lacking, so the first witness is the serial version:

> As Tess grew older, and began to see how matters stood, she felt somewhat vexed with her mother for thoughtlessly giving her so many little sisters and brothers. Her mother's intelligence was that of a happy child: Joan Durbeyfield was simply an additional one, and that not the eldest, to her own long family of seven. (Clarendon edition, 1983, p.49)[84] □

For the first edition, Gatrell notes, Hardy made three changes which involved the concept of political economy: introducing 'she felt Malthusian vexation with her mother', adding 'when it was such a trouble to nurse those that had already come', and altering 'seven' to 'nine when all were living'. These were the details he revised still further in the one-volume edition of 1892, so that the paragraph now read:

> ■ As Tess grew older, and began to see how matters stood, she felt quite Malthusian towards their mother for thoughtlessly giving her so many little sisters and brothers, when it was such a trouble to nurse and provide for them. Her mother's intelligence was that of a happy child: Joan Durbeyfield was simply an additional one, and that not the eldest, to her own long family of waiters on Providence. (p.40)[85] □

Gatrell points out that this integrates the Malthusian idea more closely into the text (Hardy added 'a' before Malthusian in the 1895 text, underlining the inference that Tess understood the term). Hardy now offers a broader socio-economic perspective of a large family and links the ideas of 'Providence' and 'provide'. Gatrell comments on the larger effects such changes have in the novel:

> ■ Of all these changes, it is the last one made in the one-volume text that reverberates longest throughout the novel. That the Durbeyfields are a 'long family of waiters on Providence' is one of Hardy's chief accusations against them, one indeed that Tess herself does not escape; and the phrase gathers force as the crucial events of Tess's life are enacted. Though a small change it has a disproportionately large significance, and this might equally well be said of the whole revision undertaken for the one-volume text.[86] □

The process of revision also gave Hardy the opportunity to reflect on the precise function in the novel that he wanted his own social class to fulfil;

his motivation, suggests Gatrell, being very much that of the 'village historian':[87]

■ There are one or two other places where Hardy's concern for the economics of rural life surfaces in one-volume changes, changes expressed also through the distanced narrative voice. One of these suggests that Hardy had done a little research between the first edition and this revision, or else that someone had told him something. It occurs at the beginning of Chapter 10, in a narratorial aside explaining why so many of Tess's contemporaries at Trantridge were married; previously the passage read: 'marriage before means was the rule here as elsewhere'. This generalised sententious comment of the superficial moralist was replaced in 1892 by an adequate economic motivation: 'a field-man's wages being as high at twenty-one as at forty, marriage was early here' (p.65). This informed and concerned perception comes from the same sector of Hardy's interests as that which had stimulated him to write his essay, 'The Dorsetshire Labourer' (some of which is incorporated into Chapter 51 of *Tess*). In reviewing in 1892 the role of 'cottagers who were not directly employed upon the land', in the relevant passage at the beginning of Chapter 51, Hardy felt the need to add that they 'had formed the backbone of the village life in the past', and that they 'were the depositaries of the village traditions' (p.339). This is his own class that he is writing about, and it is as if it took until the one-volume edition for Hardy to figure out the crucial role with which he wanted to invest that class . . . [88] □

Gatrell's linking of textual change and biographical facts is particularly revealing in showing how Hardy's changes to the 1892 text were prompted by a closer relationship with his social class, and how this creates a split within the detached narrator, who at points wants to represent his class:

■ A change in Chapter 33 is also worth considering in this context: where the narrator describes the peal of bells rung from the church in which Angel and Tess are married, the passage has been considerably revised. In the manuscript's first version 'a modest peal of four notes broke forth' . . . But the crucial change in emphasis came only in the one-volume edition – the fifth time the description had been revised – when the passage became: 'a modest peal of three bells broke forth – that limited amount of expression having been deemed sufficient for the joys of such a small parish' (p.211).[89] At once the meanness of the carillon [a set of bells] is the responsibility of some agency superior to the parish and the parishioners, and class and authority have become factors; at the same time the irony is considerably sharpened . . .

. . . I am not claiming that it was in this one-volume edition that Hardy *first* embodied in his narrator the representative of his class; what does seem to be true is that at this time something about this novel in particular, and his perception of his own fiction in general, was clarified, and stimulated the revisions I have been looking at and others like them. The 'Dorsetshire Labourer' borrowings, though lamenting, at times angrily, the decline of the artisan-craftsman class in rural areas, are written from the point of view of one who has escaped from that class-destruction into middle-class celebrity as a writer; the change to the bell-passage is made from a different point of view, that of a displaced and oppressed craftsman . . .[90] □

Gatrell notes the changes to the violation of Tess which J.T. Laird detailed (see pp.110–12 of this Guide), and also the way Hardy stresses the significance of his polemic about Tess by adding in her confession to Angel, to Tess's 'No, it cannot be more serious, certainly', the pointed 'because 'tis just the same' (pp. 221–2). Like other changes, it also makes Tess more self-aware. Similarly, the addition of the following crucial sentence helps to clarify Hardy's own understanding of Tess's state of mind when she murders Alec d'Urberville, given through the point of view of Angel Clare: 'But he had a vague consciousness of one thing, though it was not clear to him till later; that his original Tess had spiritually ceased to recognize the body before him as hers – allowing it to drift, like a corpse upon the current, in a direction dissociated from its living will' (p. 366).

Among other refocusings of this kind, there are also alterations to aspects of Angel Clare, the character about whom Hardy was most uncertain. And these changes, Gatrell suggests, involve the flexible narrative voice; both the engaged and the detached narrator:

■ There are changes made to every aspect of Angel's sense of his relationship with Tess, changes to his thoughts of her, to his physical sense of her, to his conversation with her. One of the most memorable sentences in Angel's unspoken response to Tess was only added at this stage of the novel's development: his naïve and rather priggish 'what a fresh and virginal daughter of Nature' (p. 124) was until the one-volume edition the more down-to-earth 'what a genuine daughter of nature'. The reader is, of course, aware of the ironic significance of 'virginal' at the moment that the thought passes through Angel's mind, but the irony becomes more powerful and poignant when the truth is also revealed to Angel. The capitalisation of 'Nature' is significant too, in that it reflects accurately the tendency in Angel to abstraction and idealisation, and thus helps to make his seduction by 'nature' at Talbothays more ironically effective.[91] □

Gatrell continues this exploration of the narrator's relation to Angel and to his text:

■ We also see Angel differently through the narrator's commentary. To Tess's perception – 'She was awestricken to discover such determination under such apparent flexibility' – Hardy added a narratorial view, this time directly engaged with the character, as if it were only now that he felt fully the force of the character he had created: 'His consistency was, indeed, too cruel' (p.238). On the other hand there is the addition a few pages later of: 'Some might risk the odd paradox that with more animalism he would have been the nobler man. We do not say it' (p.240). The second sentence is Hardy's narrator at the height of evasiveness, and the plural pronoun, the characteristic note of the reviewer, is quite remarkably out of place. Furthermore Hardy *does*, of course, 'say it'. The 'odd' is so clearly ironical that it ensures the reader's disbelief of the narrator's denial, and encourages the reader to see in the word 'Some' Hardy himself separating himself still further from the text that has proceeded from his pen into print.[92] □

The conclusion that Simon Gatrell arrives at, after scrupulously weighing the textual evidence, is that this one-volume edition of 1892, with the exception of Alec d'Urberville's conversion, represents 'Hardy's first final version of the novel'.[93]

The radical diversity of critical writing on *Tess of the d'Urbervilles* in the 1980s is striking. Under the scrutiny of psychoanalysis, Hardy's simultaneous creation and exploration of character is revealed as anticipating Freud and Jung; while, at the opposite pole of theoretical investigation, deconstruction concludes that all pursuit of coherence is illusory, leaving readers to produce their own meanings. During this decade, feminist criticism is especially strong. The essays included here argue that Tess resists the appropriation of the male narrator, and eludes definition by masculine language. And they demonstrate how this fractured, heteroglossic text fails to encompass Tess's sexuality. Feminist ideology also informs the materialist investigation of the way in which the text's various discourses feed into the dominant one, the social relations of production, making the reader undergo Tess's experience as a working-class woman. And this radical criticism co-exists with sophisticated examples of more traditional studies of *Tess*; the examination of Hardy's debts to visual art and solar mythology in his scrutiny of contemporary religious and ethical values; and analysis of the relationship between text and biography, which throws light on Hardy's private concern with his own class position.

The final chapter, which is devoted to the 1990s, demonstrates the continuing vigour of *Tess* criticism after more than a century, including daring developments in the areas of psychoanalytic and materialist criticism. This Guide moves full circle by concluding with a provocative post-modernist account of Hardy's deconstruction of the fundamental humanist conception of his heroine, Tess, as a unified subject.

CHAPTER SIX

Tess of the d'Urbervilles in Our Time: The 1990s

THE 1990s witnessed the continued splintering of literary criticism into theoretical and political groupings that had commenced in the 1960s, accelerated during the 1970s, and by the end of the1980s had dislodged traditional liberal humanist criticism from its dominant position. It put up a fight against the multi-faceted attack of theory, and continues to do so, and of course in the give and take of teaching and in the writing of books and essays its procedures have been greatly influenced by changes in both the theory and practice of criticism. It is now not possible to teach or write without involving insights and ideas derived from such figures as Jacques Lacan, Jacques Derrrida, Ferdinand de Saussure, Michel Foucault, Mikhail Bakhtin, or Hélène Cixous. The latest phase of post-structuralism (also often known as post-modernism) has developed apace on both sides of the Atlantic. Our time is a time of critical excitement, as fresh theoretical strategies emerge to challenge yesterday's axioms. Radical diversity has become the norm.

The momentum of *Tess* criticism slackened somewhat during the 1990s, though there was no dearth of fresh and stimulating work. The beginning of the decade saw the publication of Deborah L. Collins's *Thomas Hardy and his God* (1990), which views Hardy's fiction as a polyphonic reinterpretation of man's despairing inability to comprehend the nature of God, and the eclipse of Tess and Angel as largely due to their failures of loving kindness. Robert Langbaum's *Thomas Hardy in Our Time* (1995) reads *Tess* through the psychology of D.H. Lawrence's characters and explores the sadomasochistic nature of the relation between Tess and Alec d'Urberville. At the end of the decade Linda M. Shires's essay, 'The Radical Aesthetic of *Tess of the d'Urbervilles*', in *The Cambridge Companion to Thomas Hardy* (1999) argues, within the context of the aesthetic radicalism of the nineteeenth century, for Hardy's deliberate and consistent subversion of narrative conventions and linguistic forms in order to both enact and condemn alienated modernity.

It is clear that a good deal of recent criticism incorporates evolutionary as well as revolutionary elements; and this is true of the three essays selected here to represent significant developments in psychoanalytic, materialist and post-structuralist criticism. Once indebted to Freud, recent psychoanalytic criticism has drawn on the work of the French psychologist and theorist Jacques Lacan,[1] who sought to link the linguistic models of Saussure and Jakobson with the psychoanalytic methods of Freud, and advanced the thesis that language is a manifestation of structure in the unconscious. An interesting example of this approach is Terence Wright's *Hardy and the Erotic* (1989).

The new decade opened with a particularly stimulating Lacanian approach to *Tess of the d'Urbervilles* contained in Marjorie Garson's book, *Hardy's Fables of Integrity: Woman, Body, Text* (1991). From a feminist perspective, Garson writes with conviction and clarity about how Hardy's fictions express his desire and anxiety about wholeness, maleness and women, involving the integrity of the body, class and nature, and how his attempt to create an aesthetic wholeness is mirrored back as dissolution. In exploring these areas, Garson finds some of Lacan's concepts especially helpful, particularly the mirror, the *corps morcelé*, and the constitution of the Woman as Other, though in Hardy, Garson discovers, the Other also always includes the dimension of class; while behind his characters stands Nature, the Great Mirror.

Garson commences her discussion by pointing out Hardy's rejection of one fictional form for another. Instead of introducing the reader to a novel which, as Hardy points out in his Preface to the fifth edition, will deal with life after Tess's ruin (that is, where a conventional story of a fallen woman would end), Parson Tringham's story of the d'Urbervilles opens the novel at the point where a foundling romance would end, where the heroine discovers her true, aristocratic identity. What Garson focuses on here is the oddly contradictory impulses of a novel attacking social prejudice and conventional society on the one hand, while at the same time validating the contemporary social order through a foundling romance form. And Garson believes that this explains some of the unrealistic features of Tess's nature – her sensibility, introspection, intuition, articulateness, world-weariness and exceptional beauty. She chooses to approach her Lacanian reading of *Tess of the d'Urbervilles* through structuralism – through Fredric Jameson and A.J. Greimas.[2] Greimas, a semiotician, endeavoured to understand texts by identifying their semiotic systems. Jameson, a leading Marxist and cultural critic, found Greimas's semiotic rectangle useful in charting conflicts in ideology in the text. Garson employs this to examine the groupings of the characters in *Tess*. She relates Tess's character to Hardy's class position, and goes on to develop her structural analysis in the following passage, which incorporates diagrammatic illustrations:

■ I would argue, indeed, that the figure of Tess reflects some of the contradictions in Hardy's own feelings about social class. There are two principles or sets of values expressed in the novel which are important to Hardy's own sense of identity and which can only with difficulty be brought into alignment: 'nature' and 'aristocracy'. There is a tension between Hardy's loyalty to nature, to the countryman's life, and to his working-class roots and, on the other hand, his fascination with the upper classes, with genealogy and blood-lines. Following Fredric Jameson, I see the narrative as a symbolic resolution to a real problem: Hardy's own 'ressentiment' [resentment] about his class affiliation, especially as experienced in relation to women and to the aristocracy – his feeling of being an outsider whose real worth is not given its due because of his 'past' – and at the same time his pride in that very past, in the regional and traditional values which such people underestimate.

In *The Political Unconscious* Fredric Jameson is using structuralist means to a Marxist end, looking at the novels of, for example, Balzac, Conrad, and Stendhal by charting their characters on to Greimas's 'semiotic rectangle'. Jameson calls Greimas's system an 'ontological structuralism', one which Greimas himself believes gives insight into the logical structure of reality. Jameson, eschewing metaphysics, finds the rectangle useful instead as an emblem of the ideology which generates it. He argues that narrative is an attempt to resolve contradictions in ideology – that these contradictions actually generate characters or groups of characters. The conflicts which I have seen in Hardy, then, would be charted as in Figure 1. It can be argued that the novel does indeed take shape around character-positions which fulfil the requirements of the rectangle (see Figure 2).

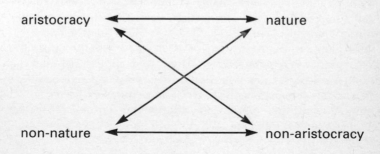

Figure 1

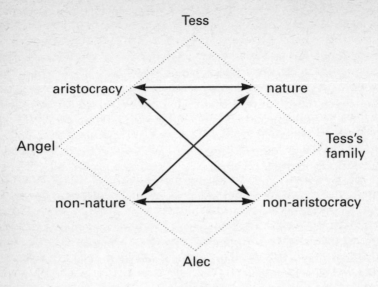

Figure 2

I see Tess's family as non-aristocratic, despite their family name and their silver spoon, for reasons already discussed: their manifest inferiority to Tess herself. I locate Angel within the category of aristocracy because he is distinguished by an alienating superiority to everyone with whom he associates: he is more intelligent than his family, and so is undervalued by them; and he is set apart from the rural people – like the prince in disguise – or as Tess herself says like Peter the Great inspecting the shipyards – during his pastoral idyll at Talbothays Dairy. Furthermore, his plain-living and high-thinking family turn out, rather unexpectedly, to be in possession of jewels which make Tess look like *her* ancestors' portraits.

This view of the novel explains a number of its aspects which seem to call for comment. For one thing, it clarifies some anomalies in Hardy's treatment of Angel and Alec. It is clear that the two men are carefully set up by Hardy in terms of their binary opposition – schematically, even alliteratively, paired. Alec appears through flames carrying a pitchfork; Angel plays the harp. One is dangerous because of his excessive sensuality, the other because of his excessive spirituality; the two together combine to destroy the heroine. The contrast generates banal, if apposite, moral conclusions: it is less an illegitimate pregnancy which destroys a woman than the self-righteousness of an attenuated and misapplied Christianity.

Yet for all the careful patterning, there is an asymmetry between

Angel and Alec as they are presented by Hardy which raises aesthetic and even ethical problems. Angel is a much more fully developed figure, and a more believable one. He is also presented with more authorial balance: although his cruelty to Tess is even more culpable than Alec's, we are consistently made to understand what made him the way he is and how he feels about what he is doing. Alec, on the other hand, is made to behave like the villain in a melodrama. Alec has to be a thorough villain if the idealised heroine is to kill him, and Tess has to kill him because Hardy has to have society kill her – but the melodramatic treatment of the character nevertheless impoverishes the novel to some extent.

Greimas's semiotic rectangle helps explain the imbalance between these apparent binary opposites. Alec is, from this perspective, not Angel's opposite but Tess's. Angel, on the other hand, is aligned with Tess, precisely in terms of the qualities they both share with Hardy. He is characterised by an innate pessimism and religious scepticism; he is intellectually superior to his own family; and he is dispossessed of the status which ought rightfully to have been his – like Tess, and like Hardy, who also never went to university. Indeed, the recognition of the parallels between Angel and Hardy himself make clearer what readers may instinctively feel: that Alec is a scapegoat, and that Hardy has some personal stake in his condemnatory and yet empathetic portrait of Angel.[3] □

Garson then discusses Hardy's ambiguous treatment of Angel Clare's feelings about the aristocracy, but she goes on to suggest, more importantly, that her reading of the text also helps to account for Tess's odd inability to think temporally, to anticipate consequences and so prevent them, even though in terms of the natural cycle and other temporal patterns she is bound into a chronological series of events. And Garson disagrees with J.T. Laird's view that Hardy's growing identification with Tess during the writing of the novel made him revise his heroine into a pure and pathetic victim:

■ . . . I see Tess's relationship to time in terms of a larger project: that dehistoricising of her which is necessary if she is to serve as a resolution of the tension between nature and aristocracy which I believe underlies the narrative.

Tess can be loved for her aristocracy only if she is felt as innocent of it – innocent of and indeed the victim of history itself. It is, I think, her innocence of history which makes readers feel that she has a mythic dimension. Her epithet – 'of the d'Urbervilles' – expresses precisely that connection in separation which links Tess with her aristocratic forebears, in such a way as to skip over her actual parents and erase all local, specific identities and allegiances. Tess inherits aristocratic glamour without being implicated in aristocratic guilt. She is like her mother but not like her father, from whom she nevertheless inherits a superiority he himself does not have. She is linked in a mystified synchronic way with her remote ancestors and condemned to suffer for their crimes; the doom does not make very much moral sense and has to be handled in a slightly unreal Gothic fashion – through winking portraits, sinister omens, and local legends. Hardy seems to be suggesting, by his discussion of Tess's rapacious ancestors, that the aristocracy of the past condemned the poor to suffer in the present; but since the figure of Tess contains both the contemporary victim and the historical victimiser, it short-circuits any serious social criticism of the contemporary class structure.

It is interesting that Tess is harassed by new social forces: by a man whose family has bought its title with new money; by the brutal technology – exemplifed by the threshing machine – which bends human life to its inhuman rhythm. But precisely how this newness is connected to history is blurred. Clearly Alec's family interest in adopting an ancient family name derives from the value such a name has acquired in a process which is not delineated. Again Alec serves as a scapegoat – mocked precisely for his newness, while the 'oldness' on which alone this newness could be parasitical is exonerated (in the figure of Tess herself) from any responsibility for creating him. The class from which Tess descends creates Alec as surely as it destroys Tess (or, one might also say, as surely as Tess destroys him) – but is not in the novel to receive the blame. It is significant that Tess is not harmed by any contemporary 'real' aristocrat: she herself usurps that position, and precludes the presentation of an old family with *contemporary* power.

Tess has value for Hardy because she is associated with the glamour of the real aristocracy; but she must not be implicated in its crimes. She must expiate them with her death, but without ever having been besmirched by them. She must retain, in the context of an implicating history, the 'purity' Hardy insists on in the subtitle. She must not operate in time – she must not operate time – but be operated upon. She must be destroyed, and yet not destroyed – victimised, and yet preserved intact. The ways in which Tess is disconnected from her past are necessary if she is to figure the unity he desires.[4] □

Garson goes on to argue that the issue of Tess's subjectivity is central in the structure of a novel so dependent on the misreading of the heroine by both Alec d'Urberville and Angel Clare. However, there is the question of the extent of Hardy's own implication in the way both Alec, and more subtly Angel, objectify Tess, as Garson explains:

■ Hardy implicates himself also, however, in Angel's idealisation of Tess as a 'fresh and virginal daughter of Nature' (p.124). There are no virgins in nature; and Hardy shows clearly how destructive to Tess this idealising will be – makes Tess protest against it – has her recognise that 'she you love is not my real self, but one in my image; the one I might have been' (p.212). And he makes clear that Angel is deceiving himself – that he is attracted to Tess precisely because she is *not* a child of nature in any simple way, because she is so much superior to the other milkmaids. Indeed it is Tess's felt alienation from nature which draws Angel to her in the first place: her musings deeply appeal to him, because they express in naïve terms precisely his own overbred pessimism. Angel exploits Tess by using her to confirm the Romantic vision of a natural life which he believes that he himself, in withdrawing from the public arena, has chosen. His outrageous treatment of her is itself a comment on the irresponsibility of the dream of pastoral innocence.

Yet Hardy, even while criticising Angel for what he does to Tess, is at the same time using Angel to do the same thing on his own behalf. Through Angel, Tess is endowed by the text with some of the very attributes which she herself explicitly disowns. By attributing to Angel an idealised vision of Tess as nature-goddess which Tess herself repudiates, Hardy is able to have it both ways. In those early mornings when the couple feel like Adam and Eve (p.134), and Angel insists on addressing Tess as Artemis and Demeter, when she becomes for him 'a visionary essence of woman – a whole sex condensed into one typical form' (pp.134–5), Hardy establishes a vision of Tess, which does not fade merely because Tess protests against it. Indeed, her protest confirms her status: what better proof that she is indeed nature's child than her uneasiness with Angel's culture-bound metaphors? The text, aware that 'nature' is itself a cultural construct, nevertheless allows the figure of Tess to draw power from the Romantic illusion.

Hardy originally thought of calling the novel 'The Body and Soul of Sue', and the novel we have is still structured around that dichotomy. Evidently Alec has possessed Tess's body but not her soul. Angel's sin against Tess is his failure to realise this. His repudiation of her causes – or deepens – a radical split in Tess, makes her separate herself from her body; it constrains Tess to define herself – while it *enables* the narrator to redefine her – along the lines of pure spirit. It is Angel's very rejection of her, in other words, which allows the text – or the narrator, or Hardy – to expiate the fascination with Tess's body expressed in the first half of the novel, and this is what it proceeds to do. Tess is increasingly spiritualised as the novel goes on. The narrator emphasises her growing dissociation from her own body, so that by the time she gives herself to Alec she has 'ceased to recognize the body before him as hers

– allowing it to drift, like a corpse upon the current, in a direction dissociated from its living will' (p. 366). But the imaginative effect of this
theoretical *division* is actually to *unify* Tess, who becomes pure spirit,
pure voice. Her final speech to Alec, a disembodied 'soliloquy' heard
through the door by Mrs Brooks, is almost operatic in its stylisation;
and her final statement – 'I am ready' (p. 382) – seems intended to have
the resonance of Shakespearian tragedy. It is as if the 'real' Tess, Tess
as she herself experiences herself, has become identical with soul: her
body has virtually become invisible before her execution.[5] □

One way of essentialising Tess, suggests Garson, is by repressing aspects
of her history, leaving gaps in our knowledge of her relationship with
Alec and Angel in the later chapters. And, as critics from Lionel Johnson
onward have remarked, Hardy's use of nature to suggest Tess's purity is
self-contradictory. In particular, in the scene in the garden at Talbothays
(see pp. 60–1 of this Guide), Garson finds an odd gap between the heavy
sexual meaning of the garden and the narrator's presentation of Tess as
unconscious of it. She proceeds to offer a Lacanian reading of the body
and nature in the following extract:

■ I see the gap . . . as revealing what most of the time remains
concealed – that *all* the natural imagery mirroring the relationship
between Tess and Angel is displaced. It is precisely because Tess does
not define her attraction to Angel as sexual that the sultry weather
'tells': the imagery would lose its point if the overt relationship
between them were as sultry as the weather. It is the repression of the
sexual nature of the attraction between them that makes the natural
imagery so powerfully metaphorical. (I want to remain ambiguous
about who is doing the repressing.) And it is also, perhaps, the sup-
pression of the whole story of the relationship between Tess and Alec,
which as it were gets told for the first time, in a kind of ponderous
slow-motion, through the Talbothays imagery – as if Tess, though
Alec's mistress and the mother of a child, had never been through this
process before. Indeed, she declares she has not: Tess defends herself
to Angel (and constitutes herself to herself) through a myth of
plenitude and presence, which depends, however, on a radical
dehistoricisation: 'What was the past to me as soon as I met you? It
was a dead thing altogether. I became another woman, filled full of
new life from you. How could I be the early one?' (p. 325).
    Natural imagery, I would argue, bears so much weight in the novel
because, while apparently mirroring Tess's experience, it in fact
restores the sequence, the temporality, the physicality, repressed in the
figure of Tess herself. The suggestion that Tess *should* have acknow-
ledged the reality figured by the garden seems from this perspective

irrelevant: Tess cannot 'see' the fissures which she herself is created to close. But there is a paradox here: Tess can be read as a pure child of nature not in spite of but *because* of her alienation from it. It is precisely because she *does not* feel what nature figures that she deserves the epithet. Attempting to constitute a 'real' Tess, a Tess who will exist to herself, Hardy has got her caught in an explicable relation with an Other which mirrors the 'body' which this 'self' represses. 'Nature' reveals the inadequacy of Tess as a figure of unity, and perhaps reflects less the relationship between the main characters than the anxieties and concerns of the author which these characters are invented to resolve.

Such concerns emerge also in the famous description of the landscape around Flintcomb-Ash, the demonic anti-Wordsworthian vision of earth and sky as 'upper and nether visages' (p.277) mirroring each other, 'the white face looking down on the brown face, and the brown face looking up at the white face' (p.277) – and neither looking at the human figures who crawl like flies between. The threat to Tess has consistently been expressed in terms of looking – both figuratively (as in the penetrating rays of the sun, to which Tess is symbolically sacrificed at Stonehenge) and literally, so that Tess has become obsessed with repelling the male gaze. Apparently, however, while to look at Tess is to violate her, not to look is worse still. The grotesque vision of the human face as featureless – as 'only an expanse of skin' (p.277) – suggests the worst threat of all: the utter extinction of the subject. It is into this context that Hardy introduces the paragraph about the Arctic birds, the most glaring and unqualified example of pathetic fallacy on the narrator's part in the novel. The attribution of human consciousness to the birds, their inexpressible 'memory' of Arctic wastelands never otherwise to be perceived, foregrounds the question of the relationship between being and perception, and suggests the anxieties of a subject dependent for sustenance on an Other which will not look, and thus vulnerable to dissolution and fragmentation.

The vision is that of a defaced or deformed or scattered body. The land around Flintcomb-Ash is imaged as an immense recumbent female, 'bosomed with semi-globular tumuli – as if Cybele the Many-breasted were supinely extended there' (p.273). Upon this gigantic but sterile mother lie scattered and relatively tiny fragments of the male body, the phallic stones which are mentioned in two different contexts by the narrator, and which Tess, characteristically, does not recognise (p.279). At Flintcomb-Ash the anxiety evoked by the idea of looking is revealed as having less to do with a female object than with a male subject.[6] □

Garson points out that both Alec and Angel misread the heroine and suffer for it. Alec is treated by Hardy as a stereotype, especially towards the end; while Angel in Brazil has become 'invisible' and returns as 'an emasculated figure'.[7] Here is Garson's forceful conclusion:

■ The pairing-off of Angel and Liza-Lu is interesting in this connection. As retribution for essentialising Tess, the text leaves Angel with an essentialised Tess, a girl who embodies, as Tess says, 'the best of me without the bad of me' (p. 380). The very fact that Tess wishes this sterile pairing to be an actual marriage underscores its antierotic character and makes the compensatory pattern ironic, Tess's dying wish into a kind of curse.

Indeed, both Alec and Angel pay a heavy price for their misreading of the heroine. Alec is treated as a cardboard villain at the end even more than at the beginning of the novel. In one curious incident, however, the text does at least raise the question of whether Alec is not Tess's victim as surely as she is his. When Alec forces Tess to swear on Cross-in-Hand that she will never again tempt him, Hardy seems to be using the encounter primarily for some rather heavy-handed foreboding ('Tis a thing of ill-omen', p. 303). But his language imbues the image with more specific associations.

Cross-in-Hand is not really a cross, but 'the stump' of what the narrator says may once have been a more 'complete erection' (p. 302). To anyone who has seen the not very impressive marker – which still stands – this seems unlikely, for the top is gently cupped rather than broken off. (The outline of the hand incised upon it is now completely obscured by lichen.) The 'rude monolith' (p. 302) is more phallic in shape than the text, with its emphasis on a broken cross, makes it sound; yet at the same time Hardy's loaded language subliminally suggests castration. Alec, who fears surrender to Tess, makes her reassure him with the ambiguous gesture – 'put your hand upon that stone hand, and swear that you will never tempt me' (p. 302) – which seems to invite the very involvement he apparently wishes to avoid. The incident may seem odd to the reader as well as to Tess; but while it suggests Alec's complicity in his own destruction, it also reminds us what the exclusive emphasis on Tess's victimisation at the end of the novel may make us forget – that fascination with Tess kills Alec.

In her discussion of the figure of the fallen woman in Victorian literature and painting, Nina Auerbach[8] points out that the stature and power the fallen woman acquires – even though she suffers for it – involves a certain triumph over the men who seduced her, renders them invisible and irrelevant. By including Tess in her discussion of this mythic pattern, Auerbach restores a meaning of the text from which we are conventionally distracted. Tess emerges as a victimiser as well as a victim, and Hardy's fable turns reflexively against itself, revealing even as it attempts to unify Tess her genesis in dissolution and fragmentation.

My theme, then, is Hardy's necessary failure to construct an aesthetic whole not subject to such dissolution. The figures of Tess and of nature, set up to supplement one another, instead subvert one another, and mirror back, to the subject attempting to constitute itself through their reflection, a fragmented body. Hardy's desire, aimed with disconcerting directness at an unresponsive 'nature', opens up the fissures in the Romantic project, and deconstructs a subject tenuously constituted in words.[9] □

The year following Marjorie Garson's penetrating Lacanian reading of *Tess of the d'Urbervilles* saw an equally striking development, this time in materialist criticism's engagement with the text, when Joe Fisher's study, *The Hidden Hardy*, was published in 1992. It is informed by feminism and by the work of the Marxist philosopher, Louis Althusser,[10] who emphasised the material determinant in the production of literary texts, and explored the ways in which ideological contradictions may be manifest in fiction through contradictions that are elements of literary production itself. Fisher's project is to reveal these partly hidden patterns in Hardy's fiction and relate them to recent Marxist and feminist writing. He therefore looks at:

■ . . . Hardy's trade as a novelist first in terms of his relation to the Victorian fiction market's production process, and secondly in terms of his own manufacturing process in creating an object to be traded in this market.[11] □

The historical context is, of course, the domination and regulation of the marketplace by Mudie and Smith, the proprietors of the circulating libraries, who decided what fiction was publishable. Drawing on the work of N.N. Feltes (*Modes of Production of Victorian Novels*, 1986), Fisher argues that Hardy involved himself in what Feltes calls the 'disruptive moment of class struggle',[12] by producing novels in his capacity as a small entrepreneur, which satisfied the 'hegemonic authority of library buyers and magazine editors',[13] offering an acceptable version of Wessex by editing its 'raw material' and using this as a bid for 'cultural power and its accompanying political platform'.[14] However, and this is the core of Joe Fisher's argument, each text contains obscure, subversive attacks on this authority. The texts subvert themselves as part of a deliberate strategy of deception, whereby the narrator seems to endorse acceptable attitudes to such matters as social class and gender, but in fact undermines them. Hardy exploits the 'gap between the trader who sells the story and the narrator who tells it to corrupt the traded object', and this is achieved through the creation of 'hostile and part-visible patterns beneath what might generally be regarded as the "surface" of the text'.[15] In the passage below, Fisher explains Hardy's strategy by analogy with the cartoon painted underneath the finished canvas:

■ ... My argument here is that ... Hardy draws a cartoon of Swiftian brutality on his empty canvas, then covers it, I believe deliberately imperfectly, with what has more usually been regarded as the 'finished' text. The presence of this hidden Hardy, and the sustained arguments to be found inside rather than outside the Trojan Horse of the 'traded' text, do much to justify and develop the suggestions made first by Roy Morrell and then more recently by Ingham and Widdowson, among others, that a new and more subversive Hardy may be found through the mechanism of his novel-writing.[16] □

From a feminist perspective, as Fisher makes clear, part of Hardy's strategy involves an assault on the patriarchal endorsement of ideas of the non-sexual 'feminine' in fiction through oblique images of sexuality that are central in the 'narrator's antithetical counter-texts',[17] and which subvert the more acceptable male voyeurism. As well as women, the narrator also writes a landscape. And here too Hardy's extensive use of myth produces an 'acceptable' system of surface allusions, which because it is composed of pre-Christian mythical elements, also provides the basis of a subversive counter-text.

Joe Fisher's complex, strenuous critical methodology is particularly challenging when it engages with *Tess of the d'Urbervilles*, in a chapter intriguingly subtitled 'Götterdämmerung' (the twilight of the gods).[18] He begins to apply his strategy of reading in the following extract:

■ ... The threats to the omniscient narrator are made by a writer who has traded himself into a position of considerable cultural power during the period of the Triumph of Fiction, so that any disruption which actually damages the surface of the traded text must be seen as an act of extremely public self-destruction. In the context of the earlier counter-texts ... the interrogation [in *Tess of the d'Urbervilles*] is not just an attack on the narrator's omniscience but a revelation of the alternative structures which have been essentially (if barely) concealed until now. The system of building a fiction with antithetical traded text and counter-text places Hardy in a uniquely strong position to disempower his traded text without weakening the novel's dramatic force, and indeed to use this surrender of omniscience to enforce more, not less, on the consumer-producer. In *Tess of the d'Urbervilles* this is a highly coherent and integrated manipulative exercise. The traded text enforces its own destruction on the reader through the unavoidable experience of Tess's life and death, and on a more minor but more overtly confrontational level through the challenges it offers to the moral code which defined a fiction acceptable for production, particularly by serial publishers . . . [19] □

Fisher finds a paradigm (a pattern, or exemplar) for Hardy's position as a powerful seller of bourgeois fictions within the class relations of the text itself:

■ The will to power represented internally by the counter-text's attacks on the traded text is not superseded, but rather now magnified, by a well-publicised attempt to trade a fiction which is openly transgressive. This entrepreneurial aggression is accompanied by a counter-text of similar scale and ferocity, which very plainly dominates the eroded dramatic/realistic narrative. The act of rape in the wilderness of the Chase, which is at the centre of the traded text's debate about purity, makes overt the fact that subordination to power relations is not a matter of choice but an unsought submission to brute force, and within the text the part-concealed, anti-realistic strategies hold a similar control. The narrator enforces his counter-fiction on the reader as Alec enforces his power over Tess.[20] □

Fisher goes on to identify Tess as a scapegoat for the sins of the community, marked by her red ribbon at the Club-walking fertility ritual, and Fisher, like J.B. Bullen when he draws on the work of Max Müller,[21] notes the connection between Tess as a sacrificial victim and the novel's systematic allusion to solar mythology:

■ . . . Tess is fused with the land she lives and works on and the sun brings her fertility to life. This fusion has been produced, impossibly, by generations of labour which have alienated the Durbeyfields from the land they once owned (at least according to Parson Tringham's fiction). In this sense Tess becomes Gaia, the land of the Greek creation myth. The world is created by the marriage of the earth (Gaia) and the sun. When the Aeschylean 'President of the Immortals' finishes his sport with Tess he is Cronos destroying Gaia. In this sense creation, of land, life and fiction, has ended when Tess dies. Angel and Tess get engaged at sunset: and this ill-starred relationship is man's inadequate attempt to intervene in the process of *Götterdämmerung*.

Angel, Tess's Christian guardian angel (complete with harp), initially seen walking between two Christian priests, has seen the start of *Götterdämmerung* at the Marlott Club-walking but failed to realise what was going on. In fact he is an impossible contradiction in terms, a post-Christian guardian angel. And you might also argue that his first perceptions of Tess and of the farm at Talbothays represent the position of the 'purchaser' of the 'traded' text naïvely consuming Wessex; so Angel's interpretative inadequacy and Tess's class and gender experience are enforced on the reader at the same time as dual tests, or proofs, of the subtitle's notions of 'purity' and 'faithful' representation.

The presence of Anglican priests at the start of the blood-letting is also engaged with the literal economic reality of the text. It is worth remembering that tithes were levied in Dorset until 1868. Having bled the land for centuries, the priests now seem to stand by and watch the result; for now the land seems to bleed spontaneously. Tess's non-Christian allusive context in the counter-text expresses their absolute irrelevance. Christian dogma and its church's failing hegemony can do nothing for working-class lives except damage them by disinformation. Even in the traded text the do-gooding Clare parents are met with contemptuous narrative satire. How are Emminster Vicarage and the sons' university education paid for if not by the same process of allegorised rape which gets Tess pregnant?

Gaia's complementary divinity is Maia, a Wild Woman usually pictured with huge, hanging breasts (like the cows at Talbothays). This links the 'high' Greek and 'low' English cultures of the counter-text, creating a fusion where in the 'traded' text there is division: Tess's position there is an impossible cultural and linguistic suspension between 'high' and 'low' . . . [22] □

What marks Tess as different from Hardy's earlier presentations of working-class character, argues Fisher, is his use of a transformation that is incomplete:

■ . . . There is nothing unconscious about the way these issues and this history are related to Tess: her two languages characterise her in terms of both sides of a long historical fight between class and class, appropriation and autonomy, capital and labour, d'Urberville and Durbeyfield (and the change from 'field' to 'ville' is, of course, the transformation of rural to urban which Tess undergoes when she becomes 'Mrs d'Urberville' of Sandbourne). Hence her spontaneous bleeding as the fight necessarily continues and hence the emergence of the scapegoat, sent out to die in the wilderness not by one side or the other but, now that Tess is a d'Urberville, by both.[23] □

The relation between traded text and counter-text in terms of myth and landscape is seen as a complex one. The legend of the white hart in the Vale of Blackmoor appears to fuse with the landscape as a proleptic metaphor for Tess's story, but it also reflects the hints of the human poverty in this abundant agricultural landscape. Similarly, as the following extracts argue, the survival of the Club-walking is part of a counter-text grounded in mythology, in which the scapegoat is finally sacrificed to the sun at Stonehenge:

■ . . . The sun rises and Tess is arrested. Christianity and post-Christian modernism, personified by the guardian Angel sent to oversee Tess's life at the point where she is chosen as scapegoat, has failed to rescue her, conceivably because the angel can no longer believe in God. Since the orphan of Paulinism [Pauline theology] has failed her (and since, not coincidentally, she has killed an ex-Pauline preacher), she is abandoned to the cruder forces of paganism and sun-worship. In the traded text the sun is presented as a benign god overseeing the harvest at Marlott, a mythic-allegorical part of Wessex's 'timeless' beauty . . . But there are two harvests here, one of the season's crop and the other of Tess's crop, the baby we see her feeding. Alec's fertilisation of Tess parallels the sun's fertilisation of Gaia; so in this sense Alec becomes also a solar surrogate.

The sun (Alec) fertilises the land (Tess/Gaia) and he thus 'makes' the text which is worked out on its subject, Tess the woman . . . So the creation of the novel is presented interrogatively as an elemental creation of the world. The unequivocal power relation between Alec and Tess is also the relation, now being dismantled, between Hardy the 'trader' and the workfolk he fictionalises. The limitations and patent artifices of Alec's characterisation are very much part of this dismantling of the traded text. He begins as a fictional cliché with an assumed sexual *droit de seigneur* [the alleged right of a feudal lord to have sexual intercourse with the bride of a vassal on her wedding-night] and the characteristics of a wicked squire in a melodrama . . . When Alec returns, transformed (or re-formed) into a preacher, the narrator says:

> The lineaments, as such, seemed to complain. They had been diverted from their hereditary connotation to signify impressions for which nature did not intend them. Strange that their very elevation was a misapplication; that to raise seemed to falsify. (p. 298)

The impressions of 'nature' are the narrative conjuring trick which created an Alec out of the 'natural' functions of land-owning and male sexual power over women, the functions which establish the 'natural' structure of the novel and the consumer's reproduction of Wessex. Alec's limited characteristics serve the structure of the counter-text, as a creative deity translated into a demon by the material structure which creates his power over Tess . . . [24] □

Drawing on the solar mythology identified by J. B. Bullen (see pp. 142–7 of this Guide), Fisher goes on to discuss the attempt by the earth (Tess) to flee the effect of the sun (Alec) on her, which is thwarted by 'the counter-text's allegorical imperatives'.[25] After the death of her baby, Tess is established as representative of a cycle; the victim of patriarchy, capitalist power relations, and of her powerful sexuality, which is disciplined by her contractual relationship with Angel Clare. Fisher then considers the implication of the Clare family as a whole in the counter-text:

■ The d'Urbervilles are temporal stewards of the land; the Clares are the spiritual stewards who have maintained the creed which maintained their power, and so created the powerlessness of the Durbeyfields. (Remember that a Christian priest tells Jack Durbeyfield that he is a d'Urberville and so begins the dramatic action.) They have also maintained the marriage contract which, although Angel tries to revise it by attempting to marry in a registry office, has maintained the structuring of sexual relations and male ownership of female fertility which suppressed Gaia and the Wild Woman, and which for the working-class Durbeyfields became the only ideology they could give their daughter. The Clare parents are 'good' in terms of the moral code *Tess of the d'Urbervilles* sets out to savage, and they are presented almost as satirical cartoons:

'But – where's your wife, dear Angel?' cried his mother. 'How you surprise us!'
'She is at her mother's – temporarily. I have come home rather in a hurry, because I've decided to go to Brazil.'
'Brazil! Why they are all Roman Catholics there, surely!'
'Are they? I hadn't thought of that.' (p. 255)

This belongs to the same disruptive-interrogative mode of characterisation as the comic Durbeyfields and the one-dimensional Alec. The Clares' spiritual engagement with the gods and the land and the people is offered up for destruction on the same basis as Jack Durbeyfield's aristocratic pretensions. *Götterdämmerung* is in progress; the land will sacrifice itself to the sky and the gods will be dead; all Pauline Christianity has produced in these circumstances is a creed with a notion of individual spiritual renewal so pernicious that it will allow Alec, who has raped the country, to become its evangelist. When Alec appears to Tess as an evangelist for a second time he is carrying the marriage contract which would give a Christian blessing to his (undeclared) first violation, unless of course you accept the implausible Christian reformation. Mr Clare's seeds, life in Angel and faith in Alec, are both used to help bleed the scapegoat to death.[26] □

Indeed, the role of Christianity is developed in Fisher's discussion of the burial of Sorrow, in which he suggests that Tess/Gaia's divinity surfaces in the context of the usurpation of the Greek creation myth by its Judeo-Christian counterpart. And this leads into a consideration of Angel Clare's relation to the Gaia myth:

▨ . . . The snobbery which makes him impressed that Tess is 'really' a d'Urberville also makes clear his continuing attachment to the class structure which makes Mrs Crick seat him apart from the workfolk to eat. His attempt to divert the Clare legacy of spirituality from university scholarship and Christian ministry to the Gaia-worship he tries to learn at Talbothays is another impossible gesture of autonomy, correct in terms of the counter-text's creative myth; he recognises what he could not see at the Marlott Club-walking, but recognition comes too late. The moral system which is still a Christian inheritance sends him away from Tess and almost ludicrously to Brazil, where he expects to find the El Dorado of Gaia and Talbothays without any blemish of the corrupting ideological history and the material violation which are his own real inheritance. Angel (and here his reader-identification is very clear) is the only character who is given all the information necessary to see Tess as Gaia and scapegoat: but his narrative of Tess collapses into an incomprehensible product of 'grotesque prestidigitation' (p. 226) when he learns about the past and the crucial violation he has not been shown.[27] □

In his trenchant conclusion, Joe Fisher sees the culmination of Hardy's counter-text as a call to ideological revolution:

■ When Tess kills Alec Gaia kills the sun god and she will be killed herself in consequence. Her guardian Angel, whose return brought about the murder, takes her to the place of her formal sacrifice at Stonehenge, where she is again met by a disruptive conjured image, this time of Stonehenge surrounded by policemen. As Bullen[28] shows, this is the conclusion of a sequence of druidical symbols which have followed Tess through the text, most strikingly in the image of (white) mistletoe on the trees on the Chase at the time of the rape and above the bed at Wellbridge. Later she contemplates suicide under mistletoe. This has an additional resonance in the sacrificial killing of Alec; in Germanic myth Loki kills the sun god Balder with a spear of mistletoe.

This *Götterdämmerung* has not ended the world but, since Gaia is dead, the earth is no longer under even the vestigial protection of the non-Christian divinities . . . But the material-ideological forces which produced Tess as their scapegoat retain their power; their representatives sentence Tess to death and hang her at Wintoncester gaol, so they are unquestionably guilty of Gaia's killing. The real overthrow demanded by this outrage can therefore now only be made in material-ideological terms, by an attack on the material-ideological 'Structure' itself.[29] □

The final example in this Guide of a contemporary *Tess of the d'Urbervilles*, created through the employment of post-modern theoretical strategies, is a stimulating essay by Peter Widdowson. Widdowson has written extensively on Hardy, from his influential book, *Hardy in History: A Study in Literary Sociology* (1989) to his latest contribution to *The Cambridge Companion to Thomas Hardy* (edited by Dale Kramer, 1999). His interest in the history and sociology of literature led him to propose what he termed 'critiography' as a method of understanding how the work of a major novelist such as Hardy is constructed for the reader by the cultural discourse which accompanies it, and by the cultural formation within which it is contained historically.

Peter Widdowson's readings of Hardy, always lively and lucid, were prompted by a reaction against the traditional humanist construction of Hardy and his timeless mythical Wessex as an icon of English culture. In common with the work of other materialist critics illustrated in this Guide, Widdowson's concerns include class, gender and anti-realism. And his re-reading of Hardy's 'minor' novels is also particularly stimulating.

The essay that is considered here is called '"Moments of Vision": Postmodernising *Tess of the d'Urbervilles*; or, *Tess of the d'Urbervilles* Faithfully Presented by Peter Widdowson' (in *New Perspectives on Thomas Hardy*, 1994, edited by Charles P. C. Pettit). It is an illuminating account of how the text deconstructs the humanist concept of character. From the perspective of class, Tess is constituted from other people's perceptions of her, and from a feminist point of view so too is her gender stereotyping. This deconstructionist approach also involves the Bakhtinian concept of dialogism,[30] the view of the text as containing a plurality of unmerged voices, the Saussurian notion of signification[31] as revealing the unstable play of language, and the idea of defamiliarisation which involves breaking with the humanist-realist convention of character as unified and stable. Widdowson discovers in *Tess of the d'Urbervilles* a post-modern text.

He begins his essay by drawing attention to the intensely visual nature of the novel and in the extract below links this to the narrator's fully ambiguous point of view of Tess:

■ It is quite possible to think . . . that *Tess of the d'Urbervilles* is actually in some way *about* seeing and representation. After all, Hardy himself describes it in the preface to the first edition – although we can never really trust that wary old ironist and least self-revealing of writers – as 'an *attempt to give artistic form* to a true sequence of things' (my italics). And he also claims, by way of the novel's hugely contentious subtitle ('appended', he would have us believe in a prefatory postscript of 1912, 'at the last moment' and with no premeditation), that his 'Pure Woman' is *faithfully presented* by Thomas Hardy' (my italics). Does the phrasing here suggest just how ironically conscious he was of representation as a potent source, precisely, of *mis*representation? Had the image, as we all now know in these post-modern times, already substantively replaced 'the thing itself' for Hardy? Was he already discrediting the notion that there is an ultimate reality, or true essence, outside of history and discourse – such as 'human nature', for example, or even perhaps: *pure woman*? . . . the 'pure woman' and her attendant debate in fact focuses the issues of seeing and representation which I have suggested the novel so insistently raises. Certainly a good deal of recent criticism emphasises these issues as crucial terms in discussing *Tess of the d'Urbervilles* – an emphasis which derives principally from two very contemporary critical sources: feminism and post-structuralism . . . [32] □

Widdowson also stresses the important contribution to this discovery of the heteroglossic nature of the text made by the scholarship of J. T. Laird and Simon Gatrell, who revealed Hardy's extensive and sometimes radical revisions to his novel. After a brief contextual review of the history of *Tess* criticism, Widdowson re-engages with the text:

■ What is happening to Hardy, as a reflex of his new critical reproduction in the 1980s and 1990s is that he is in the process of being post-modernised. The foregrounding of sexual politics in *Tess*, and of the tensions incident on a late-nineteenth-century male novelist writing so ambiguously about his 'pure woman' heroine, about the destructive maleness of his two heroes' relations with her (especially the – apparent – ambiguity of seduction and rape), and about marriage, separation, bigamy, extra-marital sex and child-birth, all imply a writer whose 'consciousness' is in some sense being recast in the mould of feminist thinking about sexuality and patriarchy.

More obviously post-structuralist in its variously stylistic, semiotic and deconstructive analyses of the complex, riven, heteroglossic textuality of *Tess*, equal amounts of contemporary criticism all point to the unstable play of the signifier as the nodal experience of the novel. In other words, we have a text which has indeed become a disruptive 'series of seemings', one which, in its destabilising formal dynamics 'disproportions' (Hardy's own word – see below, [p. 172]) reality by revealing how slippery language is, how 'meaning' (and hence ideology) is constructed within discourse, and, precisely therefore, how representation becomes *mis*representation. By disturbing and displacing 'reality' (together with its servant, Realism) in the defamiliarising discourse of his own texts, Hardy exposes (or, more exactly, as a creature of post-modernism *is made to* expose) the mystifications, natural-isations and (mis)representations by which the dominant ideology and culture sentence us all to lives of false being.[33] ☐

The essay then takes up the post-modernist implications of Hardy's ambiguous use of the phrase 'Moments of Vision' (the title of one of his later volumes of poetry) – as revelation, as a turning moment destabilis-ing perceptions; and as a breaking with the familiar and conventional. Widdowson notes that Hardy was consciously thinking about defamiliar-isation from the 1880s onward and develops his central argument from this illuminating comment in the following passage:

■ ... But it is in a couple of memoranda from 1890 (while he was com-pleting *Tess*) that his most prophetically modernist utterances are made:

> Reflections on Art. Art is a changing of the actual proportions and order of things, so as to bring out more forcibly than might other-wise be done that feature in them which appeals most strongly to the idiosyncrasy of the artist.
> Art is a disproportioning – (*i.e.* distorting, throwing out of pro-portion) – of realities, to show more clearly the features that matter in those realities, which, if merely copied or reported inventorially, might possibly be observed, but would more probably be over-looked. Hence 'realism' is not Art.[34]

It is here, I think, that the core of Hardy's fictional aesthetic is to be found, and the informing frame of reference for a reading of *Tess*: art is a 'disproportioning' of reality – realism is not art. In other words, 'vision' (abstract imaginings), swinging round its 'moment', makes visible 'essences' (the notion of a 'pure woman', for example). But at the same time, vision 'distorts', 'disproportions', those representations of reality ('copied or reported inventorially') which are the naturalised (mis)representations of Realism, in order to expose essentialist mis-representation for what it is (how can there, in fact, be 'a pure woman' or 'pure woman'?), and to illuminate another truth which those mis-representations obscure: that 'reality' is only ever *discourse* – 'seemings', 'imaginings', 'impressions'.

'My art', Hardy wrote in 1886, 'is to intensify the expression of things . . . so that the heart and inner meaning is made vividly visi-ble'.[35] *Tess*, that most 'vividly visible' of novels, may be an example of Hardy's 'intensifying the expression' in order to bring into view pre-cisely that 'expression' – the discourses of representation themselves – for scrutiny and demystification in order to exemplify the fact that 'expression' is its own very 'heart and inner meaning', that the 'reality' of an image *is* the image itself, that its only reality is what it constructs through representation. 'Expression' does not copy 'things as they really are', it forges images in its artifice. Tess may indeed be 'a pure woman', but *only as she is imaged*, only as the 'artificial' construct of representation – and who knows whether this is true or false: except, unless we miss the irony (for Hardy knows full well the claim is nonsense), when she is '*faithfully* presented by Thomas Hardy'.

Let us now turn . . . to that subtitle itself, and consider it as the pivot of a 'moment' around which *Tess of the d'Urbervilles* swings in exemplification of Hardy's disproportioning art discussed above. The two main senses of the phrase 'a pure woman' are readily evident: the ethical/sexual (the use of which in relation to Tess as fornicator-murderess so incensed Hardy's Victorian critics), and the ontological/archetypal (in which she would be, were Bob Dylan her bard, 'just like a woman' in every respect). There is also the further related sense of the generic as 'ideal' – again, perhaps, in two inflexions: both proto-typical and perfect. I am not primarily concerned here with the ethical sense, although for Hardy at the time it was clearly a strategic assault on the moral attitudes of his readers and *their perception* of purity. It is that other essentialist meaning that is of interest to me, and especially in relation to Hardy's concern with making 'visible essences' noted above. The novel is full of phrases which indicate that he was thoroughly conscious of this second sense and probably more interested in it than in the contemporary moral issue. Let me start with the two most obvious examples: at Talbothays, in the early morning idyll with Angel, Tess is described as 'a visionary essence of woman – a whole sex condensed into one typical form' (pp. 134–35); and later, as she approaches Flintcomb-Ash, the narrative, in an odd shift of tense and focus, presents her in this way: 'Thus Tess walks on; a figure which is part of the landscape; a fieldwoman pure and simple, in winter guise' (p. 272) – where the phrase 'pure and simple' *could* mean a pure, simple fieldwoman, but clearly actually implies the essential stereotype. (Much earlier, during the harvesting at Marlott, the narrative has already given us this generalisation: 'A field-man is a personality afield; a field-woman is a portion of the field; she has somehow *lost her own margin*, imbibed the *essence* of her surrounding, and assimilated herself with it' (p. 93, my italics) – so that Tess, too, the 'fieldwoman pure and simple', must also be subsumed within this characterisation – or rather, *de*characterisation.) Further, as we have seen, when Tess is first introduced in Chapter 2 she is described as 'a fine and picturesque country girl, and no more' (p. 21, note that word 'picturesque' and the phrase 'and no more'), and later again, just after the generalisation about field-women above, she is called, in an oddly contradictive phrase, 'an almost standard woman' (p. 96). Elsewhere, the narrative regularly generalises about women – for example, on Tess's 'rally' after the death of her child, it muses: 'Let the truth be told – women do as a rule live through such humiliations, and regain their spirits, and again look about them with an interested eye' (p. 110) – a sentence remarkable both for its patriarchal patronising (do men – by implication of finer sensibility – not 'regain their spirits' then?) and for that revealing phrase 'an interested eye'. Again, in relation to the dairymaids' passion for Angel at Talbothays, we are told they are involuntarily overwhelmed by 'an emotion thrust on them by cruel Nature's law'; and in an even more insulting instance of chauvinistic essentialism, 'the differences which distinguished them as individuals were abstracted by this passion, and each was but portion of one organism called sex' (p. 149) – 'pure women' indeed, and just like the field-women who have lost their 'own margin'. For Angel, of course (and for the narrator too?), Tess is archetypally this 'organism' in the famously erotic passage when she has just awoken on a summer afternoon:

> She had not heard him enter, and hardly realized his presence there. She was yawning, and *he saw the red interior of her mouth* as if it had been a snake's. She had stretched one arm so high above her coiled-up cable of hair that he could see its satin delicacy above the sunburn; her face was flushed with sleep, and her eyelids hung heavy over their pupils. The brim-fulness of her nature breathed from her. It was a moment when *a woman's soul* is more incarnate than at any other time; when the most spiritual beauty bespeaks itself flesh; and sex takes the outside place in *the presentation*. (p. 172, my italics)

Is this what Hardy means by 'a pure woman' in his subtitle? But notice again, as in all these quotations, how he seems to be doing the very opposite of establishing Tess's 'character'; that, conversely, in rendering her as essence – 'a woman's soul' – he is making her an enigma, unknowable, subject only to speculation (rather as Hardy's later disciple, John Fowles, was to do with Sarah Woodruff in *The French Lieutenant's Woman*), and inimical, therefore, to the *raison d'être* of a fictional realism which finds its very heart in well-rounded 'character'.

But, of course, it is the continuous textual 'presentation' (notice Hardy's use of the word at the end of the last quotation above) of Tess that makes the obsessive (and usually erotic) imaging of her as something to *look at*, as something *seen*, as a visual *object*, so inescapable. Space prevents a full account of the number of occasions her mouth (again, see the above quotation) is fetishistically focused upon – for example, 'To a young man with the least fire in him that little upward

lift in the middle of her red top lip was distracting, infatuating, mad-
dening' (p. 152). But her smile and her eyes also receive continual
attention ('her rosy lips curved towards a smile' (p. 43), 'a roguish curl
coming upon her mouth' (p. 184)), 'her eyes enlarged, and she involuntarily smiled in his face' (p. 63), as do her neck, her arms, her hair
and general deportment ('Tess stood there in her prettily tucked-up
milking-gown, her hair carelessly heaped upon her head' (p. 184)).
Equally heavily emphasised is the 'bouncing handsome womanliness'
(p. 21) of her figure . . . even Angel at his most idealising – in the passage where he sees her as the 'visionary essence of woman' (p. 134) – is
still aware that there weren't many women 'so well-endowed in
person as she was' (p. 134); and for Alec she is of course the true *femme
fatale* (not, by the by, necessarily a scheming woman or 'siren', merely
'irresistibly attractive'):

> . . . She had an attribute which amounted to a disadvantage just
> now; and it was this that caused Alec d'Urberville's *eyes to rivet them-
> selves upon her*. It was a luxuriance of aspect, a fulness of growth,
> which made her appear *more of a woman* than she *really* was. (p. 45)

(my emphases; note both the male gaze and the physical essentialism
implied by the phrases 'more of a woman' and 'really'). And later it is
this voluptuousness which starts the process of de-converting Alec as
preacher: 'his eyes, falling casually upon the familiar countenance and
form, remained contemplating her . . . "Don't look at me like that!" he
said abruptly' (p. 301) – an inversion which must surely be the most
brilliant evocation in fiction of male perfidy and the double standard,
for who, after all, is doing the looking? It is further worth noticing in
passing that it is not just Tess who is made into a sex-object by the
text: Car Darch, just before Alec has sex with Tess, is described thus:

> . . . she had bared her plump neck, shoulders, and arms to the
> moonshine, under which they looked as luminous and beautiful as
> some Praxitelean creation, in their possession of the faultless
> rotundities of a lusty country girl. (p. 70)

In late twentieth-century terms, the above descriptions would surely
amount to 'soft' pornography, or at least to accurate representations of
the titillatory visual devices employed therein. And the text further
emphasises this voyeuristic stance in its recurrent verbal and narrative
objectification ('the presentation') of women in the novel. The 'Club-
walking' girls in Chapter 2, for instance, are taking part in 'their first
exhibition of themselves' (p. 19, my italics here and below); the Clare
brothers are 'on-lookers' at 'the *spectacle* of a bevy of girls dancing'

(p. 22); Tess, after her first visit to Trantridge, 'became aware of the *spectacle* she presented to [her fellow-travellers'] surprised vision: 181roses at her breast; roses in her hat; roses and strawberries in her basket to the brim' (p. 47); Mrs Durbeyfield 'bedecking' Tess for the sacrifice to Alec, is so proud of 'the girl's *appearance*' that she is led to 'step back, *like a painter from his easel*, and survey her work as a whole'; and in order to let Tess 'zee' herself, she hangs a large 'black cloak [surely the 'black flag' of Tess's hanging] outside the casement, and so made a large reflector of the panes' (p. 52). On other occasions the text pans back from Tess and reduces her (once again de-characterising her in the process) to an insignificant dot on the landscape: 'Tess stood still upon the hemmed expanse of verdant flatness, like a fly on a billiard-table of indefinite length, and of no more consequence to the surroundings than that fly' (p. 110); 'the two girls crawl[ed] over the surface of [the 'desolate drab' field] like flies' (p. 277).[36] □

Widdowson's essay drives to the conclusion that, for all the intense visualisation of Tess, we cannot know her, since essential character does not exist, and she inhabits the text as an unstable post-modern construction:

■ Throughout the novel, then, Tess in particular is highly visualised as an object of 'vision' in the swinging 'moment' of the text's gaze. Only on two significant occasions does she disappear from view: once, when she is hanged, with Angel and Liza-Lu's eyes 'rivetted' (like Alec's on her body) to the gaol flag-pole, and she becomes merely 'a black flag' (p. 384); the other when, in the old phrase precisely, Alec commits 'the act of darkness' with her:

> . . . The obscurity was now so great that he could see absolutely nothing but a pale nebulousness at his feet, which represented the white muslin figure he had left upon the dead leaves. Everything else was blackness alike. (pp. 76–7)

It is as if, paradoxically and pointedly, the novel implies that the essence of the 'pure woman', can only be 'presented' as visualisations, only as she *appears*, but that the basic 'realities' of her existence (sex, death) are unknowable, unrepresentable – like those innermost secrets of 'character' that no one quite comprehends or can describe in other people, however well one knows them.

And let us be clear: we know almost nothing substantive about Tess's 'character', for the novel never attempts to penetrate her secret being. It may tell us things *about* her (she 'spoke two languages', p. 26); give us her views (about the 'blighted star' for example); and show her spirited moments of mettle (to Alex's male cliché, '"that's what every woman says"', she retorts in implicit rejection of 'pure woman' essentialism: '"did it never strike your mind that what every woman says some woman may feel?"' (p.83), just as she tells Angel to 'call me Tess' when he insists, in the 'visionary essence' scene, on idealising her with names like Artemis and Demeter (p.135)). The novel may further appear to try and characterise her state of mind – 'she looked upon herself as a figure of Guilt intruding into the haunts of Innocence . . . she fancied herself such an anomaly' (p.91) – but only, we note, at a detached psychological distance; it may try and explain her love for Angel ('its single-mindedness, its meekness; what long-suffering it guaranteed, what honesty, what endurance, what good-faith', p.211), but the more the text produces phrase after defining phrase, the more a palpable sense of her love recedes – just as earlier, despite all its words, the narrative signally fails to describe her eyes: 'neither black nor blue nor grey nor violet; rather all those shades together, and a hundred others . . . around pupils that had no bottom' (pp.95–6). For all this 'characterisation', then, we really 'know' Tess very little indeed – which is presumably why so much critical argument has raged over whether she is 'passive' or not, whether she is 'pure' or not, indeed whether she is a 'fully-rounded character' at all.

Which is, I would suggest in conclusion, to beg the question. For *Tess of the d'Urbervilles* is precisely *not* a novel attempting to offer us a 'knowable' character, but rather one which exposes *characterisation* itself as a humanist-realist mystification (producing 'visible essences') and which parades the *mis*representation that 'characterisation' involves by subjecting to irony the falsifying essentialism of 'faithfully presenting a pure woman'. In her excellent essay of 1982, 'Pure Tess: Hardy on Knowing a Woman', Kathleen Blake[37] remarks that the novel 'really scrutinises the sexual typing that plays havoc with a woman's life', while George Wotton in his book *Thomas Hardy: Towards a Materialist Criticism*, in suggesting that we recognise 'class and gender conflicts . . . as conflicts of perception in the multfarious acts of seeing of the characters who inhabit Wessex', points out that Hardy's 'production (writing) determines consumption (reading) by casting the reader in the role of seer'.[38] In other words, we may say that Hardy's 'moments of vision' disproportion characterisation and character so that we can 'see' how they function. Tess as a 'character' is no more than an amalgam – often destructively contradictory – of 'images' of her as perceived by individuals and by 'society': Angel idealises her, Alec sees her as sex-object, the narrative voice fetishises her, society regards her as prodigal, the novel 'faithfully presents' her as 'a pure woman' (with all the ironies that phrasing invokes). But Tess *has no character at all*: she is only what others (most especially the author) construct her as; and so she is herself merely a 'series of seemings' or 'impressions'. This, of course, gives the final ironic twist to the notion of her being ('a) pure woman', since there can be no such thing as 'essential character' when a woman is merely the construct of male socio-sexual images of her desired form (though my basic point here need not be limited to *gender*-stereotyping). Hardy's novel, then, well ahead of its time, seems to be dismantling the bourgeois-humanist (patriarchal and realist) notion of the unified and unitary human subject, and to be doing so by way of a discourse so self-reflexive and defamiliarising about representation, so unstable and dialogical, that it deconstructs itself even as it creates. Which is why, I believe, we can justly discover a contemporary post-modern text in *Tess of the d'Urbervilles*.[39] □

In this final chapter, as Peter Widdowson suggests, Hardy emerges as very much our contemporary and *Tess of the d'Urbervilles* as a post-modern work. Lacanian analysis reveals Hardy's anxiety about dissolution, materialist reading uncovers a subversive hidden text, and Hardy is discovered to be deconstructing the humanist conception of character as a unified subject.

The introduction to this Guide described the bizarre circumstances surrounding the publication of *Tess of the d'Urbervilles*, and the opening chapter recorded the controversy ignited by the moral and intellectual challenges that the novel posed. As each succeeding generation of critics has encountered this text, two responses have consistently stood out: a powerful reaction to the reading of *Tess* as an intense tragic experience; and a strenuous engagement in critical dispute. J. Hillis Miller, who argues that *Tess of the d'Urbervilles* resists any possibility of satisfactory explanation, feels that readers are drawn into the act of interpretation by the profound question of why Tess suffers (see pp. 121–7). And simultaneously they are lured into the arena of debate. Over a century after its publication, *Tess of the d'Urbervilles* has lost none of its capacity to stimulate argument. It still raises fundamental ideological and aesthetic issues, such as literary censorship, the status of the author, ideology, gender and sexuality, what constitutes character, and the instability of the text. It is impossible to predict the development of *Tess* criticism. History suggests that it will be both an evolutionary process and a series of new directions. Its future certainly promises to be exciting.

NOTES

INTRODUCTION

1 A character mentioned in the play *Speed the Plough* (1798) by Thomas Morton. The name has come to signify an attitude extremely critical of any breach of propriety.

CHAPTER ONE

1 Preface to *Select Poems of William Barnes* (London: Henry Frowde, 1908), p.x.

2 A group of poets who gathered to read poetry at the Cheshire Cheese in Fleet Street from 1891. It included, among others, W.B. Yeats, Lionel Johnson, Ernest Dowson, Arthur Symons, and John Davidson. Richard le Gallienne also contributed to the *Yellow Book* (1894–7), a publication devoted to literature and art.

3 Henry Arthur Jones (1851–1929), a friend and contemporary of Pinero, and encouraged by Shaw. Jones was a prolific and popular playwright, who dealt with serious social issues, and included treatment of double standards of morality and behaviour for men and women.

4 Richard le Gallienne, 'Mr Hardy's New Novel', *Star* (23 December 1891), p.4.

5 Anon., 'Mr Thomas Hardy's New Novel', *Pall Mall Gazette* (31 December 1891), p.3.

6 Henrik Ibsen (1828–1906), the Norwegian dramatist, whose earlier prose dramas were concerned with social and political themes, and whose tragedies involved ordinary people.

7 *Diana of the Crossways* (1885), a novel by George Meredith, which displays feminist sympathies.

8 Clementina Black, 'Mr Thomas Hardy's New Story', *Illustrated London News*, 100 (9 January 1892), p.50.

9 Anon., 'Novels', *Saturday Review*, (16 January 1892), p.74.

10 *Saturday Review*, p.73.

11 R.H. Hutton, 'Mr Hardy's *Tess of the d'Urbervilles*', *Spectator* (23 January 1892), pp.121–2.

12 *Spectator*, p.122.

13 *Spectator*, p.122.

14 Andrew Lang, 'Literature', *New Review*, 6 (February 1982), p.248.

15 'Whatever gods may be'. Sir William Watson is quoting from Swinburne's poem 'The Garden of Proserpine'.

16 Sir William Watson, '*Tess of the d'Urbervilles*', *Academy*, 41 (6 February 1892), pp.125–6.

17 *The History of David Grieve* (1892), was one of Mrs Humphry Ward's novels of high moral purpose. Her fiction dealt with social and religious themes.

18 Mrs Oliphant, 'The Old Saloon', *Blackwood's Magazine*, 151 (March 1892), p.465.

19 *Blackwood's Magazine*, p.464.

20 *Blackwood's Magazine*, p.465.

21 *Blackwood's Magazine*, p.472

22 *Aurora Leigh* (1857), described by Elizabeth Barrett Browning as a novel in verse, is a love story about a girl who becomes a poet, with a sub-plot involving the rape of a lower-class girl, who has a child, and who is later rescued by Aurora.

23 *Blackwood's Magazine*, pp.465–73.

24 Mowbray Morris, 'Culture and Anarchy', *Quarterly Review*, 174 (April 1892), p.321.

25 *Quarterly Review*, pp.321–2.

26 *Quarterly Review*, p.325.

27 Florence Emily Hardy, *The Life of Thomas Hardy 1840–1928* 2 vols. (London: Macmillan, 1928–30); reprinted as a single volume, 1962), p.246.

28 W.P. Trent, 'The Novels of Thomas Hardy', *Sewanee Review*, 1 (November 1892), p.19.

29 *Sewanee Review*, p.20.

30 *Sewanee Review*, p.20.

31 *Sewanee Review*, pp.20–2.

32 D.F. Hannigan, 'The Latest Development of English Fiction', *Westminster Review*, 138 (December 1892), p.655.

33 *Westminster Review*, p.657.

34 *Westminster Review*, pp.658–9.

CHAPTER TWO

1 Lionel Johnson, *The Art of Thomas Hardy* (London: John Lane, 1894), revised edition, 1923; reprinted New York: Haskell House, 1973, p.227.

2 The trilogy of Aeschylus, consisting of *Agamemnon*, *Choephoroe* and *Eumenides*.

3 Johnson, p. 228.

4 Among these philosophers, John Stuart Mill, Sir Henry Maine and Herbert Spencer were contemporaries of both Hardy and Johnson.

5 Johnson, p. 229.

6 Johnson, p. 230.

7 Johnson, p. 232.

8 William Shakespeare, *King Lear*, IV. i. 36–7.

9 Johnson, pp. 244–5.

10 The heroine of George Eliot's novel, *The Mill on the Floss* (1860).

11 Thomas à Kempis (1380–1471) was a Christian mystical writer. Johnson's reference to 'fire and water', which must be passed through to attain spiritual refreshment, is an allusion to comments from *Imitation of Christ* (c. 1447).

12 Johnson, pp. 247–8.

13 Lascelles Abercrombie, *Thomas Hardy: A Critical Study* (London: Martin Secker, 1912), p. 137.

14 Abercrombie, p. 145.

15 Abercrombie, p. 152.

16 George Bernard Shaw's play, *Candida* (1894) involves Candida, who epitomises wisdom, love and dignity, and her father, Mr Burgess, a vulgar and ignorant man.

17 Henry Charles Duffin, *Thomas Hardy* (Manchester: Manchester University Press, 1916); revised edition 1937, p. 49.

18 The tragic heroine of Hardy's *The Woodlanders* (1887).

19 Duffin, p. 58.

20 Mary Ellen Chase, *Thomas Hardy: From Serial to Novel* (Minneapolis: University of Minnesota Press, 1927); reprinted New York: Russell and Russell, 1964, p. 82.

21 Virginia Woolf, *The Common Reader: Second Series* (London: Hogarth Press, 1932); reprinted 1986, p. 253.

22 D. H. Lawrence, 'Study of Thomas Hardy', *Phoenix: The Posthumous Papers of D.H. Lawrence*, ed. Edward D. McDonald (London: Heinemann, 1936); reprinted 1970, pp. 482–3.

23 Lawrence, pp. 483–4.

24 Lawrence, p. 484.

25 Lawrence, p. 486.

26 Lawrence, p. 487.

27 Lawrence, pp. 485–6.

28 William. R. Rutland, *Thomas Hardy: A Study of His Writings and their Background* (Oxford: Basil Blackwell, 1938), pp. 232–3.

29 Rutland, p. 235.

30 Morton Dauwen Zabel, 'Hardy in Defence of his Art: The Aesthetic of Incongruity', *Southern Review*, 6 (1940), p. 126.

31 Zabel, p. 140.

32 Giles Winterborne, a character in *The Woodlanders*.

33 Zabel, pp. 147–8.

34 Donald Davidson, 'The Traditional Basis of Thomas Hardy's Fiction', *Southern Review*, 6 (1940), p. 165.

35 Davidson, p. 168.

36 Davidson, p. 170.

37 Davidson, pp. 172–3

38 Davidson, pp. 173–4.

39 Davidson, p. 177.

40 Lord David Cecil, *Hardy the Novelist* (London: Constable, 1943), p. 64.

41 Cecil, p. 32.

42 Cecil, pp. 35–6.

43 Cecil, p. 32.

44 Cecil, pp. 149–50.

45 Cecil, p. 116.

46 Cecil, p. 153.

47 Harvey Curtis Webster, *On A Darkling Plain: The Art and Thought of Thomas Hardy* (Chicago: University of Chicago Press, 1947), p. 173.

48 Webster, pp. 174–80.

49 Henry James, letter of 19 March 1892, to Robert Louis Stevenson, *The Letters of Henry James*, ed. Percy Lubbock, 2 vols. (London: Macmillan, 1920), I, p. 194; quoted in F. R. Leavis, *The Great Tradition* (London: Chatto and Windus, 1948), p. 22.

50 Leavis, p. 23.

51 Leavis, p. 124.

52 Albert J. Guerard, *Thomas Hardy* (Cambridge, Massachusetts: Harvard University Press, 1949); reprinted London: New Directions, 1964, p. 2.

53 Guerard, p. ix.

54 Guerard, p. 3.

55 Guerard, p. 41.

56 Guerard, pp. 17–18.

57 Guerard, p. 19.

58 Guerard, p. 74.

59 Guerard, p. 19.
60 Guerard, pp. 74–5.
61 Guerard, p. 81.
62 Guerard, pp. 80–1.

CHAPTER THREE

1 John Holloway, *The Victorian Sage* (London: Macmillan, 1953), p. 11.
2 Holloway, pp. 10–11.
3 Holloway, p. 13.
4 Holloway, p. 252.
5 Holloway, p. 259.
6 Holloway, p. 262.
7 Holloway, pp. 264–5.
8 Holloway, p. 266.
9 Holloway, pp. 269–70.
10 Holloway, p. 277.
11 Holloway, pp. 278–9.
12 Holloway, p. 281.
13 Holloway, p. 281.
14 Holloway, pp. 285–6.
15 Dorothy Van Ghent, *The English Novel: Form and Function* (New York: Rinehart & Company, 1953); reprinted New York: Harper & Row, 1967, p. 17.
16 Van Ghent, p. 17.
17 Van Ghent, p. 17.
18 Van Ghent, p. 18.
19 Van Ghent, p. 238.
20 Van Ghent, p. 238.
21 Van Ghent, p. 239.
22 Van Ghent, p. 240.
23 Van Ghent, p. 241.
24 Van Ghent, p. 242.
25 Van Ghent, p. 244.
26 Van Ghent, p. 244.
27 Van Ghent, p. 245.
28 Van Ghent, pp. 246–7.
29 Van Ghent, pp. 248–50.
30 Van Ghent, pp. 252–3.
31 Van Ghent, p. 254.
32 Van Ghent, pp. 254–5.
33 Arnold Kettle, *An Introduction to the English Novel* 2 vols. (London: Hutchinson, 1953), vol. II, pp. 45–6.
34 Kettle, II, p. 47.
35 Kettle, II, pp. 47–8.
36 Kettle, II, p. 48.
37 Kettle, II, p. 50.
38 Kettle, II, p. 49.
39 Kettle, II, p. 49.
40 Kettle, II, p. 50.
41 Kettle, II, p. 50.
42 Kettle, II, p. 51.
43 Kettle, II, p. 52.
44 Kettle, II, p. 52.
45 Kettle, II, p. 53.
46 Kettle, II, p. 52.
47 Kettle, II, p. 55.
48 Kettle, II, pp. 55–6.
49 Douglas Brown, *Thomas Hardy* (London: Longmans, Green and Co., 1954), pp. 30–1.
50 Brown, pp. 89–90.
51 *The Woodlanders.*
52 Brown, pp. 91–2.
53 Brown, pp. 92–3.
54 Brown, pp. 94–6.
55 Brown, p. 96.
56 Brown, pp. 97–8.

CHAPTER FOUR

1 Roy Morrell, *Thomas Hardy: The Will and the Way* (Kuala Lumpur: University of Malaya Press, 1965), pp. 1–2.
2 Morrell, p. xiii.
3 Morrell, p. 16.
4 Morrell, p. 11.
5 Morrell, pp. 17–18.
6 Morrell, pp. 18–19.
7 Morrell, p. 91.
8 Morrell, pp. 32–4.
9 Morrell, p. 40.
10 Irving Howe, *Thomas Hardy* (London: Weidenfeld and Nicolson, 1968), p. 110.
11 Howe, p. 130.
12 Dorothy Van Ghent, *The English Novel: Form and Function* (New York: Rinehart & Company, 1953); reprinted New York: Harper & Row, 1967, p. 240.
13 Tony Tanner, 'Colour and Movement in Hardy's *Tess of the d'Urbervilles*', *Critical Quarterly*, 10 (1968), p. 220.
14 Tanner, p. 219.
15 Tanner, p. 220.
16 Tanner, p. 220.
17 Tanner, pp. 220–1.
18 Tanner, p. 222.
19 Tanner, p. 223.
20 Tanner, p. 225.
21 Tanner, p. 226.
22 Tanner, pp. 228–9.
23 Tanner, p. 232.
24 Tanner, pp. 236–7.
25 David Lodge, *Language of Fiction*

(London: Routledge and Kegan Paul, 1966), p. 47.

26 Lodge, p. 170.

27 William Empson, poet and critic, whose work included his influential book, *Seven Types of Ambiguity* (London: Chatto and Windus, 1930).

28 William Shakespeare, *Romeo and Juliet*, II. v. 9.

29 Robert Liddell, *A Treatise on the Novel* (London: Jonathan Cape, 1947), p. 118.

30 John Holloway, *The Victorian Sage* (London: Macmillan, 1953), p. 263.

31 Lodge, pp. 184–6.

32 Lodge, p. 187.

33 Richard Carpenter, *Thomas Hardy* (New York: Twayne, 1964), p. 125.

34 Carpenter, p. 135.

35 Jean R. Brooks, *Thomas Hardy: The Poetic Structure* (London: Elek, 1971), pp. 237–8.

36 Dale Kramer, *Thomas Hardy: The Forms of Tragedy* (London: Macmillan, 1975), pp. 113–14.

37 Kramer, p. 115.

38 Kramer, pp. 116–17.

39 Kramer, p. 121.

40 Kramer, p. 122.

41 Kramer, p. 122.

42 Kramer, p. 128.

43 Kramer, p. 131.

44 Kramer, p. 134.

45 Kramer, pp. 134–5.

46 Ian Gregor and Brian Nicholas, *The Moral and the Story* (London: Faber and Faber, 1962).

47 Gregor, 'What Kind of Fiction did Hardy Write?', *Essays in Criticism*, 16 (1966), pp. 290–308.

48 Florence Emily Hardy, *The Life of Thomas Hardy 1840–1928* 2 vols. (London: Macmillan, 1928–30); reprinted as a single volume, 1962), p. 177.

49 Gregor, *The Great Web: The Form of Hardy's Major Fiction* (London: Faber and Faber), 1974, p. 33.

50 Gregor, p. 26.

51 Gregor, p. 27.

52 Gregor, p. 29.

53 Gregor, p. 32.

54 Gregor, p. 33.

55 Gregor, p. 41.

56 Gregor, p. 179.

57 Gregor, p. 185.

58 Gregor, pp. 187–8.

59 Gregor, p. 191.

60 Gregor, p. 192.

61 William Shakespeare, *Hamlet*, V. ii. 233–6.

62 Gregor, pp. 196–7.

63 Gregor, pp. 201–2.

64 William Shakespeare, *The Two Gentlemen of Verona*, I. ii. 111–12. Gregor, pp. 203–4.

65 David J. De Laura, '"The Ache of Modernism" in Hardy's Later Novels', *ELH*, 34 (1967), pp. 380–1.

66 Letter of 14 December 1852, *The Letters of Matthew Arnold to Arthur Hugh Clough*, ed. Howard Foster Lowry (London: Oxford University Press, 1932), p. 126.

67 See Matthew Arnold's discussion of Hebraism and Hellenism in *Culture and Anarchy* (London: Smith, Elder and Co., 1869).

68 De Laura, pp. 395–6.

69 De Laura, p. 397.

70 De Laura, pp. 396–7.

71 Raymond Williams, *The English Novel from Dickens to Lawrence* (London: Chatto and Windus, 1970); reprinted London: Hogarth Press, 1984, p. 100.

72 Williams, p. 102.

73 Williams, p. 106.

74 Williams, pp. 107–8.

75 Williams, p. 110.

76 Williams, pp. 110–11.

77 Williams, p. 112.

78 Williams, p. 113.

79 Williams, pp. 114–15.

80 Williams, p. 115.

81 Merryn Williams, *Thomas Hardy and Rural England* (London: Macmillan, 1972), p. 170.

82 M. Williams, p. 170.

83 M. Williams, p. 171.

84 J.T. Laird, *The Shaping of 'Tess of the d'Urbervilles'* (Oxford: Clarendon Press, 1975), p. 122.

85 Laird, p. 175.

86 Laird, pp. 175–6.

87 Laird, pp. 176–8.

88 Mary Jacobus, 'Tess: The Making of a Pure Woman', in *Tearing the Veil: Essays on Femininity*, ed. Susan Lipshitz (London: Routledge and Kegan Paul, 1978), p. 78.

89 Jacobus, p. 78.

90 Jacobus, p.79.
91 Jacobus, p.80.
92 Jacobus, p.81.
93 [*Jacobus's Note:*] Folio references, in the case of quotations from manuscript, refer to the final pagination system adopted by Hardy in the manuscript preserved in the British Museum; asterisks denote leaves belonging to the earliest phase of composition. In quoting from ms., the text presented is that of the earliest readings, unless changes were clearly made at the same time.
94 Jacobus, pp.87–8.
95 Jacobus, p.90.
96 Laird, p.4.

CHAPTER FIVE

1 [*Sumner's Note:*] I am indebted to Lennart Björk for this information, which is partly derived from his edition of *The Literary Notebooks of Thomas Hardy* (Götenborg: Acta Universitatis Gothoburgensis, 1974), and also from his lecture on the influence of Fourier on Hardy's social and psychological thinking given at the 1975 Hardy Summer School. [*Editor's Note*: see *Budmouth Essays on Thomas Hardy: Papers Presented at the 1975 Summer School* ed. F.B. Pinion (Dorchester: Thomas Hardy Society, 1976).]
2 Rosemary Sumner, *Thomas Hardy: Psychological Novelist* (London: Macmillan, 1981), p.132.
3 Carl Jung, *Two Essays in Analytical Psychology, The Collected Work of C.J. Jung*, ed. Sir Herbert Read et al. (London: Routledge and Kegan Paul, 1953–71), Vol. 7, p.188.
4 Jung, *Aion, Collected Works*, Vol. 9, (ii) p.13.
5 Jung, *The Development of the Personality, Collected Works*, Vol. 17, p.198.
6 Sumner, pp.133–4.
7 Sigmund Freud, *Delusions and Dreams in Jensen's 'Gradiva'* (1907); *Standard Edition of the Complete Psychological Works of Sigmund Freud*, ed. James Strachey (London: Hogarth Press, 1953–74), Vol. 9, p.83.
8 Freud, p.89.
9 Sumner, pp.134–5.
10 Sumner, p.135.
11 Freud, *The Taboo of Virginity* (1917); *Standard Edition*, Vol. 16, p.199.
12 Freud, *On Narcissism* (1914); *Standard Edition*, Vol. 14, p.80.
13 Sumner, pp.135–6.
14 Freud, *Group Psychology, 8, Being in Love and Hypnosis* (1921); *Standard Edition*, Vol. 18, p.112.
15 Sumner, pp.136–7.
16 Sumner, p.142.
17 Freud, *Civilisation and its Discontents* (1930); *Standard Edition*, Vol. 21, p.112.
18 Sumner, p.142.
19 Sumner, p.139.
20 Jacques Derrida's radically sceptical theory of deconstruction, applied to literary texts, undermines the structuralist principle – based on the relationship between linguistic signs and what they represent – of binary opposition (man/woman, light/dark, order/anarchy). These boundaries, which suppport ideology (patriarchy in the case of man/woman) are eroded by the arbitrariness of the sign, and by what Derrida identifies as the continual play of difference (*différance* – difference and deferral). Derrida thus seeks to reveal the inherent indeterminacy of meaning. He also employs the strategy of pursuing marginal details in texts, and exposes their systems of thought as containing inherent contradictions.
21 The Yale school of criticism, influenced by Derrida and founded by Paul de Man, established a distinctively American approach to deconstruction, of which J. Hillis Miller is a major exponent. Its sceptical close reading demonstrates the impossibility of the text saying anything that it does not itself undermine.
22 J. Hillis Miller, *Fiction and Repetition: Seven English Novels* (Oxford: Basil Blackwell, 1982), pp.116–18.
23 Miller, p.120.
24 Miller, pp.120–1.
25 Miller, p.121.
26 Miller, p.122.
27 Miller, p.123.
28 Miller, p.126.
29 Miller, pp.126–7.
30 Miller, p.128.
31 Overdetermination, originally a Freudian concept used to describe how some

elements of dreams have multiple determinants, was taken up by the Marxist theorist, Louis Althusser, to explain the structural articulation of contradictions and determinations in a social formation. Miller's deconstructive approach uses the term to reveal how the text may be seen to generate contradictions determined by multiple causes.

32 Miller, pp. 140–1.

33 Penny Boumelha, *Thomas Hardy and Women: Sexual Ideology and Narrative Form* (Brighton: Harvester Wheatsheaf, 1982), p. 120.

34 Boumelha, p. 119. For the relationship between feminism and poststructuralism, see Chris Weedon, *Feminist Practice and Poststructuralist Theory* (Oxford: Basil Blackwell, 1987).

35 For example by Tony Tanner, 'Colour and Movement in Hardy's *Tess of the d'Urbervilles*, *Critical Quarterly*, 10 (1968), pp. 219–39.

36 Henry James, letter to Robert Louis Stevenson, 17 February, 1893, *Letters*, I, p. 205.

37 Boumelha, pp. 120–2.

38 Boumelha, p. 123.

39 Boumelha, pp. 123–6.

40 Heteroglossia is a term created by Mikhail Bakhtin to describe the many discourses within language. Elements of this multivocal discourse are outside the control of the author.

41 Boumelha, p. 128.

42 Boumelha, pp. 129–130.

43 John Bayley, *An Essay on Hardy* (Cambridge: Cambridge University Press, 1978), p. 189.

44 Boumelha, p. 132.

45 Patricia Ingham, *Thomas Hardy: A Feminist Reading* (Hemel Hempstead: Harvester Wheatsheaf, 1989), pp. 6–7.

46 Ingham, p. 68.

47 Ingham, pp. 72–4.

48 Ingham, p. 86.

49 Ingham, pp. 87–9.

50 Materialism seeks to understand the literary text as rooted in history, but also as an on-going process, and involved with political struggle.

51 John Goode, *Thomas Hardy: The Offensive Truth* (Oxford, Basil Blackwell, 1988), p. 111.

52 Goode, pp. 111–12.

53 John Ruskin (1819–1900), the renowned writer on art and architecture, also lectured and wrote prolifically against supporters of capitalism. William Morris (1834–96), in addition to revolutionising domestic design, was a prominent socialist and published lectures on politics. Both men believed in the importance of labour affording pleasure.

54 Goode, pp. 125–6.

55 Goode, p. 127.

56 Goode, p. 128.

57 Goode, p. 129.

58 Goode, p. 129.

59 Goode, p. 130.

60 Goode, p. 131.

61 Goode, p. 131.

62 Goode, p. 132.

63 Goode, p. 134.

64 Goode, p. 136.

65 Goode, pp. 134–5.

66 Goode, p. 137.

67 Goode, p. 137.

68 J.B. Bullen, *The Expressive Eye: Fiction and Perception in the Work of Thomas Hardy* (Oxford: Clarendon Press, 1986), p. 12.

69 Florence Emily Hardy, *The Life of Thomas Hardy 1840–1928* 2 vols. (London: Macmillan, 1928–30); reprinted as a single volume, 1962), p. 216.

70 Bullen, pp. 197–8.

71 Frédéric Brunetière, 'Symbolistes et Decadens', *Revue des Deux Mondes*, 90 (1888), pp. 217–18.

72 Bullen, pp. 203–4.

73 Bullen, pp. 204–6.

74 Max Müller, 'Comparative Mythology', *Chips from a German Workshop*, second edition (London: Longmans, Green and Co., 1868), ii. p. 132.

75 Müller, p. 132.

76 Müller, p. 132.

77 Bullen, pp. 211–12.

78 Walter Pater, 'Apollo in Picardy', *Miscellaneous Studies* (London: Macmillan, and Co., 1895). Second edition, 1904. [*Bullen's Note*: Though *Tess of the d'Urbervilles* was published in 1891, and 'Apollo in Picardy' not until 1893, the rate at which Pater usually worked makes it

quite possible that he discussed his ideas for 'Apollo' even before Hardy began writing his novel.]

79 Bullen, p. 215.

80 James Cotter Morison (1832–88), a Positivist and historian, was on the staff of the *Saturday Review*. Thomas Henry Huxley (1825–95), was a friend and influential supporter of Charles Darwin, and wrote widely on science and ethics.

81 Bullen, p. 216.

82 Bullen, p. 221.

83 Simon Gatrell, *Hardy the Creator: A Textual Biography* (Oxford: Clarendon Press, 1988), p. 101.

84 Gatrell, pp. 101–2.

85 Gatrell, p. 102.

86 Gatrell, p. 103.

87 Gatrell, p. 103.

88 Gatrell, p. 103.

89 Gatrell notes that 'by the church builders' was added after 'sufficient' in the 1900 paperback and the 1912 Wessex editions, p. 104.

90 Gatrell, pp. 103–4.

91 Gatrell, p. 105.

92 Gatrell, p. 106.

93 Gatrell, p. 110.

CHAPTER SIX

1 Jacques Lacan challenged the humanist conception of the integrated subject. In its place he postulated the subject as the fragmented product of unconscious desire articulated in language. He suggested that desire, rather than being sexual, as Freud had argued, is directed towards the realisation of unity. This can never be attained because of a psychic split at the 'mirror' stage of development, when the ego misrecognises its image in a mirror as representing its own unity. The 'I' then enters the symbolic order, socialised through language, which enacts the repressive system of the father, the realm of law and institution. Unconscious desire, or lack, originates in relation to the absent Other, the locus of signification, where identity is established. This Other may be woman, who assists in affirming man's selfhood. Marjorie Garson's feminist approach employs Lacan's psychoanalytic theory to analyse Hardy's anxieties about the unity of the self, women, social class, the integrity of the body, and nature. She also demonstrates how this text, which aims for aesthetic wholeness, serves instead to mirror dissolution. See Elizabeth Grosz, *Jacques Lacan: A Feminist Introduction* (London and New York: Routledge, 1990).

2 Fredric R. Jameson is a Marxist cultural critic, who regards history as a narrative of humankind, to be understood as text, parts of which, such as the collective struggle for freedom, have been suppressed into the political unconscious. For Jameson, literary narrative is a 'socially symbolic act', which also requires interpretation, primarily in terms of its representation of class structure, and its historical context. See John Frow, *Marxism and Literary History* (Cambridge, Massachusetts: Harvard University Press, 1986). Jameson draws on the work of, among other theorists, A. J. Greimas, who sought to systematise semiotics (the study of signs) as a science. He regarded a literary text as including several semiotic systems, analysis of which depends on a complex descriptive methodology. Jameson makes use of Greimas's 'semiotic rectangle', for his own investigation of ideology. See Jonathan Culler, *Structural Poetics* (London: Routledge and Kegan Paul, 1975).

3 Marjorie Garson, *Hardy's Fables of Integrity: Woman, Body, Text* (Oxford: Clarendon Press, 1991), pp. 133–7.

4 Garson, pp. 138–40.

5 Garson, pp. 141–3.

6 Garson, pp. 146–8.

7 Garson, pp. 148–9.

8 Nina Auerbach, 'The Rise of the Fallen Woman', *Nineteenth-Century Fiction*, 35 (1980), pp. 34–5, 40–6.

9 Garson, pp. 149–51.

10 Louis Althusser was a Marxist philosopher, whose concept of social formation (the structural complexity of social reality) describes the relationship between literature and society. He argues that literature produces, yet is detached from, ideology (a system of thought that accounts for the social world), since the writer is relatively autonomous. Althusser's methodology of symptomatic reading (analysing the pres-

ence of ideology in texts) uncovers the text's buried problematic (its body of thought) by focusing on its contradictions, omissions and distortions, which may be elements of literary production itself. See Ted Benton, *The Rise and Fall of Structural Marxism: Althusser and His Influence* (London: Macmillan, 1984).

11 Joe Fisher, *The Hidden Hardy* (London: Macmillan, 1992), p. 3.

12 N.N. Feltes, *Modes of Production of Victorian Novels* (Chicago and London: University of Chicago Press, 1986), p. 63.

13 Fisher, p. 4. Hegemony (power) is a concept developed from the work of the Italian Marxist philosopher, Antonio Gramsci. For him the bourgeoisie exerts hegemony over other classes in capitalist societies, a dominance maintained in democracies through consent, and he analyses the play of social forces within the literary text. Here Fisher is referring to the way middle-class hegemony is achieved at the level of culture and aesthetics by capitalist circulating libraries and magazines. See Walter L. Adamson, *Hegemony and Revolution: A Study of Antonio Gramsci's Political and Cultural Theory* (Berkeley: University of California Press, 1980).

14 Fisher, p. 5.

15 Fisher, p. 7.

16 Fisher, p. 8.

17 Fisher, p. 13.

18 *Götterdämmerung*: the twilight of the gods, popularised by its employment by Wagner as the title of the last opera of the Ring cycle. Here it is used figuratively to denote the downfall of an entire world.

19 Fisher, p. 154.

20 Fisher, pp. 154–5.

21 See particularly *An Introduction to the Science of Religion* (London: Longmans, Green and Co., 1873).

22 Fisher, pp. 157–8.

23 Fisher, p. 159.

24 Fisher, pp. 164–6.

25 Fisher, pp. 166–7.

26 Fisher, p. 169.

27 Fisher, pp. 170–1.

28 J.B. Bullen, *The Expressive Eye: Fiction and Perception in the Work of Thomas Hardy* (Oxford: Clarendon Press, 1986), p. 192.

29 Fisher, p. 173.

30 Dialogism is the existence within a literary text of a polyphonic heterogeneity, a plurality of cultural voices, representing a variety of ideological positions, none of which is privileged. Mikhail Bakhtin identified this as operating within the writing of Dostoevsky.

31 For the linguist, Saussure, language was a system held together by the mechanism of signification, each sign being composed of a 'signifier' (spoken or written word) and a 'signified' (concept or meaning). He saw the relationship between these as being relatively arbitrary. Also arbitrary is the relationship between the sign and what it refers to. Post-structuralists argued further that there is no firm distinction between signifiers and signifieds, since each signifier in turn becomes a signified, in an endless sequence. They conclude, therefore, that language and meaning are inherently unstable.

32 Peter Widdowson, '"Moments of Vision": Postmodernising *Tess of the d'Urbervilles*; or, *Tess of the d'Urbervilles* Faithfully Presented by Peter Widdowson', *New Perspectives on Thomas Hardy*, ed. Charles P.C. Pettit (London: Macmillan, 1994), p. 82.

33 Widdowson, pp. 87–8.

34 Florence Emily Hardy, *The Life of Thomas Hardy 1840–1928* 2 vols. (London: Macmillan, 1928–30); reprinted as a single volume, 1962), pp. 228–9.

35 F.E. Hardy, p. 177.

36 Widdowson, pp. 91–6.

37 Kathleen Blake, 'Pure Tess: Hardy on Knowing a Woman', *Studies in English Literature*, 22 (1982), pp. 689–705.

38 George Wotton, *Thomas Hardy: Towards a Materialist Criticism* (Goldenbridge: Gill & Macmillan, 1985), p. 4.

39 Widdowson, pp. 96–8.

SELECT BIBLIOGRAPHY

Novels

This list notes the chronological appearance of Hardy's novels in serial form, followed by details of their first publication in Britain.

The Poor Man and the Lady. Written in 1868; unpublished.

Desperate Remedies. 3 vols. London: Tinsley, 1871.

Under the Greenwood Tree. 2 vols. London: Tinsley, 1872.

A Pair of Blue Eyes. Serialised in *Tinsley's Magazine*, September 1872–July 1873. 3 vols. London: Tinsley, 1873.

Far from the Madding Crowd. Serialised in the *Cornhill*, January–December 1874. 2 vols. London: Smith, Elder, 1874.

The Hand of Ethelberta. Serialised in the *Cornhill*, July 1875–May 1876. 2 vols. London: Smith, Elder, 1876.

The Return of the Native. Serialised in *Belgravia*, January–December 1878. 3 vols. London: Smith, Elder, 1878.

The Trumpet-Major. Serialised in *Good Words*, January–December 1880. 3 vols. London: Smith, Elder, 1880.

A Laodicean. Serialised in *Harper's New Monthly Magazine*, December 1880–December 1881. 3 vols. London: Sampson Low, 1881.

Two on a Tower. Serialised in *Atlantic Monthly*, May–December 1882. 3 vols. London: Sampson Low, 1882.

The Mayor of Casterbridge. Serialised in the *Graphic*, January–May 1886. 2 vols. London: Smith, Elder, 1886.

The Woodlanders. Serialised in *Macmillan's Magazine*, May 1886–April 1887. 3 vols. London: Macmillan, 1887.

Tess of the d'Urbervilles. Serialised in the *Graphic*, July–December 1891. 3 vols. London: Osgood, McIlvaine, 1891.

Jude the Obscure. Serialised in *Harper's New Monthly Magazine*, December 1894–November 1895. 1 vol. London: Osgood, McIlvaine, 1895.

The Well-Beloved. Serialised in the *Illustrated London News*, October–December 1892. 1 vol. London: Osgood, McIlvaine, 1897.

Editions of *Tess of the d'Urbervilles*

Elledge, Scott, ed. *Tess of the d'Urbervilles*. New York: Norton, 1965. Second edition 1979.

Furbank, P.N., ed. *Tess of the d'Urbervilles*. New Wessex edition. London: Macmillan, 1974.

Grindle, Juliet, and Gatrell, Simon, eds. *Tess of the d'Urbervilles*. Oxford: Clarendon Press, 1983.

Grindle, Juliet, and Gatrell, Simon, eds. *Tess of the d'Urbervilles*. Oxford World's Classics series. Oxford: Oxford University Press, 1983; reissued 1998. This contains the authoritative Clarendon text.

Skilton, David, ed. *Tess of the d'Urbervilles*. Penguin Classics. Harmondsworth: Penguin, 1978; reissued 1985.

Letters
Purdy, R. L., and Millgate, Michael, eds. *The Collected Letters of Thomas Hardy*. 7 vols. Oxford: Oxford University Press, 1978–88.

Working notes
Björk, Lennart, ed. *The Literary Notebooks of Thomas Hardy*. 2 vols. London: Macmillan, 1985.

Orel, Harold, ed. *Thomas Hardy's Personal Writings*. Kansas: University of Kansas Press, 1966; London: Macmillan, 1967; revised edition, 1990.

Taylor, Richard H., ed. *The Personal Notebooks of Thomas Hardy*. London: Macmillan, 1978.

Bibliographies of criticism
Draper, Ronald. P., and Ray, Martin. S. *An Annotated Critical Bibliography of Thomas Hardy*. London: Harvester Wheatsheaf, 1989.

Purdy, R. L. *Thomas Hardy: A Bibliographical Study*. Oxford: Clarendon Press, 1954; revised edition 1968.

Journals
Page, Norman, ed. *Thomas Hardy Annual*. London: Macmillan, 1982– .

Studies of Hardy's working methods, critical reputation, publishing history
Chase, Mary Ellen. *Thomas Hardy: From Serial to Novel*. Minneapolis: University of Minnesota Press, 1927.

Gatrell, Simon. *Hardy the Creator: A Textual Biography*. Oxford: Clarendon Press, 1988.

Jacobus, Mary. 'Tess's Purity'. *Essays in Criticism*, 26 (1976), pp. 318–38. Reprinted with alterations as 'Tess: The Making of a Pure Woman'. Susan Lipshitz, ed. *Tearing the Veil: Essays on Femininity*. London: Routledge & Kegan Paul, 1978, pp. 77–92; and also in Bloom (1987) pp. 44–60.

Laird, J. T. *The Shaping of 'Tess of the d'Urbervilles'*. Oxford: Clarendon Press, 1975.

Biographies
Gibson, James. *Thomas Hardy: A Literary Life*. London: Macmillan, 1996.

Gittings, Robert. *Young Thomas Hardy*. London: Heinemann Educational, 1975.

Gittings, Robert. *The Older Hardy*. London: Heinemann Educational, 1978.

Hardy, Florence Emily. *The Early Life of Thomas Hardy, 1840–1891*. London and New York: Macmillan, 1928; and *The Later Years of Thomas Hardy*,

1892–1928. London and New York: Macmillan, 1930; reprinted in one volume as *The Life of Thomas Hardy, 1840–1928*. London: Macmillan; New York: St Martin's Press, 1962.

Millgate, Michael, ed. *The Life and Work of Thomas Hardy by Thomas Hardy*. London: Macmillan, 1985.

Millgate, Michael. *Thomas Hardy: A Biography*. London: Oxford University Press, 1982; reissued 1992.

Orel, Harold. *The Final Years of Thomas Hardy, 1912–1928*. London: Macmillan; Kansas: University of Kansas Press, 1976.

Seymour-Smith, Martin. *Hardy*. London: Bloomsbury, 1994.

Stewart, J.I.M. *Thomas Hardy: A Critical Biography*. London: Longman, 1971.

Turner, Paul. *The Life of Thomas Hardy: A Critical Biography*. Oxford: Blackwell, 1998.

Weber, Carl J. *Hardy of Wessex: His Life and Literary Career*. New York: Columbia University Press; London: Routledge & Kegan Paul,1940; revised edition 1965.

General critical works on Hardy

Abercrombie, Lascelles. *Thomas Hardy: A Critical Study*. London: Martin Secker, 1912.

Bayley, John. *An Essay on Hardy*. Cambridge: Cambridge University Press, 1978.

Beach, Joseph Warren. *The Technique of Thomas Hardy*. Chicago: University of Chicago Press, 1922; reprinted New York: Russell & Russell, 1962.

Blunden, Edmund. *Thomas Hardy*. London: Macmillan, 1942.

Boumelha, Penny. *Thomas Hardy and Women: Sexual Ideology and Narrative Form*. Brighton: Harvester Wheatsheaf, 1982.

Brooks, Jean R. *Thomas Hardy: The Poetic Structure*. London: Elek, 1971.

Brown, Douglas. *Thomas Hardy*. London: Longmans, Green and Co, 1954. Extracts in Draper (1975), pp.158–64.

Bullen, J.B. *The Expressive Eye: Fiction and Perception in the Work of Thomas Hardy*. Oxford: Clarendon Press, 1986.

Butler, Lance St John. *Thomas Hardy*. Cambridge: Cambridge University Press, 1978.

Carpenter, Richard C. *Thomas Hardy*. English Authors series. New York: Twayne, 1964.

Casagrande, Peter J. *Unity in Hardy's Novels: 'Repetitive Symmetries'*. London: Macmillan, 1982.

Cecil, Lord David. *Hardy the Novelist: An Essay in Criticism*. London: Constable, 1943.

Chew, Samuel C. *Thomas Hardy: Poet and Novelist*. Bryn Mawr College, New York: Longmans, Green and Co., 1921.

Collins, Deborah L. *Thomas Hardy and his God*. Basingstoke: Macmillan, 1990.

Duffin, H.C. *Thomas Hardy*. Manchester: Manchester University Press, 1916; revised 1921 and 1937.

Enstice, Andrew. *Thomas Hardy: Landscapes of the Mind*. London: Macmillan, 1979.

Firor, Ruth. *Folkways in Thomas Hardy*. Philadelphia: University of Pennsylvania Press, 1931; reprinted New York: Russell & Russell, 1968.

Fisher, Joe. *The Hidden Hardy*. Basingstoke: Macmillan, 1992.

Garson, Marjorie. *Hardy's Fables of Integrity: Woman, Body, Text*. Oxford: Clarendon Press, 1991.

Garwood, Helen. *Thomas Hardy: An Illustration of the Philosophy of Schopenhauer*. Philadelphia: John C. Winston, 1911.

Goode, John. *Thomas Hardy: The Offensive Truth*. Oxford: Basil Blackwell, 1988.

Gregor, Ian. *The Great Web: The Form of Hardy's Major Fiction*. London: Faber & Faber, 1974.

Grundy, Joan. *Hardy and the Sister Arts*. London: Macmillan, 1979.

Guerard, Albert J., *Thomas Hardy: The Novels and Stories*. Cambridge, Massachusetts: Harvard University Press, 1949; revised edition London: New Directions, 1964.

Hands, Timothy. *Thomas Hardy*. Writers in their Time series. Basingstoke: Macmillan, 1995.

Howe, Irving. *Thomas Hardy*. London: Weidenfeld and Nicolson, 1968.

Ingham, Patricia. *Thomas Hardy: A Feminist Reading*. Hemel Hempstead: Harvester Wheatsheaf, 1989.

Johnson, Bruce. *True Correspondence: A Phenomenology of Thomas Hardy's Novels*. Tallahassee, Florida: Florida State University Press, 1983.

Johnson, Lionel. *The Art of Thomas Hardy*. London: John Lane, 1894; revised edition, 1922.

Kramer, Dale. *Thomas Hardy: The Forms of Tragedy*. Detroit, Michigan: Wayne State University Press; London: Macmillan, 1975.

Langbaum, Robert. *Thomas Hardy in Our Time*. Basingstoke: Macmillan, 1995.

Miller, J. Hillis. *Thomas Hardy: Distance and Desire*. Cambridge, Massachusetts: Harvard University Press, 1970.

Millgate, Michael. *Thomas Hardy: His Career as a Novelist*. London: Bodley Head, 1971.

Morgan, Rosemarie. *Women and Sexuality in the Novels of Thomas Hardy*. London: Routledge, 1988.

Morrell, Roy. *Thomas Hardy: The Will and the Way*. Kuala Lumpur: University of Malaya Press, 1965.

Page, Norman. *Thomas Hardy*. London: Routledge & Kegan Paul, 1977.

Pinion, Frank B. *A Hardy Companion*. London: Macmillan, 1968.

Pinion, Frank B. *Thomas Hardy: Art and Thought*. London: Macmillan, 1977.

Rutland, William R. *Thomas Hardy: A Study of His Writings and their Background*. Oxford: Basil Blackwell, 1938.

Southerington, F.R. *Hardy's Vision of Man*. London: Chatto & Windus, 1971.

Sumner, Rosemary. *Thomas Hardy: Psychological Novelist*. London: Macmillan, 1981.

Thurley, Geoffrey. *The Psychology of Hardy's Novels: The Nervous and the Statuesque*. St Lucia, Queensland: University of Queensland Press, 1975.

Vigar, Penelope. *The Novels of Thomas Hardy: Illusion and Reality*. London: Athlone Press, 1974.

Webster, Harvey Curtis. *On A Darkling Plain: The Art and Thought of Thomas Hardy*. Chicago: University of Chicago Press, 1947.

Widdowson, Peter. *Hardy in History: A Study in Literary Sociology*. London and New York: Routledge, 1989.

Williams, Merryn. *A Preface to Hardy*. London: Longman, 1976.

Williams, Merryn. *Thomas Hardy and Rural England*. London: Macmillan, 1972.

Williams, Merryn and Williams, Raymond. 'Hardy and Social Class'. Norman Page, ed. *Thomas Hardy: The Writer and His Background*. London: Bell & Hyman, 1980.

Wotton, George. *Thomas Hardy: Towards a Materialist Criticism*. Goldenbridge: Gill & Macmillan, 1985.

Wright, T.R. *Hardy and the Erotic*. Basingstoke: Macmillan, 1989.

Critical books on *Tess of the d'Urbervilles*

Gibson, James. *Tess of the d'Urbervilles*. Master Guides series. London: Macmillan, 1986.

Handley, Graham. *Tess of the d'Urbervilles*. Critical Studies series. Harmondsworth: Penguin, 1991.

Kramer, Dale. *Tess of the d'Urbervilles*. Landmarks of World Literature series. Cambridge: Cambridge University Press, 1991.

Other books that discuss Hardy and *Tess of the d'Urbervilles*

Hardy, Barbara. *Tellers and Listeners: The Narrative Imagination*. London: Athlone Press, 1975, pp.175–205.

Holloway, John. *The Victorian Sage*. London: Macmillan, 1953, pp.244–89. Extracts in Guerard (1963), pp.52–62.

Schorer, Mark, ed. *Modern British Fiction*. New York: Oxford University Press, 1961, pp.30–44.

Watt, Ian, ed. *The Victorian Novel: Modern Essays in Criticism*. London: Oxford University Press, 1971, pp.407–31.

Essay/review collections
On Hardy in general:

Butler, Lance St John, ed. *Thomas Hardy After Fifty Years*. London: Macmillan, 1977.

Cox, R.G. *Thomas Hardy: The Critical Heritage*. London: Routledge & Kegan Paul, 1970.

Drabble, Margaret, ed. *The Genius of Thomas Hardy*. London: Weidenfeld & Nicolson, 1976.

Draper, R.P., ed. *Hardy: The Tragic Novels*. Casebook series. London: Macmillan, 1975; revised edition 1991.

Guerard, Albert J., ed. *Hardy: A Collection of Critical Essays*. Englewood Cliffs,

New Jersey: Prentice Hall, 1963.

Higgonet, Margaret R., ed. *The Sense of Sex: Feminist Perspectives on Hardy*. Urbana, Illinois: University of Illinois Press, 1993.

Kramer, Dale, ed. *Critical Approaches to the Fiction of Thomas Hardy*. London: Macmillan, 1975.

Kramer, Dale, ed. *The Cambridge Companion to Thomas Hardy*. Cambridge: Cambridge University Press, 1999.

Lerner, Laurence and Holstrom, John, eds. *Thomas Hardy and his Readers: A Selection of Contemporary Reviews*. London: Bodley Head, 1968.

Page, Norman, ed. *Thomas Hardy: The Writer and His Background*. London: Bell & Hyman, 1980.

Pettit, Charles P.C., ed. *New Perspectives on Thomas Hardy*. Basingstoke: Macmillan, 1994.

Pettit, Charles P.C., ed. *Reading Thomas Hardy*. Basingstoke: Macmillan, 1988.

Smith, Anne, ed. *The Novels of Thomas Hardy*. London: Vision Press, 1979.

On *Tess of the d'Urbervilles*:

Bloom, Harold, ed. *Thomas Hardy's 'Tess of the d'Urbervilles'*. New York: Chelsea House, 1987.

LaValley, Albert J., ed. *Twentieth-Century Interpretations of 'Tess of the d'Urbervilles'*. Englewood Cliffs, New Jersey: Prentice Hall, 1969.

Widdowson, Peter, ed. *Tess of the d'Urbervilles*. New Casebook series. London: Macmillan, 1993.

Reviews of *Tess of the d'Urbervilles*

Anon. 'Mr Thomas Hardy's New Novel'. *Pall Mall Gazette* (31 December 1891), 3.

Anon. 'Novels'. *Saturday Review* (16 January 1892), 73–4.

Black, Clementina. 'Mr Thomas Hardy's New Story'. *Illustrated London News*, 100 (9 January 1892), 50.

Hannigan, D.F. 'The Latest Development of English Fiction'. *Westminster Review*, 138 (December 1892), 655–9.

Hutton, R.H. 'Mr Hardy's *Tess of the d'Urbervilles*'. *Spectator* (23 January 1892), pp.121–2.

Lang, Andrew. 'Literature'. *New Review*, 6 (February 1892), pp.243–51.

Lang, Andrew. 'At the Sign of the Ship'. *Longman's Magazine*, 21 (November 1892), p.100.

Le Gallienne, Richard. 'Mr Hardy's New Novel'. *Star* (23 December 1891), p.4.

Morris, Mowbray. 'Culture and Anarchy'. *Quarterly Review*, 174 (April 1892), pp.317–44.

Oliphant, Mrs. 'The Old Saloon'. *Blackwood's Magazine*, 151 (March 1892), pp.455–74.

Trent, 'W.P. 'The Novels of Thomas Hardy'. *Sewanee Review*, 1 (November 1892), pp.1–25.

Watson, Sir William. '*Tess of the d'Urbervilles*'. *Academy*, 41 (6 February 1892), pp. 125–6.

Essays in journals and books
General essays on Hardy:

Eagleton, Terry. 'Thomas Hardy: Nature as Language'. *Critical Quarterly* 13 (1971), pp. 155–62.

Gilmour, Robin. 'The Ache of Modernism'. *The Novel in the Victorian Age*. London: Edward Arnold, 1986, pp. 185–95.

Gregor, Ian. 'What Kind of Fiction did Hardy Write?' *Essays in Criticism*, 16 (1966), pp. 290–308.

King, Jeannette. 'Thomas Hardy: tragedy ancient and modern'. *Tragedy in the Victorian Novel*. Cambridge: Cambridge University Press, 1978, pp. 112–19.

Lawrence, D. H. 'Study of Thomas Hardy'. *Phoenix: The Posthumous Papers of D. H. Lawrence*. Ed. Edward D. McDonald. London: Heinemann, 1936, pp. 398–516. Extracts in LaValley (1969), pp. 69–73.

Liddell, Robert. *A Treatise on the Novel*. London: Jonathan Cape, 1947, pp. 115–21.

Lucas, John. 'Hardy's Women'. *The Literature of Change: Studies in the Nineteenth-Century Provincial Novel*. Brighton: Harvester Press, 1977, pp. 119–91.

Williams, Raymond. 'Thomas Hardy'. *The English Novel from Dickens to Lawrence*. London: Chatto & Windus, 1970; reprinted Hogarth Press, 1984, pp. 95–118; reprinted with alterations from 'Thomas Hardy'. *Critical Quarterly*, 6 (1964), pp. 341–50.

Stubbs, Patricia. *Women and Fiction: Feminism and the Novel 1880–1920*. Brighton: Harvester Press, 1979; paperback London: Methuen, 1981, pp. 58–87.

Woolf, Virginia. 'The Novels of Thomas Hardy'. *The Common Reader: Second Series*. London: Hogarth Press, 1932; reissued 1986, pp. 245–57.

Essays and articles on *Tess of the d'Urbervilles*:

Adamson, Jane. '*Tess of the d'Urbervilles*: Time and its Shapings'. *Critical Review*, 26 (1984), pp. 18-36.

Blake, Kathleen. 'Pure Tess: Hardy on Knowing a Woman'. *Studies in English Literature 1500–1900*, 22 (1982), pp. 689–705; reprinted in Bloom (1987), pp. 87–102.

Blank, Paula C. '*Tess of the d'Urbervilles*: The English Novel and the Foreign Plot'. *Mid-Hudson Language Studies*, 12 (1989), pp. 62–71.

Bonica, Charlotte. 'Nature and Paganism in Hardy's *Tess of the d'Urbervilles*'. *Journal of English Literary History* 49 (1982), pp. 849–62.

Brick, Allan. 'Paradise and Consciousness in Hardy's *Tess of the d'Urbervilles*'. *Nineteenth-Century Fiction* 17 (1962), pp. 115–34.

Brown, Suzanne Hunter. '"Tess" and Tess: An Experiment in Genre'. *Modern Fiction Studies*, 28 (1982), pp. 25–44.

Buckley, Jerome H. 'Tess and the d'Urbervilles'. *Victorian Institute Journal*, 20 (1992), pp. 1–12.

Campbell, Elizabeth. '*Tess of the d'Urbervilles*: Misfortune Is a Woman'. *Victorian Newsletter*, 76 (1989), pp. 1–5.

Claridge, Laura, 'Tess: A Less than Pure Woman Ambivalently Presented'. *Texas Studies in Literature and Language* 28 (1986), pp. 324–38; reprinted in Widdowson (1993), pp. 63–79.

Daleski, H. M. '*Tess of the d'Urbervilles*: Mastery and Abandon'. *Essays in Criticism*, 30 (1980), pp. 326–45.

Davidson, Donald. 'The Traditional Basis of Thomas Hardy's Fiction'. *Southern Review*, 6 (1940), pp. 162–78; reprinted in Guerard (1963), pp. 10–23.

De Laura, David J. '"The Ache of Modernism" in Hardy's Later Novels'. *ELH*, 34 (1967), pp. 380–99. Extracts in LaValley (1969), pp. 85–92.

Eakins, Rosemary L. 'Tess: The Pagan and the Christian Traditions'. Anne Smith, ed. *The Novels of Thomas Hardy*. London: Vision Press, 1970, pp. 107–25.

Ebbatson, Roger. 'The Plutonic Master: Hardy and the Steam Threshing-Machine'. *Critical Survey*, 2 (1990), pp. 63–9.

Freeman, Janet. 'Ways of Looking at Tess'. *Studies in Philology* 79 (1982), pp. 311–23.

Gose, Elliot B. 'Psychic Evolution: Darwin and Initiation in *Tess of the d'Urbervilles*'. *Nineteenth-Century Fiction* 18 (1963), pp. 261–72.

Gregor, Ian. 'The Novel as Moral Protest: *Tess of the d'Urbervilles*'. Ian Gregor, and Brian Nicholas. *The Moral and the Story*. London: Faber & Faber, 1962, pp. 123–50. Extracts in LaValley (1969), pp. 30–47.

Hazen, James. 'Angel's Hellenism in *Tess of the d'Urbervilles*'. *College Literature*, 4 (1977), pp. 129–35.

Higonnet, Margaret R. 'Fictions of Feminine Voice: Antiphony and Silence in Hardy's *Tess of the d'Urbervilles*'. Laura Claridge and Elizabeth Langland, eds. *Out of Bounds: Male Writers and Gender(ed) Criticism*. Amherst: University of Massachusetts Press, 1990, pp. 197–218.

Holloway, John. '*Tess of the d'Urbervilles* and *The Awkward Age*'. *The Charted Mirror: Literary and Critical Essays*. London: Routledge & Kegan Paul, 1960, pp. 108–17.

Humma, John B. 'Language and Disguise: The Imagery of Nature and Sex in *Tess*'. *South Atlantic Review*, 54 (1989), pp. 63–83.

Johnson, Bruce. '"The Perfection of Species" and Hardy's Tess'. U. C. Knoepflmacher and G.B. Tennyson, eds. *Nature and the Victorian Imagination*. Berkeley: University of California Press, 1977, pp. 259–77; reprinted in Bloom (1987), pp. 25–44.

Kelly, Mary Ann. 'Hardy's Reading in Schopenhauer: *Tess of the d'Urbervilles*'. *Colby Library Quarterly* 18 (1982), pp. 183–98.

Kettle, Arnold. '*Tess of the d'Urbervilles*'. *An Introduction to the English Novel*. Vol. 2. London: Hutchinson University Library, 1953, pp. 45–56.

Kettle, Arnold, *Tess of the d'Urbervilles*. 'The nineteenth-century novel and its legacy', Units 17–18, prepared by A.K. Milton Keynes: Open University Press, 1982.

Kincaid, James. '"You Did Not Come": Absence, Death and Eroticism in *Tess*'. Regina Barreca, ed. *Sex and Death in Victorian Literature*. Bloomington: Indiana University Press, 1990, pp. 9–31.

Laird, J. T. 'New Light on the Evolution of *Tess of the d'Urbervilles*'. *Review of English Studies*, 31 (1980), pp. 414–35.

Lodge, David. 'Tess, Nature, and the Voices of Hardy'. *Language of Fiction*. London: Routledge & Kegan Paul, 1966, pp. 164–88. Extracts in LaValley (1969), pp. 74–84, and in Draper (1975), pp. 165–81.

Lothe, Jakob. 'Hardy's Authorial Narrative Methods in *Tess of the d'Urbervilles*'. Jeremy Hawthorn, ed. *The Nineteenth-Century British Novel*. London: Edward Arnold, 1986, pp. 157–70.

Miller, J. Hillis. 'Fiction and Repetition: *Tess of the d'Urbervilles*'. Alan Warren Friedman, ed. *Forms of Modern British Fiction*. Austin and London: University of Texas Press, 1975, pp. 43–71; reprinted as '*Tess of the d'Urbervilles*: Repetition as Immanent Design'. J. Hillis Miller, *Fiction and Repetition: Seven English Novels*. Oxford: Basil Blackwell, 1982, pp. 116–46; and also under the same title in Bloom (1987) pp. 61–86.

Morrison, Ronald D. 'Reading and Restoration in *Tess of the d'Urbervilles*'. *Victorian Newsletter* 82 (1992), pp. 27–35.

Paris, Bernard J. '"A Confusion of Many Standards": Conflicting Value Systems in *Tess of the d'Urbervilles*'. *Nineteenth-Century Fiction* 24 (1969), pp. 57–79.

Parker, Lynn. '"Pure Woman" and Tragic Heroine? Conflicting Myths in Hardy's *Tess of the d'Urbervilles*.' *Studies in the Novel*. 24 (1992), pp. 273–81.

Shires, Linda M. 'The Radical Aesthetic of *Tess of the d'Urbervilles*'. Dale Kramer, ed. *The Cambridge Companion to Thomas Hardy*. Cambridge: Cambridge University Press, 1999, pp. 145–163.

Silverman, Kaja. 'History, Figuration and Female Subjectivity in *Tess of the d'Urbervilles*'. *Novel* 18 (1984), pp. 5–28; reprinted in Widdowson (1993), pp. 129–46.

Sommers, Jeffrey. 'Hardy's Other *Bildungsroman*: *Tess of the d'Urbervilles*'. *English Literature in Transition*, 25 (1982), pp. 159–68.

Tanner, Tony. 'Colour and Movement in Hardy's *Tess of the d'Urbervilles*'. *Critical Quarterly*, 10 (1968), pp. 219–39; reprinted in Draper (1975), pp. 182–208; Watt (1971), pp. 407–31; and Bloom (1987), pp. 9–24.

Thompson, Charlotte. 'Language and the Shape of Reality in *Tess of the d'Urbervilles*'. *Journal of English Literary History*, 50 (1983), pp. 729–62; reprinted in Widdowson (1993), pp. 109–28.

Tomlinson, T. B. 'Hardy's Universe: *Tess of the d'Urbervilles*'. *Critical Review*, 16 (1973), pp. 19–38.

Van Ghent, Dorothy 'On *Tess of the d'Urbervilles*'. *The English Novel: Form and Function*. New York: Holt, Rinehart & Winstan, 1953; reprinted New York: Harper, 1961, pp. 195–209; reprinted in Schorer (1961), pp. 30–44; Guerard (1963), pp. 77–90; and LaValley (1969), pp. 48–61.

Wickens, G. Glen. 'Hardy and the Aesthetic Mythographers: The Myth of Demeter and Persephone in *Tess of the d'Urbervilles*'. *University of Toronto*

Quarterly, 53 (1983–4), pp.85–106.

Wickens, G. Glen. 'Victorian Theories of Language and *Tess of the d'Urbervilles'. Mosaic,* 19 (1986), pp.99–115.

Widdowson, Peter. '"Moments of Vision": Postmodernising *Tess of the d'Urbervilles;* or, *Tess of the d'Urbervilles* Faithfully Presented by Peter Widdowson'. Charles P.C. Pettit, ed. *New Perspectives on Thomas Hardy.* London: Macmillan, 1994, pp.80–100.

Wright, Terence. 'Rhetorical and Lyrical Imagery in *Tess of the d'Urbervilles', Durham University Journal* 24 (1972), pp.79–85.

Zabel, Morton Dauwen. 'Hardy in Defence of his Art: The Aesthetic of Incongruity'. *Southern Review,* 6 (1940), pp.125–49. Extract in Guerard (1963), pp.24–45.

Essays on other topics with a significant mention of Hardy, or *Tess of the d'Urbervilles*

Feltes, N.N., *Modes of Production of Victorian Novels.* Chicago and London: University of Chicago Press, 1986.

Leavis, F.R., *The Great Tradition.* London: Chatto and Windus, 1948.

Films and television productions of *Tess of the d'Urbervilles*

Films:

Tess of the d'Urbervilles (1913). Famous Players Film Co./Monopol Film Co. (America). Directed by J. Searle Dawley. Black and white. Silent. With Minnie Maddern Fiske as Tess Durbeyfield.

Tess of the d'Urbervilles (1924). Metro-Goldwyn. (America). Directed by Marshall Neilan. Black and white. With Blanche Sweet as Tess Durbeyfield, Conrad Nagel as Angel Clare and Stuart Holmes as Alec d'Urberville.

Tess (1979). Claude Berri and Timothy Burrill. Screenplay by Gerard Brach, John Brownjohn and Roman Polanski. Directed by Roman Polanski. (France/Britain). With Nastassia Kinski as Tess Durbeyfield, Peter Firth as Angel Clare and Leigh Lawson as Alec d'Urberville.

Television

Tess of the d'Urbervilles (1998). BBC. Ian Sharp. Screenplay by Ted Whitehead. With Justine Waddell as Tess Durbeyfield, Oliver Milburn as Angel Clare and Jason Flemyng as Alec d'Urberville. Available as a commercial video.

Roman Polanski's film has attracted considerable critical attention:

Constanzo, William V. 'Polanski in Wessex . . . filming *Tess of the d'Urbervilles'. Literature/Film Quarterly,* 9 (1981), pp.72–9.

Marcus, Jane. 'A Tess for Child Molesters'. *Jump Cut,* 26 (December 1981), p.3.

Totterdell, Ann. 'Tess, a second view'. *Films*, 1 (June 1981), p. 39.
Sarne, Mike. 'Tess'. *Films*, 1 (May, 1981), p. 35.
Widdowson, Peter. *Hardy in History: A Study in Literary Sociology*. London and New York: Routledge, 1989, pp. 115–25; reprinted as 'A "Tragedy of Modern Life"? Polanski's Tess' in Peter Widdowson, ed. *Tess of the d'Urbervilles*. New Casebook series. Basingstoke: Macmillan, 1993, pp. 95–108.

ACKNOWLEDGEMENTS

The editor and publisher wish to thank the following for their permission to reprint copyright material: Heinemann (for material from *Phoenix: The Posthumous Papers of D.H. Lawrence*); University of Chicago Press (for material from *On a Darkling Plain: The Art and Thought of Thomas Hardy*); Harvard University Press (for material from *Thomas Hardy*); Macmillan (for material from *The Victorian Sage*; *Thomas Hardy and the Forms of Tragedy*; *Thomas Hardy: Psychological Novelist*; *The Hidden Hardy*; and '"Moments of Vision": Post-modernising *Tess of the d'Urbervilles*; or, *Tess of the d'Urbervilles* Faithfully Presented by Peter Widdowson', in *New Perspectives on Thomas Hardy*); Harper and Row (for material from *The English Novel: Form and Function*); Hutchinson (for material from *An Introduction to the English Novel*); Longmans, Green (for material from *Thomas Hardy*); University of Malaya Press (for material from *Thomas Hardy: The Will and the Way*); Weidenfeld and Nicolson (for material from *Thomas Hardy*); *Critical Quarterly* (for material from 'Colour and Movement in Hardy's *Tess of the d'Urbervilles*'); Routledge (for material from *Language of Fiction*; and 'Tess: The Making of a Pure Woman', in *Tearing the Veil: Essays in Femininity*); Faber (for material from *The Great Web: The Form of Hardy's Major Fiction*); *ELH* (for material from 'The "Ache of Modernism" in Hardy's Later Novels'); Hogarth Press (for material from *The English Novel from Dickens to Lawrence*); Clarendon Press (for material from *The Shaping of 'Tess of the d'Urbervilles'*; *The Expressive Eye: Fiction and Perception in the Work of Thomas Hardy*; *Hardy the Creator: A Textual Biography*; and *Hardy's Fables of Identity: Woman, Body, Text*); Basil Blackwell (for material from *Fiction and Repetition: Seven English Novels*; and *Thomas Hardy: The Offensive Truth*); Harvester Wheatsheaf (for material from *Thomas Hardy and Women: Sexual Ideology and Narrative Form*; and *Thomas Hardy*).

There are instances where we have been unable to trace or contact copyright holders before our printing deadline. If notified, the publisher will be pleased to acknowledge the use of copyright material.

The editor wishes to thank the staff of the Library of the University of Reading for their unfailing assistance in obtaining copies of the array of material consulted in the compilation of this Guide.

Geoffrey Harvey is Senior Lecturer in English at the University of Reading. He has published widely on nineteenth- and twentieth-century writers in journals in Britain and America. His books include *The Art of Anthony Trollope* (1980) and *The Romantic Tradition in Modern English Poetry* (1986). He has also edited novels of Trollope, Galsworthy and Jerome K. Jerome for Oxford University Press. An edition of Trollope's *The Warden* is forthcoming from Broadview Press. He is currently working on a book on Hardy.

INDEX